A Proficiency Course in E[nglish]
with key

F. V. Bywater, M.A.

Edward Arnold
A division of Hodder & Stoughton
LONDON   MELBOURNE   AUCKLAND

© 1982 F. V. Bywater

New edition with key first published 1982
Nineteenth impression 1989

British Library Cataloguing in Publication Data

Bywater, F. V.
    A proficiency course in English, with key.
    1. English language—Text-books for foreigners.
    I. Title
    428.2'4   PE1128

    ISBN 0 340 28628 8

Printed and bound in Great Britain for Edward Arnold, the
educational, academic and medical publishing division of Hodder
and Stoughton Limited, 41 Bedford Square, London WC1B 3DQ by
Biddles Limited, Guildford and King's Lynn

Contents

[handwritten annotation next to item 6:] Excersicopy: 41

Introduction

This book has a very specific purpose. Between the Cambridge First Certificate and Cambridge Proficiency Examinations, students have to build up a far greater knowledge of idiomatic English and they have to learn to eliminate grammatical and stylistic mistakes. This involves a systematic revision of all the most important aspects of grammar and construction, and this book is designed to help in this task. In compiling it, I have had only one criterion: I have considered what, in the light of some years' experience of teaching English to foreign students, seem to be the things that advanced students still have difficulty with, and I have given most of my attention to these things. The Cambridge Examiners themselves have pointed out the vast number of mistakes with constructions after verbs (which I have called government of verbs) and so I have dealt with these in considerable detail, partly by giving lists for reference of the commonest expressions followed by a particular construction and, above all, by setting a large number of exercises to give students practice in using these constructions.

Apart from the government of verbs the following seem to me the most usual sources of mistakes: uncountable nouns, phrasal verbs (which I have usually called compound verbs), tenses, articles and word order. These are therefore the things that have been gone into most fully.

This book, however, is not meant to be a comprehensive grammar book, and on many other aspects of grammar—such as the Passive, Relative Pronouns, Indirect Speech and Auxiliary Verbs—it assumes that the students have already studied the subject and merely draws attention to some salient points that may have been overlooked or not properly grasped.

I may, with some justification, be accused of over-simplification in grammatical expositions. This is at least partly deliberate. As I have no wish to bog the student down in a mass of minor intricacies, everything not essential has been omitted. My aim throughout has been to present the grammar simply enough for the student to be able to get a clear, overall picture of it. Where teachers think the over-simplification too scandalous, there is nothing to stop them filling in further details. Everyone has his hobby-horse and no book completely suits anyone except its writer. Books are aids to teachers, not tyrants over them. Allowing for such filling-in, however, I do intend the book to be worked through systematically.

Here, perhaps, a little advice about how to use it in class may not come amiss. It is obviously impossible for the teacher to read through the grammar sections with the pupils in class: nothing could be more sleep-inducing. It is suggested, therefore, that the teacher (with his book open) should do his best to elicit the information required by questioning the pupils (with their books closed). Thus, for example, in section 1 the teacher would point out the first principle mentioned and then ask members of the class to give some examples of it. Then he would ask one student to make up a sentence using 'advise'. Another student would be asked to make up another one using a different construction, then a third student, and so on. Subsequently, the grammar of the section can be given to read for homework as a preface to the students' writing the exercise(s) on it. Similarly in sections 2 and 3 questions will be put about the use of the Present Simple and Continuous, Present Perfect and Simple Past etc. so that, as far as possible, the information contained in those sections can be gleaned from the pupils themselves. Afterwards the teacher can fill in this method of class participation and it can be applied to all sections, except 14 (on the gerund) and 15 (on the infinitive), where the lists are most obviously for reference. Here the teacher will probably limit himself to making sure that the students understand the meaning of the less common words. Throughout the book, this may be necessary, as the vocabulary used is quite extensive and in no way specially selected as simple. In short, the grammar sections will be mainly useful for reference after the essential contents have been taught in the way suggested. This method will ensure that the teacher is teaching, not merely acting as a kind of 'medium' to transmit messages from me—a disembodied spirit to all except my own pupils—to the class.

Because the book is meant to be worked through systematically I have not grouped all the grammar and exercises on a particular subject together. It looks neat, but is, for practical purposes, absurd to have a whole lot of exercises on one point together and then never another mention of the point. Even the grammar on the government of verbs, tenses and phrasal verbs has been split up into a number of sections in an attempt to avoid mental indigestion. All the exercises on grammar follow the expositions and so are prepared beforehand, but revision exercises are found throughout the book. Exercises on vocabulary and comprehension, however, are inserted and have not been prepared beforehand. I do not see how they can be prepared without giving away all the answers.

A number of the points dealt with in this book do not seem to have been tackled in other books that I have seen for foreign students. I have therefore had little precedent to guide me and have indeed been driven to writing this by the very real gaps that I have noticed in grammar books for advanced students. I hope, therefore, that the shortcomings here will not be as severely censured as they would be if I were covering only well-known ground.

Finally, a word on grammar rules. There is no justice in this life and all examiners are on the look-out for lapses of grammar. When Dickens wrote: 'The clerk's fire was so very much smaller that it looked like one coal', he, in common with every Englishman who has not taught English to foreigners, had never heard of an uncountable noun. The unfortunate foreigner writing the same sentence would have marks deducted for not knowing his grammar. Grammar rules, therefore, serve only to help the student to play safe. They are empirical, not absolute. Only a vast amount of reading of English literature will give the student a 'feel for the language' that will enable him to snap his fingers at the rules. If he has already reached that stage, this book has nothing to teach him. If not, I hope it may help him to reach it.

F. V. Bywater

1: The constructions with basic verbs A—C

An important principle of English construction is that most verbs are followed by the same preposition before an ordinary noun and before a gerundive noun. (For a detailed study of the gerund construction see Section 14, page 74.)
He insists on that course of action. (ordinary noun)
He insists on behaving so outrageously. (gerundive noun)
I praised the boy for his courage.
I praised the boy for acting so courageously.
She is quite used to English life.
She is quite used to living in England.
A lot of children are fond of music.
A lot of children are fond of singing and dancing.
That man saved me from an unpleasant death.
That man saved me from drowning.

If there is no preposition before an ordinary noun, there is no preposition before a gerundive noun either.
He denied all knowledge of it.
He denied stealing the money.
Hampton Court is well worth a visit.
Hampton Court is well worth taking the trouble to visit.
I hope you do not mind a salad for lunch.
I hope you do not mind having just a salad for lunch.
A number of very common verbs, however, have a lot of different prepositions and constructions after them, and this section (which is divided up to make it easier to digest) deals with some fifty of these basic verbs in alphabetical order. This basic principle of construction will be noticed in studying most of these verbs.

Advise

1. *I wouldn't advise that course of action.* (No preposition before an ordinary noun.)
2. *I wouldn't advise taking that course of action.* (No preposition before a gerundive noun.)
3. *I wouldn't advise you to take that course of action.* (If a personal object is inserted the gerund is replaced by the infinitive. As will be noted, *advise* is not the only verb with which this happens.)
4. *I wouldn't advise your taking that course of action.* (This is an alternative to 3, but less common. The possessive adjective is always used with the gerund when the person doing the gerund is different from the subject of the sentence. See Section 14, page 74.)

5. *I advised them against that course of action.* (Note the preposition. The meaning is: *I advised them not to do it.*)
6. *I advised them against taking that course of action.* (The same meaning and preposition as in 5.)

Agree

1. *I agreed to that suggestion.* (Note the preposition.)
2. *I agreed with him on/about politics.* (Note the prepositions.)
3. *They agree in their tastes.* (Note the preposition.)
4. *They agreed to doing that.* (The same preposition as in 1 before a gerundive noun. *To* with the gerund is as common as any other preposition. For other expressions see pages 86 and 87.)
5. *They agreed to do that.* (This is an alternative to 4. In this case usage breaks the usual rule.)
6. *I agreed to his doing that.* (A different person is doing the gerund from the subject of the sentence.)
7. *Do you agree with allowing children to do as they like?* (The same preposition as in 2 before a gerund. The meaning is: *Do you approve of the principle of allowing children to do as they like?*)
8. *They failed to agree on/about going to Corsica for their holiday.* (The same preposition as in 2 before a gerund.)
9. *They failed to agree on how to do it.* (The same preposition as in 2, plus an infinitive phrase. Infinitive phrases can also be introduced by: *when, whom, what, where, whether* and *which.*
They failed to agree on when to do it/whom to choose/what to say/where to emigrate to/whether or not to do it/which colour to choose. For a list of verbs followed by these see Section 15, pages 92 and 93.)
10. *They agreed in wanting a change of government.* (The same preposition as in 3 before a gerund.)
11. *I agreed that he should do it.* (The clause is an alternative to 6.)

Allow

1. *I don't allow argument in here.* (No preposition before an ordinary noun.)
2. *I don't allow arguing in here.* (No preposition before a gerundive noun.)
3. *I don't allow anyone to argue in here.* (If a personal object is inserted the gerund is replaced by the infinitive, as with *advise* 3.)
4. *They allowed me £5 on my old radio.* (Note the preposition. The meaning is: *They took £5 off the price of the new radio in return for my handing them my old one.*)
5. *I didn't allow for a delay.* (Note the preposition. The meaning is: *I didn't think of a possible delay when I made my plans.*)

6. *I didn't allow for being delayed.* (The same preposition as in 5 used before a gerund, and the same meaning.)

7. *I made allowances for his being very young.* (The same preposition is used before a gerund after the noun *allowances*. The meaning is: *I took his extreme youth into consideration in judging him.*)

8. *His father makes him an allowance of £70 a week* (A different meaning of *allowance* and a different preposition after it. The meaning is: *His father sends him £70 a week to live on.*)

Apologise

1. *I apologised (to her) for my lateness.* (Note the prepositions.)

2. *I apologised (to her) for being late.* (The same preposition before a gerundive noun.)

Ask

1. *She asked him a searching question.* (Note the absence of prepositions.)

2. *She asked to leave early* (*To* is only a sign of the infinitive and is not a real preposition in this sentence.)

3. *She asked if she could leave early.* (The clause is an alternative to 2.)

4. *She asked me to leave early.* (The object and the infinitive.)

5. *She asked me if I would leave early.* (The clause is an alternative to 4, but is, in fact, ambiguous. It could mean the same as 4: *She requested me to leave early*, or it could mean: *She wanted to know if I intended to leave early.* Unless the context makes the meaning clear, this ambiguity should be avoided.)

6. *He asked the waiter for the bill.* (Note the preposition.)

7. *That job is yours for the asking.* (An idiom, using the same preposition as in 6 before a gerund. The meaning is: *All you have to do is to apply for the job and you will automatically get it.*)

8. *That is asking a lot of me.* (Another idiom. The meaning is: *It is almost too much to expect of me because I don't think I am clever or virtuous enough to do it.*)

9. *Stop to ask yourself a simple question.* (The reflexive use of *ask*.)

10. *I asked how to get there, etc.* (*How* plus an infinitive phrase. See *agree* 9 for other introductory words to infinitive phrases.)

Believe

1. *She believes in her husband.* (Note the preposition.)

2. *She believes in telling her husband the truth.* (The same preposition before a gerundive noun.)

3. *She believes that her husband is intelligent.* (A clause.)

4. *She believes her husband (to be) intelligent.* (This is an alternative to 3. It is the Latin accusative and infinitive construction and is rather literary in English. As in Latin, the infinitive can be omitted.)
5. *I believe so.* (i.e. *that it is true.*) *I believe not.* (i.e. *that it is not true.*) (See also Section 17, page 103.)

Concentrate

1. *You must concentrate on your work.* (Note the preposition.)
2. *You must concentrate on doing your work.* (The same preposition before a gerund.)
3. *You must concentrate to do this.* (The infinitive indicates purpose. See Section 15, page 93. The meaning is: *You must concentrate in order to do this.*)

Consider

1. *I considered the matter carefully.* (No preposition before an ordinary noun.)
2. *I considered going to live abroad.* (No preposition before the gerund.)
3. *I considered his going to live abroad.* (The possessive adjective indicates a different person considering and going there.)
4. *I consider that he is a fool.* (A clause.)
5. *I consider him to be a fool.* (A rather literary alternative to 4. As in Latin, the infinitive can be omitted.)
6. *I consider so. I consider not.* (Rather literary.)
7. *I considered how to do it, etc.* (An infinitive phrase. See *agree* 9.)
8. *He has no consideration for others.* (Note the preposition after the noun.)
9. *No consideration of personal gain entered his head.* (Note the preposition.

EXERCISES

a. Put in the missing prepositions:
1. *You must make allowances ...... his having been in England such a short time.*
2. *How much did they allow you ...... your old car?*
3. *Some people do not believe ...... teaching formal grammar.*
4. *Do you agree ...... nationalising basic industries?*
5. *Why did you advise me ...... marrying that girl?*
6. *They knew it needed doing but failed to agree ...... how to do it.*
7. *He was concentrating so hard ...... his detective story that he didn't hear me come in.*

8. *It is asking a lot ...... me to come to your wedding to someone else when you know I am in love with you myself.*
9. *I agree ...... you ...... Jane; she ought not to have behaved like that.*
10. *He was late because he didn't allow ...... having to wait so long for a train.*

b. Explain the difference in meaning between:
1. *How is she?*
   How does she look?
   What is she?
   What is she like?
2. *They are looking at the house.*
   They are watching the house.
3. *a paper*
   a piece of paper
4. *to sue someone*
   to prosecute someone
5. *to support a policy*
   to put up with a policy
6. *They needn't have gone.*
   They didn't need to go.
7. *He's engaged with her.*
   He's engaged to her.
8. to get over it
   to get it over
9. In a short time you can go there.
   In a short time you will be able to go there.
10. *I must hand it over to the police.*
    I must hand it to the police.
11. *What do you make it of ?*
    What do you make of it ?

c. Use the following idiomatic expressions in sentences of your own. (The teacher may think it advisable to explain the meaning of these idioms first.)

1. *bits and pieces*	2. *cut and dried*	3. *house and home*
4. *pure and simple*	5. *wind and weather*	6. *far and wide*
7. *dead and buried*	8. *fast and furious*	9. *odds and ends*
10. *out-and-out*	11. *rough and ready*	12. *all and sundry*
13. *high and dry*	14. *by and by*	15. *spick and span*
16. *hard and fast*	17. *free and easy*	18. *flesh and blood*
19. *few and far between*	20. *song and dance*	21. *might and main*
22. *wear and tear*	23. *the rank and file*	24. *meek and mild*
25. *now and then*		

2: Pattern of verb tenses (excluding conditionals)

SIMPLE	active	passive	use	Examples active	passive
1 past	I did	it was done	You are thinking of when it happened, whether you say when or not.	What did you do last weekend? Columbus discovered America.	The crime was committed between 9 and 10 p.m.
2 present	I do	it is done	This is used for habit or permanent state.	What do you do for a living? The Thames flows through London.	Every year a few cinemas are closed. Most furniture is made of wood.
3 future	I shall do	it will be done	You are thinking of when it will happen in the future.	I shall go there next Thursday.	Your complaint will be dealt with as soon as possible.

CONTINUOUS

4 past	I was doing	it was being done	You are thinking of the action in the middle of happening when something else happened.	Dickens was writing a book when he died. The orchestra was playing a pretty tune as we came in.	An important operation was being performed when the lights went out. What tune was being played as we came in?
5 present	I am doing	it is being done	You are thinking of what is in the middle of happening now.	Look! A cow is coming in through the French window. Go and see what he is doing	The whole matter is being investigated at at this moment. Nothing is being done about it at present.
6 future	I shall be doing		You are thinking of what will be in the middle of happening at a certain time in the future.	This time next week he will be flying to Spain. Next week you will be lying in the sun on some coral-fringed island.	

	active	passive	use	Examples active	passive
PERFECT					
7 past	I had done	it had been done	You are thinking of the completion of one action before another in the past.	He had learnt English before he came here. My girl friend had left before my wife got home.	The house had been demolished before the Preservation Society could intervene.
8 present	I have done	it has been done	You are thinking of the result into the present of the completion of the action.	I have lost my pen; may I borrow yours? I have seen that film, so I don't want to see it again so soon.	The matter has been discussed; now let us put it to the vote.
9 future	I shall have done	it will have been done	You are thinking of the completion of the action by a certain time in the future.	I shall have finished work by 5 o'clock.	I think the vote will have been taken before he arrives.

PERFECT
CONTINUOUS

10 past	*I had been doing*	You are thinking of *the length of time taken* by one action before *another in past.*	*He had been living there for 20 years before he decided to move.*
11 present	*I have been been doing*	You are thinking of *the length of time taken up to the present or with a result into the present.*	*I have been wanting to go there ever since I was a child. I have been waiting nearly half an hour; if she doesn't come in five minutes I'm going home.*
12 future	*I shall have been doing*	You are thinking of *the length of time that will have been taken by a certain time in the future.*	*Next year he will have been working here for fifty years.*

EXERCISES

a. Put the verbs in brackets into the right tense.
1. *I do not know Portugal; I (never be) there.*
2. *I (not go) to Portugal when I (be) in Spain last year.*
3. *Go and see what John (do), will you?*
4. *If you (live) in London for nearly a year now I expect you know where the Royal Academy is.*
5. *She (play) the piano when I (knock) on her door last night.*
6. *I wonder who (make) that dreadful row.*
7. *You do not need to describe her; I (meet) her several times.*
8. *After he (eat) an enormous dinner, he (fall) asleep and (dream) peacefully when a lump of coal (fall) on to the hearth and (wake) him up.*
9. *I (live) in that flat for several years before I (decide) to look round for something more central.*
10. *Imagine it! This time next week you (live) in the lap of luxury in a first-class hotel.*
11. *I (finish) the book in about twenty minutes' time; can't you wait until then?*
12. *When you last (see) your sister?*
13. *I (long) to meet you for ages. I (hear) so much about you.*
14. *The Incas (beat) in battle by the Spanish conquistadores and, after (hold) in captivity for some time, their Emperor (murder).*
15. *When I (get) home last night I (find) a note from my wife saying that she (run) away with a friend of mine.*
16. *He (soon complete) thirty years in that job.*
17. *This time tomorrow you (sit) here again doing some more exercises.*
18. *A new cinema (build) here. They hope to finish it next month.*
19. *A new block of flats (build) just opposite where I live. I am not too pleased about it.*
20. *The whole house is in confusion because preparations (make) for this evening's dance.*
21. *Many people (send) to prison for less than that!*
22. *You (see) my glasses? I can't find them anywhere.*
23. *Just as I (luxuriate) in a really hot bath the telephone (ring).*
24. *When I (get) home I (find) that nothing (do) about clearing up the mess.*
25. *When I (arrive) on the field yesterday, preparations (be) in full swing for the Fair which opens today: tents (put) up, swings (erect), people (rush) about in all directions carrying strange objects, cars (churn) up the mud, booths (put) together and (fix) in the ground and a group of policemen (stroll) about keeping an eye on things.*
26. *Why nothing (do) to stop the blood pouring out?*
27. *I was feeling very tired because I (work) very hard in the garden all day.*
28. *I assure you that the matter (attend) to as quickly as possible. Have a little patience.*

29. Tolstoy (try) for some time to educate his serfs but after he (work) at it for about twenty years he (get) discouraged and (give) it up.
30. I (meet) your sister yesterday and I (think) she (look) very well.

b. Use these words in sentences so as to bring out their meaning clearly:

to deceive	historic	inane	a break
to disappoint	historical	insane	a breach
			breakages
to rise	parting	obscure	
to raise	departure	dark	unconnected
to rouse			disconnected
to arouse	urban	wave	
to arise	urbane	waive	

c. Explain the meaning of the italicised words.
1. He lives in a very nice *flat*.
2. He was driving *flat* out.
3. That singer was horribly *flat*.
4. The joke fell *flat*.
5. He *flatly* refused to have anything to do with it.
6. A *flat* surface is necessary for drawing.
7. A *flat* voice is a handicap to a public speaker.
8. What is the *mean* annual rainfall?
9. A row of *mean* houses blocked the view.
10. I have been *meaning* to do it for a long time.
11. Exploring a new country in the olden days *meant* putting up with considerable hardship.
12. What is your favourite *means* of transport?
13. He has private *means*.
14. Can you think of a *means* of doing it?
15. By all *means* do it if you want to.
16. Does the end justify the *means*?
17. I do not like *meanness* in people.
18. That *bar* has a lot of atmosphere.
19. He was called to the *Bar* last year.
20. A few *bars* of chocolate are included in most emergency rations.
21. He hummed a few *bars* of a tune.
22. No holds are *barred* in that contest.
23. They all went *bar* me.
24. He bent two *bars* and forced his way between them.
25. Will the prisoner at the *bar* kindly answer the questions?
26. The police *barred* the way.
27. The American Administration is doing its best to break down *the colour bar* in the United States.
28. On what *grounds* are you applying for a divorce?
29. All aeroplanes of that type have been *grounded* until further notice.
30. The house stood in extensive *grounds*.

3: Notes on the uses of basic tenses

1. Certain verbs whose meanings suggest permanence and which therefore cannot really be applied to what is happening now, at this moment, are never used in the present continuous or in any other continuous tense. Such verbs are: *to resemble, to look like*, to mean* (in the sense of *signify*), *to belong to, to contain, to hold* (in the sense of *contain*), *to be fond of, to possess, to know, to consist of, to be* (but see page 153 for details of this verb).

2. A few verbs are only used in the continuous form if their meaning is different from their normal meaning.
The Headmaster *is seeing** a student. *(interviewing him)*
Are you *supposing* him to be honest? *(assuming)*
He *is hearing** a case. *(judging it in a court of law)*
He *is appearing* in the new play. *(acting in it)*
He *is forgetting* his German. *(little by little)*
He *is remembering* his vocabulary better. *(little by little)*

3. Adverbs like *always, forever, perpetually, continually* and *constantly* are frequently used with the present continuous or past continuous to suggest annoyance. The simple present or simple past would indicate philosophical calm.
My car *is always breaking* down just when I need it most.
She *was constantly asking* silly questions and really got on my nerves.
Why *are* you *perpetually getting* into debt?
They *were continually squabbling* over trifles.

4. If there is an adverbial expression to indicate futurity, the present continuous can be used instead of the future, if the matter is one of personal choice.
The Prime Minister *is flying* to Iraq *tomorrow.*
The Government *is meeting on Monday* to discuss the matter.

5. The present continuous is used for habit when it is clear that the habit is only a temporary one.
At the moment he *is attending* school every afternoon, but he is starting a job next month and will have to transfer to a twice-weekly evening class.

6. The difference between the simple past and the present perfect is extremely important. If you use the simple past you are thinking of

*See note 13 page 23

when something happened or you are *narrating a sequence of events at a given time*. The simple past is the only narrative tense in English. If you use the present perfect tense you are thinking, *not* of when it happened, but of its *result into the present* or of *some knowledge that you have as a result of its happening*.

Compare and contrast the following sentences:

'*I read the book* War and Peace *at the age of seven*.' *(i.e. When I was only seven; wasn't it clever of me to read it when I was so young?)*

'*I have read the book* War and Peace.' *(So I have some knowledge of Tolstoy's work, Napoleon's campaign in Russia, etc.)*

'*When did you last see your wife? (It is very important to remember the exact time: it may help the police to trace her.)*

'*I have seen your wife and I must say I think she is very charming indeed.' (I have some knowledge and some personal impression of her.)*

'*I have seen that film so I have made up my own mind and do not agree at all with the critics.' (My personal knowledge of the film puts me in a position to disagree with the critics.)*

'*Did you sleep well?' (Did you have a good night? Did anything disturb you? Were you warm enough? Did you have pleasant dreams?)*

'*Have you slept well?' (Last night you were tired and had a headache. How do you feel now after your night's rest?)*

Consequently a sentence like: '*I have seen her yesterday*' is impossible. It would mean: '*I know what she is like yesterday*'—which is nonsense.

7. The present perfect tense (simple or continuous) is also used for something that has happened within a period of time not yet finished.
I *have been working* hard *this week*.
She *has had* two holidays so far *this year*.
I *have had* a cold all *this month*.

8. *Already*, *yet* and *just* (meaning *a short time ago*) are *never* used with the simple past. The present perfect simple is the tense most frequently used with them, though others are possible.
I *have just run* the bath for you.
Haven't you *finished* reading the chapter *yet*?
The speaker *was already addressing* the crowd when I arrived.
Just, however, can also mean *only* and in this case it is used with the simple past.
I *just came in* to say goodbye.

9. The present perfect continuous tense can never be used for inter-mittent actions: an idea of continuity is implied in it.
It is correct to say:
I *have been teaching* here for several years.
She *has been wanting* to visit India all her life.
It is not correct to say:
I *have been going* to three films this week.

Sometimes, however, if an action is intermittent but has become a habit, the present perfect continuous is used.

I *have been going* to the cinema ever since I was ten years old.

He *has been writing* letters to newspapers ever since I have known him.

I *have been popping* in to see her two or three times a week for some time now.

10. The past continuous indicates that an action was not completed. It was either interrupted in the middle of happening or prevented from even starting.

I *was hoping* to go last week, but unfortunately I couldn't manage it.

He *was going* to see his uncle on Saturday, but he was taken ill and couldn't.

11. The past perfect tense must be used for an action that is finished before another in the past *if there is a logical connection between the two actions.*

Many European Kings *felt* happier after Napoleon *had disappeared* from the scene.

If there is no logical connection the past perfect need not be used.

Napoleon *died* before my grandfather *was born.*

12. *Shall* and *will.*

a. In modern English *shall* is never used in the second person. Whereas a Victorian mother might have said: 'If you are a good girl you *shall* go to the zoo', a modern one would say: 'If you are a good girl *I'll take you* to the zoo' or 'If you are a good girl you *can* go to the zoo'.

b. *Shall* nowadays is used in the third person only for *legal or formal undertakings or guarantees.*

A condition of publication is that the book *shall* not contain offensive material.

The tenant *shall* hereafter be held responsible for all internal repairs and decorations.

No-one *shall* be allowed in unless he can give the password.

Notices *shall* be put in conspicuous places announcing the date from which this is to be a smokeless zone.

c. *Shall* is always used in the first person singular and plural in the interrogative *(Shall I?, Shall we?)* and in statements where there is *no suggestion whatever of willingness.*

I *shall* be 65 next birthday.

Willingness (e.g. at the marriage service) is expressed by *will.*

'*Will* you take this woman to be your wedded wife . . . ?' 'I *will.*'

d. Determination is conveyed nowadays not by using *shall* or *will* differently but by emphasising the *auxiliary* instead of the *infinitive.*

I shall/will *gó*
I'll *gó*   (Future)

I *shåll/wíll* go   (Determination)

13. Another use of the future (both simple and continuous) is to indicate *I suppose*, though the words *I suppose* are often inserted as well (unnecessarily but to make quite sure there is no ambiguity). It should be noted that in this kind of sentence the future continuous is very commonly used even with such verbs as *see, hear* and *look like.*
You'll be the boy my daughter has told me so much about.
You *will be seeing* your parents at Christmas, I suppose.
They *will be hearing* their examination results soon, poor things!
You'll be feeling lonely now that your circle of friends has split up.
He'll be wondering where on earth we have got to.
I *shall be looking* like a tramp by the time I get there.
The future perfect simple and continuous can also be used in this way.
You'll have heard people talking about him, no doubt.
He'll have been seeing quite a lot of Mary recently, I daresay.
They'll have been playing pranks on everyone as usual, I suppose.

14. It is only fair to say that, although in my pattern of tenses I have marked the future continuous passive and all the perfect continuous passives as missing because I think their use very rare (and possibly dialect English), some grammarians disagree and declare that they use them not infrequently. They therefore admit such forms as: 'Next week it *will be being put* to the vote and there is nothing you can do about it' or: 'It *has been being done* like that for years and I'm not going to change it'. I, personally, would not recommend these forms to foreign students. I must add, however, that there is actually nothing to prevent one from using an auxiliary verb with *be* in the continuous form. I recently came across the following sentence in a very reputable newspaper. 'There is reason to suppose that those flats *may be being built* with their foundations insufficiently deep'.

15. Never use the future (or, in sentences in the past, the conditional) in adverbial clauses after such words as *before, as soon as, as long as, unless, on condition that, after, in case, provided that, etc.*
Write to me *as soon as* you *get* home.
After you *have finished* that book will you lend it to me?
I won't go there *unless* you *want* me to.
The same rule applies to *if* and *when* in adverbial clauses. *If* and *when*, however, can be used in noun clauses which are the object of a verb. In noun clauses they are used with the future or conditional.
Write to me when you *get* home.
There is no reason why you shouldn't telephone me *if* you *want* to.
I don't know his plans/*when* he *will come* (Noun clause)
I didn't hear that remark/*when* he *would be* coming back/*if* he *would do* it or not. (Noun clause)
N.B. In studying the conditional further exceptions to the main rule will be noted.

16. *Is going to* can be used instead of *shall* or *will* to indicate:
a. That it is your will or intention to do something:
I am going to study Russian next year.
b. That an action is imminent:
I think it *is going to* rain in a few minutes.
17. The future continuous can be used to convey the idea that something is not at all exceptional but quite a normal happening.
'I *shall see* the Queen tomorrow' indicates that it is a special day in your life.
'I *shall be seeing* the Queen tomorrow and I'll tell her what you said' indicates that this is quite normal; you are a relation, a close friend or a member of her household.
Indeed, it could be said that, although there are immense subtleties in the use of the future continuous, it generally has a greater idea of informality that the future simple. For example: 'What time will you be coming tomorrow?' is much friendlier and less aggressive than 'What time will you come tomorrow?'

EXERCISES
a. Put the verbs in brackets into the right tense.
1. *How can I ever concentrate if you (continually interrupt) me with idiotic questions?*
2. *I am afraid the Director cannot see you at present. He (see) a candidate for a vacancy.*
3. *He (hope) to go to University next year but his parents (decide) that they will not be able to afford it unless he (succeed) in getting a Government grant.*
4. *He (know) her a long time before he (marry) her.*
5. *When you (finish) with that book, just pop it in my pigeon-hole, will you?*
6. *Come and look what (happen) in the street: a woman (rob) of her handbag and (point) to a man who (chase) along the street by a policeman. I wonder if he (catch).*
7. *I expect you (see) the Headmaster in the normal course of events, so you can tell him then.*
8. *I am not sure whom that house (belong) to now but I do know that a few years ago it (live) in by a strange old recluse.*
9. *I (teach) English for several years before I (realise) why students of certain nationalities (make) certain mistakes.*
10. *I (go) to see him as soon as I (receive) his wife's telegram yesterday, but he already (relapse) into a coma before I (get) there.*

b. Explain the difference of meaning between:
1. *What is he doing?*
   What does he do?
2. *They talked as I came in.*

They were talking as I came in.
3. *He had learnt English before he came to England.*
   He had been learning English before he came to England.
4. *You are very stupid.*
   You are being very stupid.
5. *Tell me when he comes.*
   Tell me when he will come.
6. *A new cinema is being built there.*
   A new cinema has been built there.
7. *Last year he wrote a book.*
   Last year he was writing a book.
8. *He is always going to Paris.*
   He always goes to Paris.
9. *My car always breaks down.*
   My car is always breaking down.
10. *Have you seen that film?*
    Did you see that film?
11. *I shall go to Paris next month.*
    I will go to Paris next month.

c. Give the opposite of:
1. profound. [superficial] 2. deep. [shallow] 3. bigoted. [tolerant]
4. a *plain* tie: [patterned] 5. hand-made : [machine made] 6. manufactured goods: [natural]
   [demobilized]
7. to be called up. [rookie / raw recruit] 8. to embark. [disembark] 9. ready-made: [tailor-made]
10. free will : [compulsion] 11. a *busy* day. [slack] 12. to infuriate. [calm]
13. a *veteran* soldier. 14. contempt. [esteem] 15. apathetic. [concern / interest]
16. to follow. [turn away / lead] 17. a misanthropist. [philanthropist] 18. fictitious: [true]
19. to bequeath. [inherit] 20. to repel. [enact] 21. to smile. [scowl]
22. religious. 23. *densely* populated: [sparsely populated] 24. a *slack* rope. [taut rope]
25. to forgive : 26. a *strict* teacher. 27. respectable
28. inflammable. [non-inflammable] 29. cautious. [incautious / rash] 30. a *sentimental* [unsentimental] person.

Dare

1. In an affirmative sentence *dare* is always used as a principal verb and is therefore used with *to* before the infinitive.
He dares to say that, does he?
2. In questions and negatives, however, in the present simple tense, *dare* can be used either as a principal or an auxiliary verb, without any change of meaning. If it is a principal verb it is (like almost all other principal verbs) used with *do* and followed by *to* before the infinitive. If it is an auxiliary verb it is (like other auxiliary verbs) used without *do* and without *s* in the third person singular, and without *to* before the infinitive.

Does he dare to do it? (principal)
Dare he do it? (auxiliary)
He doesn't dare to do it (principal)
He daren't do it (auxiliary)
3. *I dared him to jump over the ditch.* (The meaning is: *I challenged him to jump over it.*)
4. *I did it for a dare.* (The meaning is: *...because I had been challenged to do it.*)
5. *I daresay you know this already.* (This exists only in the first person singular and means *I expect.*)

Decide

1. *I decided on Paris for my holiday.* (Note the preposition.)
2. *I decided against Paris for my holiday.* (Note the preposition. The meaning is: *I decided not to go.*)
3. *I decided on going to Paris for my holiday.* (The same preposition as in 1 before a gerund.)
4. *I decided against going to Paris for my holiday.* (The same preposition as in 2 before a gerund.)
5. *I decided the matter then.* (No preposition before an ordinary noun, the direct object.)
6. *I decided to go to Paris then.* (No preposition here. *To* only indicates the infinitive. This is an alternative construction to 3.)
7. *I decided how to do it.* (Infinitive phrase.)
8. *I decided that I would go to Paris.* (The clause is an alternative to 3 and 6.)

Enjoy

1. *He enjoyed that party.* (No preposition before an ordinary noun.)
2. *He enjoyed going to that party.* (No preposition before a gerundive noun.)
3. *He enjoyed himself at that party.* (The reflexive use.)

Excuse

1. *Please excuse my lateness.* (No preposition before an ordinary noun.)
2. *Please excuse my being late.* (No preposition before a gerundive noun.)
3. *Please excuse me for my lateness.* (An alternative to 1. Note the preposition.)
4. *Please excuse me for being late.* (An alternative to 2. The same preposition is used before a gerundive noun.)
5. *There is no excuse for such behaviour.* (The same preposition after the noun *excuse.)*

Explain

1. *I explained the construction to him.* (No preposition before the direct object, *to* before the indirect object.)
2. *I couldn't explain being found on the premises.* (No preposition before a gerundive noun. The meaning is: *I could not satisfactorily explain why I was in the building.)*
3. *I explained (to him) how to do it.* (Infinitive phrase.)
4. *Please explain why you did that.* (Clause.)
5. *He explained that he had been taken ill.* (Clause.)
6. *Please explain yourself.* (The reflexive use. The meaning is: *Please make your meaning clear.)*

Expect

1. *She expected a letter this morning.* (No preposition before an ordinary noun.)
2. *She expected to get a letter this morning.* (No preposition before a verb. *To* only indicates the infinitive.)
3. *She expected me to get a letter.* (The object and infinitive.)
4. *She expected that I would get a letter.* (Clause. An alternative to 3.)
5. *Your expectations of coming into a lot of money have not been fulfilled.* (The noun *expectations* is followed by *of* and the gerund. This is

the most usual construction after nouns. For a list of some of the commonest nouns followed by *of* and the gerund see pages 79-80.)

6. *That film did not come up to my expectations.* (An idiom. The meaning is: *That film was not as good as I expected it to be.*)

7. *I expect so: I expect not.*

Fancy

This verb has two quite distinct meanings—*to like* and *to think*. In the meaning of *like:*

1. *I don't fancy the prospect of a night in the open.* (No preposition before an ordinary noun.)

2. *I don't fancy spending the night in the open.* (No preposition before a gerundive noun.)

3. *I don't fancy your spending the night in the open.* (A different person is doing the action of the gerund from the subject of the sentence.)

4. *She rather fancies herself.* (Reflexive use. The meaning is: *She has a very high opinion of herself.*)

5. *I took a fancy to him at once.* (A colloquial idiom. The meaning is: *I liked him immediately.*)

In the meaning of *think:*

6. *I fancy that he is clever.* (Clause.)

7. *I fancy him to be clever.* (This is the Latin accusative and infinitive construction, which is rather literary in English. In this case it is better not to omit the infinitive.)

Find

1. *I found the course of study (to be) difficult.* (No preposition before an ordinary noun. This is the same construction as the last one with *fancy*, but here it is much commoner to omit the infinitive.)

2. *I found learning Latin difficult.* (No preposition before a gerundive noun.)

3. *I found his learning Latin inexplicable.* (A different person is finding and learning.)

4. *I found it difficult to learn Latin./learning Latin.* (This is an alternative to 2. The infinitive construction is the commoner of the two. The *it* is a kind of extra or pleonastic object preceding the real object, which is the infinitive or gerund. For a fuller explanation of the use of *it*, see page 73.)

5. *I found that he was wrong.* (Clause.)

6. *I found out how to do it.* (Note the preposition before the infinitive phrase.)

7. *The findings of the court have not been made public.* (The meaning is: *The results of the court enquiry...*)

Forget

1. *I forgot that appointment.* (No preposition before an ordinary noun.)
2. *I forgot to keep that appointment.* (No preposition before the verb. *To* is only a sign of the infinitive.)
3. *I shall never forget seeing that film.* (No preposition before the gerund. The gerund is only used after *forget* to indicate that something made an indelible impression on your mind.)
4. *I forgot that I had to keep that appointment.* (Clause as an alternative to 2.)
5. *I forget now why I did it.* (Clause.)
6. *I forgot how to do it.* (Infinitive phrase.)

Get

1. *I got him to do it for me.* (This is the causative use of *get* and is commoner than the alternative construction with *have (I had him do it for me).* The meaning is: *I asked him to do it for me.)*
2. *I got it done yesterday.* (This is also the causative use of *get* but with the passive construction. The alternative with *have (I had it done yesterday)* is equally common with the passive construction. See also *have* page 39 and the exercise on this construction, pages 148 and 149.)
3. *He got drowned trying to swim these straits.* (This is a form of the passive that is most commonly used in the case of misfortune, i.e. *he got robbed, he got sacked (dismissed), he got told off, etc.*)
4. *Get moving: get cracking: get going.* (This is a form of the imperative and is the only occasion when *get* is followed by the gerund. It is colloquial. *Get cracking* is slang.)
5. *I got to know her at John's party.* (The meaning is: *I made her acquaintance there.* It is important to remember that *to know* in English is only a verb of state, never a verb of action, so that *get to know* will often be necessary to translate *know* in, for example, Romance languages.)
N.B. When not used in the above mentioned constructions *get* has five principal meanings:

a. *to receive*   *I didn't get a letter this morning.*
b. *to become*   *He's getting quite old now.*
c. *to fetch*   *Go and get a doctor quickly.*
d. *to buy*   *I got it at the Antique Fair.*
e. *to arrive*   *I got here late this morning.*

EXERCISES

a. Do what is necessary to the verbs in brackets. They will be in the infinitive or present participle. It may be necessary for you to add prepositions or put the possessive adjective before the gerund.

1. *Why don't you concentrate (learn) these? They are very important.*
2. *It was rash of you not to allow (miss) the train.*
3. *His mother doesn't fancy (he marry) a girl of such a different background.*
4. *I shall never forget (go) abroad for the first time.*
5. *He could not explain (be) found in possession of the stolen articles.*
6. *She looked for him everywhere and eventually found him (sleep) in the shade of some bushes.*
7. *She agreed (institute) divorce proceedings.*
8. *What a pity that you forgot (meet) me yesterday as arranged.*
9. *Why do you always expect (I take) an interest in your love-affairs?*
10. *Queen Victoria did not allow (smoke) in her presence; she only allowed her son (smoke) if he lay on the floor with his head in the fireplace.*
11. *You must get (go) if you want to catch that train.*
12. *I found (she be) a very superficial person.*
13. *Why won't you consider (share) a flat with me?*
14. *Would you advise (I book) accommodation in advance?*
15. *I do hope you will excuse (I be) so late; I am dreadfully sorry.*
16. *A lot of people do not believe (teach) formal grammar; I do not agree with them.*
17. *I tried to make allowances (she be) young and inexperienced; nonetheless her inefficiency in running the house irritated me.*
18. *Some boys enjoy (live) in a community at boarding school, but others hate it.*
19. *Your expectations (pass) the examination have not, unfortunately, been fulfilled.*
20. *I thought you liked Paris. What made you decide (go) there this year?*
21. *I dared (he walk) down Piccadilly in a sack.*
22. *They agree (want) a change of government, but do not fancy (have) a socialist government.*
23. *I apologised (mislead) them.*
24. *Would you consider Shakespeare (be) the greatest European dramatist?*
25. *She asked (I buy) some fruit on the way home.*
26. *I advised him (go) to Spain last week: it is much too hot at this time of year.*

b. Choose the right word(s) from those in brackets, and use the words that are wrong in these contexts in sentences of your own.
1. *When he was absent from work, his employers (deduced, subtracted, deducted) three days' wages from his pay (packet, parcel, pocket).*
2. *There is a lot of excitement in the Bennett family in* Pride and Prejudice *when two (illegible, illegal, elected, eligible) bachelors take a house in the vicinity.*
3. *As it was a (delightful, delicious, lovely) spring day we (could, were able to) (go for, go on, take) a walk.*

4. *I am afraid the results of the X-ray examination are quite (undecided, indecisive, inconclusive, unfinished, irresolute).*
5. *Generally it is a skin (disease, decease) that is (infectious, contagious, contiguous, intangible).*
6. *That pupil has worked very (indigently, diligently, conscientiously) (all over, throughout) his time at the school.*
7. *Some children are absolutely (inexhaustible, indefatigable).*
8. *The Council have decided not to (destroy, abolish, pull down, do away with, demolish) that lovely old house but to (restore, rebuild, renew, repair) it to its former glory.*
9. *He sat there (cackling, chuckling, clucking, chucking) to himself.*
10. *The sun was (glimmering, sparkling, glinting, glistening) on the lake.*

c. Certain groups of words are naturally used together. Insert the right verbs in the following sentences. In certain cases more than one is possible. In that case put the alternatives.
1. *That letter has certainly …… my mind at rest.*
2. *Witnesses must …… evidence on oath.*
3. *It is advisable to …… precautions against burglars. Have you …… out an insurance policy?*
4. *The Prime Minister …… tribute to his late colleague's devotion to duty.*
5. *I tried hard to …… the taxi-driver's attention.*
6. *Usually the English are not good at …… compliments.*
7. *I hope you are …… steps to …… the matter right.*
8. *He …… a vote of censure on the Government.*
9. *If I …… orders I naturally expect them to be …… out by my subordinates.*
10. *Christ …… pity on the cripple and healed him.*
11. *Wolsey …… into disgrace in the end, but he had had a good run for his money.*
12. *Shakespeare …… a curse on anyone who might move his remains from Stratford.*
13. *May I …… you company as far as the end of the road?*
14. *Unfortunately that Company …… bankrupt last year.*
15. *If you insist on behaving like that you must be prepared to …… the consequences.*
16. *He swore to …… his revenge on me for making him suffer so much.*
17. *I hear you are …… for Parliament in the next election! Good luck to you!*
18. *That was a dirty trick to …… on your wife.*
19. *Please don't …… offence at what I am saying*
20. *It …… me great pleasure to announce my daughter's engagement to Mr Peter Magnus.*
21. *I can't …… a football pool; I don't know how to …… one in!*
22. *Did that candidate …… a good impression on you?*

23. *I ...... call on Aunt Jane in the hope of ...... on her to lend me £5.*
24. *I wish you would tell me why you ...... a grievance against me.*
25. *To everyone's surprise the jury ...... in a verdict of not guilty.*

5: Conditionals

It must be remembered that in any kind of conditional sentence the continuous tense must be used for an action in the middle of happening. There are basically four kinds of conditional sentences in English and the combination of tenses in each group is of the greatest importance. Normally the barriers between the four kinds cannot be crossed. Composite conditionals are only possible when quite different circumstances apply to each half. For example: *I apologise if I was snoring just now.* The snoring and the apology are not simultaneous.

Combinations of tenses in conditional sentences (What is sometimes called the basic type is written in capital letters.)

1. Present conditionals which are quite possible or probable: completely open conditions.

present		**imperative**
or	with	**future**
present		or
perfect		**present**

If you are enjoying the party, don't go home yet.
If you see him, give him this.
If you call him, he comes.
IF HE COMES, I SHALL BE SURPRISED.
If you have been there, you will not need a guide.
If you have been living here for twenty years, I expect you have a wide circle of friends.
If that cinema is finished next month, I shall be surprised.
If you have done your homework, give it to me.

2. Present conditionals which are possible but very improbable.

simple past		**present conditional**
or	with	or
past continuous		**simple past**

IF HE CAME NOW, I SHOULD BE SURPRISED.

If he was snoring, he wouldn't realise it.
If I was hurrying, I shouldn't notice anyone in a crowd.
If that crime was committed by my brother, I should be amazed.

3. Conditionals which refer to the present but which are impossible or unfulfilled. They are mere hypotheses.

subjunctive   **present conditional**
of 'be'   with
IF I WERE YOU, I WOULD NOT DO THAT.
IF LONDON WERE SMALLER, IT WOULD BE NICER.
If he were intelligent, he wouldn't be always getting into debt.
If I were rich, I would be lying in the sun on some tropical island.
If that food were eaten, it would cause intense discomfort.

4. Past conditionals. These are also mere hypotheses, but they refer to what might have happened in the past but did not, in fact, happen.

past perfect with   **past conditional**
IF HE HAD COME YESTERDAY, I SHOULD HAVE BEEN SUR-PRISED.
If he had been working when I went to see him last week, I shouldn't have disturbed him.
If I had known the truth of the matter sooner, I would not have been talking like that.
If Napoleon had not been born, European history would have been very different.
If the matter had been settled before I arrived, I should have been very angry.

EXERCISES

a. Put the verb in brackets into the right tense.
1. *Go and tell him that if he (make) a nuisance of himself he must stop it.*
2. *If I (have) enough money I (spend) three months in the south of France next summer.*
3. *If he (ask) you for the money yesterday, what you (say)?*
4. *If you (finish) doing this test, give it to me to mark.*
5. *If she (be) better dressed she would be more popular.*
6. *It (not be) funny if you (see) him last week?*
7. *If you (be) to Paris, do tell me about it.*
8. *If I (see) him next week I (tell) him what you said.*
9. *If I (listen) to that symphony concert on the radio last night I certainly (not hear) you knock.*
10. *If he (tell) me that last week I (be) saved a lot of trouble.*

b. Complete the following:
1. *If you were in my place ......*

2. *Will you lend me £5 if* ᴵ.ᵗʰⁱⁿᵏ ʸᵒᵘ ?
3. *...... would you have paid the bill?*
4. *I should have had my photograph taken if ......*
5. *Surely if you ...... he would understand.*
6. *If he had told you everything ......*
7. *If you have finished with that book ......*
8. *Would you have told him the truth if ......?*
9. *I should not like to be in his shoes if ......?*
10. *Wouldn't it have been extraordinary if ......*
11. *If I were Prime Minister ......*
12. *If you ...... it last week ......*
13. *If he ...... that he deserved whatever came to him.*
14. *...... if she were rich?*
15. *If William the Conqueror ......*
16. *If you have been gardening all day ......*
17. *Tell me something of prison life if ......*
18. *Would European thought now be different if Rousseau ......?*
19. *I shall not be at all surprised if ......*
20. *If I have offended you ......*

Additional points about conditional sentences.

1. In *polite requests only* the present conditional or, less formally, the future can be used in both halves of the sentence. The conditional in both halves is especially common in business letters.
I should be grateful if you would send me your estimate as soon as possible.
I should appreciate it if you would put the matter in hand at your earliest convenience.
I will carry in the tea things if you will bring the teapot.

2. *Should* and *were to* are used in conditional sentences in all persons to suggest extreme improbability. *Were to* can be used only with a verb suggesting action, not state.
If he should arrive after supper, please show him to his room.
If you should not have been satisfied with the meal, kindly inform the manager at once.
If he were to ask you for the money tomorrow, whatever would you do?
N.B. *Were to* could not be used in the second example, because it is state, not action.

3. In past conditionals and those with *should* or *were to, if* can be omitted if an inversion is used instead.
If he had come/Had he come I would have given him a black eye.
If you should wish/Should you wish to complain, the address of the manufacturers is on the packet.

If I had known/Had I known the real situation I would have acted differently.

4. Past conditionals are sometimes avoided by using *but for*.
If he had not plunged in to save me/But for his plunging in to save me I should have been drowned.
If I had not helped you/But for my help you would never have done it.

5. Several other auxiliary verbs besides *would* are used to suggest nuances of uncertainty.
If she were rich he might marry her.
He could have got there on time if he had had a bicycle.
He should/ought to have got it right if he had had it explained to him.
You need not have made that mistake if you had thought a bit more about it.
Mightn't he have risked imprisonment if he had done that?
Mustn't he have been a fool if he talked to a policeman like that?

6. The infinitive can be used to replace one half of a conditional sentence.
I shouldn't be surprised if he came/to see him.
Wouldn't you have been frightened if you found yourself in such a situation?/to find yourself in such a situation?
Mustn't he have been a fool if he did that?/to do that?

7. Other words besides *if* can be used in conditional sentences. The commonest are: *unless (= if not), on condition that, provided that, supposing* and *as long as*.
Unless you work harder you will get the sack.
He agreed to do it on condition that he got paid in advance.
As long as you let me know when you will arrive, I will come and meet you.
Supposing he had asked you for the money immediately, what would you have done?
Provided that she were sincere with me, I should forgive her a lot.

EXERCISES

a. Put the verbs in brackets into the right tense.
1. *I will hold the ladder if you (try) to reach the cat.*
2. *If someone were to leave me £5,000 I (be) able to fulfil my lifelong ambition.*
3. *Don't you think you ought to have done it if he (ask) you to?*
4. *If you (see) my puppy anywhere, please tell me.*
5. *You (be) amused if he had impersonated Mr Churchill.*
6. *If I (offend) you, I do apologise.*
7. *If she were to marry him, what (be) your reaction?*

8. *I should be grateful if you (raise) the matter with the Managing Director.*

9. *Mightn't he have fallen if he (try) to climb over the roof to the sky-light?*

10. *If it (not snow) I will go for a brisk walk.*

11. *He would not agree to it unless I (be) prepared to make considerable concessions.*

12. *Provided that she (tell) me, I wouldn't have minded.*

b. Substitute another construction for the part of the sentence that is italicised.

1. You would have been annoyed *if you had seen* how he reacted.

2. *If you had not sprung* to my defence, I should have been overpowered.

3. *If they had not been really stuck* for someone to do it, I would never have volunteered.

4. My wife would have been shocked *if she had seen* how her children behaved at that party.

5. *If he had not had a* very strong constitution, that operation would have killed him

6. The fire would have gutted the house completely *if I had not lived* almost next door to the Fire Station.

7. *If he had not made* a complete confession of his crime no-one would have suspected him.

8. I should have been thunderstruck *if I had received* such a message.

9. *If the Government had not intervened promptly*, chaos would have ensued.

c. Use the following words in sentences so as to bring out their meaning clearly:

to gleam	faction	statue	to glare at
to glow	fraction	status	to stare at
to shimmer	fracture	statute	to gaze at
to glint	friction	stature	to peep at
to glimmer	fiction	stratum	to peer at
to glitter		state	to glance at
			to glimpse

d. Choose the correct idiomatic words from those in brackets at the end of the sentence.

1. *For the first time in my life I really ...... him napping. (found, caught, observed) (colloquial)*

2. *Things have come to a ...... pass when he insults his wife in public. (strange, bad, pretty) (colloquial)*

3. *I am amazed at people who think that any political party will offer them the ...... for all evils. (panacea, cure, answer)*

4. *I am delighted that such a ...... of virtue should have been shown to have normal human weaknesses. (example, paragon, epitome)*

5. *I decided to* ...... *his tongue with the help of a little alcohol. (grease, loose, loosen)*

6. *We are surprised that such a well-known author should use such a* ...... *phrase. (hackneyed, usual, cliché)*

7. *Modern writers are not afraid of calling a* ...... *a* ...... *(thing, fact, spade) (colloquial)*

8. *I resorted to a little judicious flattery before* ...... *the subject of a possible loan. (broaching, breaching, opening)*

9. *It was only when the figure vanished into* ...... *air that I realised it was a ghost. (blue, dim, thin)*

10. *The famous man is now 95 and sinking into his* ...... *(senility, dotage, decline)*

11. *As there were no* ...... *circumstances the criminal was given the maximum sentence. (extenuating, excusing, pardonable)*

12. *I was feeling quite ill but I am as right as* ...... *now. (possible, usual, rain)*

13. *She was* ...... *her brains to remember the man's name. (racking, beating, exhausting)*

14. *Many political problems are so complicated that the layman cannot see the wood for the* ...... *(hills, trees, confusion)*

15. *Criminals generally think of an* ...... *before committing a crime. (alibi, alias, answer)*

16. *Once you have finished painting the ceiling of a room the rest is* ...... *sailing. (easy, straightforward, plain)*

17. *You needn't worry about him. He knows which side his bread is* ...... *(toasted, baked, buttered) (colloquial)*

18. *Don't you think you have been sitting on the* ...... *long enough? (wall, fence, chair) It is time you* ...... *down on one side or the other. (jumped, came, plunged)*

19. *Burglars are liable to* ...... *up rough if they are disturbed. (cut, finish, limber) (slang)*

20. *Policemen on* ...... *duty control traffic at crossroads. (beat, point, ordinary)*

6: The constructions with basic verbs H−I

Hate

1. *She hates the theatre.* (No preposition before an ordinary noun.)
2. *She hates going to the theatre.* (No preposition before a gerundive noun. This indicates general taste.)
3. *She would hate to see that play.* (This refers to one particular occasion only.)
4. *She hates my going to the theatre.* (The same construction as in 2, but a different person *hating* and *going.)*
5. *She hates me to go to the theatre.* (A commoner alternative to 4.)
6. *She hates it if I go to the theatre.* (Another alternative to 4 and 5. Here we have the extra or pleonastic *it* which we saw in *find* 4, followed by a clause.)
7. *She has a hatred of cruelty.* (Note the preposition after the noun *hatred*.)
8. *She has a hatred of being criticised.* (The same proposition as in 7 before a gerundive noun.)

Have

1. *He has to do it.* (The meaning is: *It is compulsory.*)
2. *He does not have to do it.* (It is voluntary.)
3. *He has not got to do it.* (An alternative to 2 that is very common in speaking but not considered good style in writing.)
4. *He had it done yesterday.* (The causative use of *have*. The same as *get* 2.)
5. *He had his leg broken playing football.* (He was the victim of an unfortunate accident. This is similar in use to *get* 3 but different in construction in that there is a direct object between *had* and the past participle.)
6. *You had better make a full confession.* (Note that there is no *to* before the infinitive, and note also that this is a present tense. In this meaning *(It would be better if you made a full confession) had better* is invariable.)
7. *I cannot have you behave like that.* (Note that again there is no *to* before the infinitive. The meaning is: *I cannot allow you to behave like that.*)
8. *I cannot have you behaving like that.* (A common alternative to 7.)
9. *Have* is very often used with nouns formed from verbs.
e.g. *to have a swim, to have a try, to have a rest, to have a sit down, to have a walk, to have a sleep, to have a go at it.* (The last expression means *to try to do it.*)

10. *Have* is used as a principal verb and therefore is conjugated with *do* in negatives and questions:

a. In its causative sense:

I didn't have my house painted last year.

Did you have your photograph taken yesterday?

b. If used for habit:

Do you have a clean shirt every day?

Do you have time to answer questions at the end of your lessons?

c. Whenever it is really used as a substitute for some other verb.

Did you have (= eat) a large breakfast?

I won't have (= allow) that kind of behaviour.

11. *Have* is, therefore, used as an auxiliary verb in its literal meaning, when it refers to one occasion and for something permanent.

Has he a nice flat?

He hasn't a chance of passing the examination.

I haven't a clean handkerchief on me today.

Help

1. *I helped that man.* (No preposition before a noun.)

2. *I helped to do it.* (No preposition before a verb. *To* merely indicates the infinitive.)

3. *I helped that man to do it.* (A combination of the two previous constructions.)

4. *I helped that man with his work.* (Note the preposition which is used only before an ordinary noun and not before a gerund.)

5. *I helped that man by lending him some money.* (*By* and the gerund here, as usually, indicates the method(s) used. See pages 87 and 88.)

6. *I can't help laughing to think of it.* (*Can't help* is always followed by the gerund.)

7. *Help yourself to some more tea.* (The reflexive use. Note also the preposition.)

8. *You have been of great help to me.* (Note the preposition.)

9. *There is no help for it.* (Note the preposition. The meaning is: *It is unavoidable.*)

10. *Thank you for your help in making the party a success.* (Note the preposition used here to pinpoint the nature of the help.)

11. *Don't be longer than you can help.* (An idiom meaning:...*than is strictly necessary.*)

12. *Don't give me a large helping, please.* (The meaning is: *portion of food.*)

Hope

1. *He hopes to do that.* (The infinitive.)

2. *He hopes that he will be able to do that.* (A clause as an alternative to 1.)
3. *There is little hope of success.* (Note the preposition after the noun *hope.*)
4. *There is little hope of (his) succeeding.* (The same preposition before a gerundive noun.)
5. *I hope so: I hope not.*

Imagine

1. *I imagined the whole thing.* (No preposition before an ordinary noun.)
2. *I imagined living in Russia.* (No preposition before a gerundive noun.)
3. *I cannot imagine your living in Russia.* (A different person is *imagining* and *living.*)
4. *I imagined that I was living in Russia.* (A clause used as an alternative to 2.)
5. *I imagined myself to be living in Russia.* (The Latin accusative and infinitive construction. This is a rather literary alternative to 2 and 4.)
6. *I cannot imagine why you want to live there.* (A clause).
7. *I imagine so: I imagine not.*
8. *I cannot imagine how to do it, etc.* (Infinitive phrase.)

Intend

1. *I don't intend to do it/doing it.*
(There is a free choice between the infinitive and gerund, which is quite rare in English.)
2. *I don't intend her to do it.* (The object and infinitive construction.)
3. *I have no intention of doing it.* (Note the preposition used before the gerund after the noun *intention.*)
4. *That gift was intended for you.* (Note the preposition.)

Interest

1. *I interested him in philosophy.* (No preposition before the personal pronoun. Note the use of *in.*)
2. *I am interested to learn of your success.* (No preposition before the infinitive. This is used when you are talking about something that interests you on one particular occasion.)
3. *I am interested in studying philosophy.* (The same preposition as in 1. This is used when you are talking about something that always interests you.)

4. *The man took no interest in philosophy.* (Note that the same preposition is used after the noun *interest.*)
5. *That is of great interest to me personally.* (Note the preposition.)

EXERCISES

a. Rewrite the following with the passive form of the causative use of *have* or *get:*
e.g. *I had someone to do it.* (Active)
　　I had it done. (Passive)
　　I got it done. (Passive)
1. *I must get someone to take my photograph.*
2. *Get a chambermaid to bring your breakfast in bed.*
3. *He told me he was getting someone to paint his portrait.*
4. *It is time you got someone to repaint your house.*
5. *Unfortunately someone burgled his house while he was away on holiday.*
6. *Why don't you get the butcher to deliver your meat every day?*
7. *He does not have anyone to clean his flat for him.*
8. *I advised him to get his tailor to make him a new suit.*
9. *I have broken this valuable vase. Do you think I can get someone to repair it for me?*
10. *Someone picked my pocket during the rush hour yesterday.*
11. *He is getting a well-known firm of landscape gardeners to lay out his new garden.*
12. *The lights have fused. We must get someone to put them right.*
13. *The police searched his pockets at the police station.*
14. *I hear that some publishers have recently brought out his new book.*
15. *The escaped prisoner got someone to dye his hair for him.*
16. *It is time we got someone to decorate this room.*
17. *Someone knocked his hat off in the skirmish.*
18. *I must find someone to let out this jacket.*
19. *It is advisable to get some Company to insure the contents of your flat.*
20. *His motor-car was completely wrecked in that accident.*

b. Do what is necessary to the words in brackets adding prepositions if necessary:
1. *What a pity you hate (swim). It is a lovely day for a swim.*
2. *I am not in the least interested (watch) football matches.*
3. *There is little hope (she change) her mind.*
4. *She has little intention (follow) my advice.*
5. *You had better (leave) before I throw you out!*
6. *I cannot have you (idle) about all day.*
7. *I don't intend my wife (know) anything about that weekend.*
8. *Most people hate (be) made to look small.*
9. *Thank you for your help (clean) up the place.*

10. *She can't help (laugh) whenever I try to speak French.*
11. *The children did not help me (get) on (get) under my feet all the time.*
12. *I cannot imagine what (do) in this dreadful situation.*
13. *He took little interest (educate) his children.*
14. *She is hoping (go) abroad next year.*
15. *He had better (not say) such a thing here.*

c. Choose the right word(s) from those in brackets and use those that are wrong in this context in sentences of your own.
1. *His single-mindedness has proved a (priceless, invaluable, valueless) (asset, assert, ascent).*
2. *His wife has no children because she is (sterile, barren, impregnable, infertile).*
3. *Everyone was stirred by his (impassioned, passionate) speech.*
4. *Many people (regard, look at, consider) a television set as a(n) (fundamental, indispensable) article of furniture.*
5. *The novel I bought the other day is (illiterate, illegible, illegal, unreadable, illicit).*
6. *Many people, especially men, are keenly interested in (actual, current, topical, nowadays) affairs.*
7. *The shock of that moment made an (indelible, inedible, lasting, ever-lasting) impression on my mind.*
8. *You must choose the best man (irrespective, unresponsive, disrespectful, regardless, heedless) of his political (affinities, affiliations).*
9. *That is an (iniquitous, ubiquitous, injurious) law that should be done away with.*
10. *That kind of diet is very (injurious, harmful, unwholesome, inordinate) to the health.*

7: Points to remember about using the passive in English

1. The passive is used when the action is more important than the person who does it. Consequently *by* and the agent are put in only when they are absolutely necessary to the meaning.
English is spoken here.
A new block of flats has been built here.
Another cinema was closed last week.
That book was written by Dickens.
(There is no meaning without the agent in the last sentence.)

2. Following from the dominance of the action over the person who does it is the common use of the gerund (and sometimes the infinitive) with a passive meaning as a way of entirely suppressing the doer of the action. This may lead to the sentence ending with a preposition, but prepositions have changed their use so much since the days of the Roman Empire that there is now no objection in English to a preposition at the end.

That photograph wants touching up.
She enjoys being admired.
She is not looking forward to being operated on.
There was nothing whatever to see.
I don't like being read to.
The matter needs looking into.
He is tired of being sponged on.
Some people object to being called up.
He left without being noticed.
I do not see anything to make a fuss about.
There is something to admire in him.
She loves being flirted with.
Most politicians cannot bear being laughed at.
Few people like being ignored.
It is silly to take exception to being found fault with.

N.B. It should be noted that the gerund always replaces the passive infinitive after *need, want, require* and *deserve*, all verbs that are followed by the infinitive in an active sense.

The matter requires going into.
My shoes want cleaning.
His advice deserves acting on.
This room needs decorating.

It should further be noted that the infinitive in this kind of sentence can only be used after pronouns like *nothing, anything, something, someone, etc.* Furthermore, the passive infinitive is sometimes used after these, where an active infinitive is employed in German, French, Italian, etc. Sometimes the meaning will be different if the wrong from is used.

Music is to be enjoyed.
There was nothing to be seen.
Nobody is to blame/to be blamed for that.
There is something to be said for that.
There is nothing to do. (i.e. *No entertainments are provided.*)
There is nothing to be done. (i.e. *It is too late now; what has been done cannot be undone.*)

3. Some verbs which are really passive in meaning have an active form in English.

This soup tastes nice.
Those new houses are selling well.
That material wears well.

4. If there are two objects in the active, a personal indirect object and a thing direct object, the personal indirect object always becomes the subject of the passive unless any special emphasis is required.

They gave me that vase.
I was given that vase.
He sent her a present.
She was sent a present.
They offered my uncle a job.
My uncle was offered a job.
but: *That vase was given to me not to you; I want it back at once.* (Special emphasis)

5. Verbs followed necessarily by prepositions or compound verbs (sometimes called 'verbs followed by adverbial particles') can be used in the passive, on condition that the preposition is left in. This is because the verb and preposition are considered as one idea and, in fact, often replace a simple verb.

Subject	Verb	Object
active		
The robbers	attacked/set upon	the travellers
Fifty students	passed/succeeded in	the examination
The men	noticed/looked at	the pretty girl
The Town Council	have abolished/have done away with	trams
They	have cancelled/taken off	that train

Subject	Verb	Agent
passive		
The travellers	were attacked/were set upon	by the robbers
The examination	was passed/was succeeded in	by fifty students
The pretty girl	was noticed/was looked at	by the men
Trams	have been abolished/have been done away with	by the Town Council
That train	has been cancelled/has been taken off	(by them)

6. Remember from the pattern of tenses that the present continuous and the past continuous exist in the passive and are used just the same as in the active: for an action *in the middle of happening*.

They are now building a new cinema there.
A new cinema is now being built there.
Dinners are now being served.
What tune were they playing as we came in?
What tune was being played as we came in?
I assure you that your complaint is being investigated.

7. It is permissible and quite common to put adverbs rather earlier in the passive than in the active. This is not, however, compulsory.
They fed the soldiers very well.
The soldiers were very well fed.
She played that piece beautifully.
That piece was beautifully played.

EXERCISES

a. Put into the passive.
1. *His grandfather left him about £10,000.*
2. *The hooligans set upon the old man and beat him up.*
3. *She doesn't like it if people criticise her.*
4. *They have done away with trams in England.*
5. *I do not think the police are doing anything about it.*
6. *They were giving a concert in that hall when a large piece of plaster fell down from the ceiling. It injured about fifty people seriously enough for the ambulance men to take them to hospital.*
7. *I gave him a cheque for the amount required.*
8. *The magistrate let him off with a severe reprimand.*
9. *They had evacuated Chichester Cathedral before the spire collapsed, so it did not hurt anyone.*
10. *They look after you very well in that hotel.*
11. *The police eventually gave up the search for the missing man.*
12. *Some girls love it if men pay them compliments.*
13. *Someone gave me this fountain-pen for Christmas.*
14. *Everyone was listening to the news bulletin with avid interest.*
15. *They told him curtly to go away.*
16. *Someone sent my sister a Valentine card last week.*
17. *Some people object if others make them work hard.*
18. *Have you paid for that television set yet?*
19. *I hate it when people make fun of me, though I don't mind it if they tease me.*
20. *My sister's fiancé is cooking dinner tonight. It smells all right anyway.*

b. Put in the right verbs
1. *That film ...... short of my expectations.*
2. *He ...... up courage to ask for a rise.*
3. *I shall certainly ...... you to that promise.*
4. *The charwoman soon ..... the room to rights.*
5. *The Government has not felt ..... upon to ...... any action yet.*
6. *My curiosity was ...... by what I had glimpsed and I could not ...... myself away until it had been ......*
7. *He is ...... trial on the charge of embezzlement.*
8. *Richard I was ...... to ransom by the Duke of Austria.*

9. *If my wife has found out everything I had better go back home and ...... the music.*
10. *Never ...... into the temptation of underestimating your opponent.*
11. *If one has not much money one must ...... do and .....*
12. *Perhaps it is a good thing to ...... absurdities up to ridicule.*
13. *Fearing a shortage of sugar she ...... in a good stock of it.*
14. *You cannot ...... wrong if you ...... the instructions on the packet.*
15. *He is ...... up a plan to ...... London's traffic problems.*
16. *I feel that I ...... you an apology for my rudeness the other night.*
17. *It is becoming much less common than it used to be for children to ...... in their father's footsteps.*
18. *Children may have certain obligations to ...... to their parents.*
19. *What a shock to hear that he had ...... suicide! Who was asked to ...... the news to his wife?*
20. *I can't ...... out much hope of your getting that job.*
21. *The police ...... a trap for the blackmailer.*
22. *We ...... our destination in good time.*
23. *I wonder what proportion of people ...... their ambition in life.*
24. *'If you have ...... your bed you must ...... on it.'*
25. *She ...... me to task about the state of my flat.*
26. *Tell me where you ...... his acquaintance.*
27. *You are ...... disaster by behaving like that.*
28. *Did you have any difficulty in ...... admittance?*
29. *The French monarchy was temporarily ...... in the revolution of 1789.*
30. *Don't ...... your own trumpet!*

c. Put the verbs in brackets into the right tense.
1. *This meat (cook) for nearly two hours: it should be tender by now.*
2. *As he (cross) the narrow bridge he suddenly (feel) dizzy and (fall) into the water. Its coldness (revive) him and he (splash) about trying to reach the bank when a passer-by (glimpse) him, (dive) in and (pull) him out. I think he (drown) if nobody (be) about.*
3. *Look! There is a whole crowd of people over there. Go and see what (be) sold and if it (be) a bargain, buy it.*
4. *His wife (always nag) him these days but fortunately he is good at shutting out unwanted noise, so he (not hear) a single word of her tirades!*
5. *I (be) brought to an ancient chateau and when the lights (fail) and I (be) alone in a vast room with only one guttering candle I (not be) at all surprised to see a ghost at any moment. The fact, however, that the French (not believe) in ghosts (reassure) me a little.*
6. *In two years' time you (work) here for ten years. I (never know) you stay in the same job for so long.*
7. *As soon as you (wash) up the dinner things you can go home.*
8. *(You be) surprised if I (arrive) yesterday without letting you know I (come)?*
9. *Yesterday she (promise) to leave me in peace for the whole after-*

noon, but I (not work) more than ten minutes before she (burst) in to say that she (pick) up a valuable Chinese vase to dust it, (drop) it and (break) it into smithereens.
10. *What on earth (you do)? You are covered with mud from head to foot.*

d. Use the following words in sentences so as to bring out their meaning clearly.

blunder	*except*	*goal*	*grief*
plunder	*to expect*	*gaol*	*grievance*
pander	*to accept*		
		steak	*to meddle*
livid	*survivor*	*stake*	*medal*
lively	*surveyor*	*stark*	*medley*
vital	*supervisor*	*stank*	*motley*

8: The constructions with basic verbs K–N

Keep

1. *He keeps a dog to guard the house.* (No preposition before an ordinary noun. The infinitive here indicates purpose. See page 93.)
2. *He keeps on with his work.* (Note the prepositions.)
3. *He keeps talking about the dog.* (No preposition before a gerundive noun.)
4. *He keeps on talking about the dog.* (An alternative to 3 using the same preposition as in 2.)
5. *I could not keep the news from her any longer.* (Note the preposition.)
6. *I could not keep her from finding out about it any longer.* (The same preposition as in 5 before a gerund.)
7. *Please keep it to yourself.* (In this idiom which means: *Do not tell anyone else about it,* a kind of reflexive construction is used.)

Know

1. *I know him as/for a fool.* (Note the prepositions.)
2. *I know him as being a fool.* (A rare alternative to 1 using the gerund.)
3. *I know him to be a fool.* (An alternative to 1 and 2 but more literary because it is the Latin accusative and infinitive construction. In this case the infinitive cannot be omitted.)

4. *I know that he is a fool.* (The clause is the commonest way of expressing this idea.)
5. *I know why you did that.* (Another clause construction.)
6. *I know how to do that, etc.* (An infinitive phrase.)
7. *I have known him say/to say things like that.* (This construction is equally common with and without *to*. It is not really the same as 3, in which it would be impossible to omit *to*. This construction appears to be used only when the verb is in the simple past, present perfect or past perfect tense.)
8. *I know of your past indiscretions.* (Note the preposition.)
9. *If you are in the know, you might tell me.* (A colloquial idiom meaning: *If you have been told the facts.*)
10. *There is no knowing what may happen in that case.* (This idiom means: *It is impossible to foresee.)*
11. *He is very knowing in business.* (The adjective means: *shrewd.*)
12. *He has not gone there to the best of my knowledge.* (A common idiom meaning: *As far as I know.*)

Laugh

1. *They laughed at the joke.* (Note the preposition.)
2. *They laughed about the joke.* (Note the preposition. The meaning is not the same. In this case they laughed in retrospect, i.e. *when they looked back on it.*)
3. *They laughed at being expected to do such a thing.* (The same preposition as in 1 before a gerund.)
4. *They laughed about being expected to do such a thing.* (The same preposition as in 2 before a gerund. As in 2 they laughed in retrospect.)

Let

1. *I let him come in.* (Note that there is no *to* before the infinitive.)
2. *Let* has no passive. The meaning can be conveyed with: *He was allowed/permitted to come in.*

Like and Love

Love of course is stronger than *like* but as they are very similar in meaning and have exactly the same constructions they can be treated together.
1. *I like/love compliments.* (No preposition before an ordinary noun.)
2. *I like/love being paid compliments.* (No preposition before a gerundive noun. This indicates general taste.)
3. *I would like/love to be paid a compliment like that.* (The infinitive

with *would like* and *would love* indicates that it refers only to one particular occasion.)

4. *I like/love you to pay me compliments.* (The object and infinitive construction.)

5. *I like/love your paying me compliments.* (The gerund with a possessive adjective is a less common alternative to 4.)

6. *I like/love it when you pay me compliments.* (The pleonastic *it* and a clause. An alternative to 4 and 5.)

7. *I like/love you for saying that.* (Note the preposition. As is usually the case *for* with the gerund means: *because you did it.* See page 76.)

Make

1. *He made a mess of it.* (No preposition before an ordinary noun.)

2. *He made me do it.* (No preposition, not even *to*, before the infinitive in the active.)*

3. *I was made to do it.* (Note that *to* is used before the infinitive in the passive.)*

4. *That makes understanding the problem hard.* (No preposition before a gerundive noun.)

5. *That makes it hard to understand the problem.* (The same pleonastic *it*, adjective and infinitive as in *find* 4—see page 28. This is a much commoner construction than 4.)

6. *I can make myself understood in Italian.* (This is a kind of reflexive construction. Note the use of the past participle here.)

7. *This is a film in the making.* (This is an idiom meaning: *In the process of being made.*)

8. *He has the makings of a good citizen.* (Another idiom meaning: *He is potentially a good citizen.*)

Mean

When it is possible to use a verb after *mean* it has two distinct meanings: *a. intend*; *b. necessitate.* An ordinary noun or an infinitive is used after it in the meaning of *intend.*

1. *I meant a house not a bungalow.* (This is not very common except in clearing up misunderstandings.)

2. *I meant to get it but I forgot.*

3. *I meant you to get it but I forgot to tell you.*

And ordinary noun or a gerundive noun is used after it in the meaning of *necessitate.*

4. *It means a three-mile walk.*

---

*It should be noted that another verb with exactly the same construction as make 2 and 3 is *bid* (which means *order*). *He bade me do it. I was bidden to do it.*

5. *It means walking three miles.*
6. *It means your walking three miles.*
(This is a different use of the possessive adjective before the gerund from the one we have previously had. Here it is used to limit the gerund to the activity of one particular person. In 5 the gerund applied to a general necessity. See page 74 for further examples.)
7. *What do you mean by behaving like that?* (This is an idiomatic use of *mean* and is equivalent to: *How dare you behave like that?*)

Need

1. *He needs a book.* (No preposition before an ordinary noun.)
2. *He needs to buy a book.* (No preposition before the infinitive. *To* is merely a sign of the infinitive.)
3. *He needs me to help him.* (The object and infinitive construction.)
4. *The room needs painting.* (No preposition before the gerund. The gerund is only used after *need* to replace the passive infinitive—*to be painted.* See page 43.)
5. When *need* is intransitive and is in the present tense it can be used either as a principal or an auxiliary verb in questions and negatives. The use of it as a principal verb normally indicates habit and as an auxiliary verb one particular occasion.
Do you need to spend so much on clothes? (A principal verb: habit.)
Need you make so much noise? (An auxiliary verb: on this particular occasion.)
I don't need to take a bus to get to work. (A principal verb: habit.)
I needn't leave just yet. (An auxiliary verb: on this particular occasion.)
Note that when *need* is a principal verb it is used with *do* and followed by *to* before the infinitive. When it is an auxiliary verb it has neither *do* nor *to*.
6. *There is no need to cry.* (The infinitive is used after the noun *need*.)
7. *There is a need for that kind of book.* (Note the preposition. This preposition is not used before a gerund after *need*.)
8. *She is in need of help.* (Note the preposition.)
9. *She is in need of being looked after.* (The same preposition as in 8 before a gerund. This is not nearly so common as construction 4—*She needs looking after.*)

EXERCISES

a. Do what is necessary to the words in brackets, adding prepositions if necessary.
1. *She laughed (be) told she was a flirt.*
2. *What a lot of houses need (paint) in this road!*
3. *She would not let him (kiss) her.*

4. *I would love (go) to that exhibition with you, though in general I don't like (see) things set out in lines.*
5. *I asked him what he meant (behave) so abominably to our guests.*
6. *If it means (sacrifice) any of his pleasures, he is not prepared to work hard.*
7. *I don't like (you go) out with Tom. I don't trust him.*
8. *What on earth made you (say) such a thing?*
9. *I could not keep the police (search) the house.*
10. *She loves (organise) outings to places of interest.*
11. *The matter needs (investigate) and I intend (see) that something is done about it.*
12. *I know (he be) an authority on old silver.*
13. *He can make himself (like) in any group of people.*
14. *She bade me (hold) my tongue.*
15. *I loved her (show) such sympathy for someone in trouble.*
16. *The other day we had a good laugh (I be) a 'chaperon' to her ten years ago.*
17. *He should be made (apologise) for his rudeness.*
18. *He keeps (tell) me how much he loves her.*
19. *I meant (you be) the first to hear the news.*
20. *I have never known (he be) late in all these years.*

b. Put the verbs in brackets into the right tense.
1. *Where (you be)? I (look) for you all afternoon.*
2. *I wonder if you (sit) here in the same room doing the same job this time next year.*
3. *Everyone (know) what a large proportion of British cars (produce) in the Midlands, but not everyone (realise) what a difficult time the industry (go) through at the moment.*
4. *Tell me what first (strike) you about the house as soon as you (see) it.*
5. *I (turn) on the radio to listen to the news. It (not be) on for more than a few moments when it suddenly (blow) up. I (never have) such a shock in my life.*
6. *If you (learn) English for six years I must say you (have) a very poor grasp of its construction.*
7. *At the moment His Honour (hear) a case but we expect the court to rise in about half an hour.*
8. *Really women (be) the limit; you (nag) me for weeks to mend this fire and now I (do) so you (keep) on interrupting me.*
9. *I (save) up for some time now and next year I (really go) to India for three months.*
10. *You (have) your ear to the keyhole a few minutes ago. You (hear) what time Charles (come) home?*
11. *I (go) to spend my holidays in Italy next year but the price of everything (rather put) me off the idea. Perhaps I (go) to Spain instead.*
12. *My school (be) moved just as the war (break) out, so you can imagine what chaos (ensue).*

13. *I (be) to Paris several times but I (not recollect) that particular spot.*
14. *Why (you look) at me in that funny way? Someone (spread) scandal about me behind my back?*
15. *We (hear) a great many different points of view. If everyone who (want) to say anything (already do) so, we (put) the matter to the vote?*

c. Explain the difference in meaning between:
1. *to do time* (colloquial)
   to make time
   to mark time
   to beat time
   to kill time
2. *I gave him an example.*
   I set him an example.
   I held him up as an example.
   I made an example of him.
   I pointed to him as an example.
3. *She swept out the room.*
   She swept out of the room.
4. *He's mad to buy it.*
   He's mad about buying it.
5. *to swear at someone*
   to swear by someone
   to swear someone in
6. *It is in the north-west of London.*
   It is to the north-west of London.
7. *matters of moment*
   matters of the moment
8. *to take place*
   to take one's place
9. *to go on a walk*
   to go for a walk
   to take a walk
   to go on foot
10. *I haven't time to answer questions.*
    I don't have time to answer questions.
11. *It is time to go to bed.*
    There is time to go to bed.
12. *I don't think much of Shakespeare*
    I don't think much about Shakespeare.

d. Give the past simple form and the past participle of the following verbs.
e.g. *to do   did   done*

1. *to flow*	2. *to flee*	3. *to swell*
4. *to fell*	5. *to slay*	6. *to hold*
7. *to beseech*	8. *to raise*	9. *to lie (down)*

10. *to fall*	11. *to beat*	12. *to tread*
13. *to lay*	14. *to rid*	15. *to saw*
16. *to seek*	17 *to lie (not to speak*	18. *to stroke*
19. *to fly*	*the truth)*	20. *to slide*
21. *to weave*	22. *to strike*	23. *to wreak*
24. *to fine*	25. *to founder*	26. *to run*
27. *to sneeze*	28. *to forsake*	29. *to thrive*
30. *to bear*	31. *to bid*	32. *to fight*
33. *to ride*	34. *to bet*	35. *to sling*

9: The subjunctive

The real reason for the existence of the subjunctive is to convey ideas that are not facts. This should be borne in mind throughout our study of the subjunctive.

Kinds of subjunctives

1. The subjunctive in *wishes.*
a. Without using any auxiliary verb:
God save the Queen!
Devil take you!
Long live the Queen
God bless you!
b. Using *may:*
Long may you live to enjoy your retirement.
Long may the Queen rule over us.
May you enjoy a ripe old age!

2. The subjunctive of *be* in unfulfilled or impossible conditionals:
If she were less plain he might propose to her.
If he were here all would be well.

3. The subjunctive after *propose* and *suggest,* either without an auxiliary verb or with *should:*
I suggest he be/should be asked to resign.
I propose it be/should be done at once.

4. The subjunctive with *may* or *might*.

a. To indicate purpose:

In order that he might have more time to study, he gave up his job.

b. In hypotheses, especially when introduced by *however*, *whatever*, *wherever*, etc.

However poor one may be, one can always find something to be thankful for.

Whatever may be the results of that policy, I support it on principle.

He swore to catch up with him, wherever he might be.

Try as I might, I could not do it.

5. The subjunctive that looks like a simple past tense (unless it is the verb *be*) but isn't, mainly used after certain impersonal constructions, in wishes and suppositions:

I wish I had my revolver here.

I wish I knew how to do it.

I wish she were here with me.

If only I had more time to think about it.

It is time that child went to school.

If only he weren't so thick-skinned!

I would rather you went home now.

I had sooner you didn't tell him.

It is high time you learnt to correct that mistake.

Suppose he were to ask/asked for the money back at once.

Sometimes this subjunctive looks like a conditional:

I wish you would look where you are going!

If only he would not eat so much garlic!

If you are wishing that something had been different in the past, this subjunctive looks like a past perfect tense:

I wish I had had your opportunities when I was young.

If only he had taken my advice years ago!

If only he had told you the truth months ago!

6. The subjunctive with *should*, principally used after expressions of emotion (this is voluntary but gives emphasis to the strength of the emotion), propriety, impropriety, impossibility, command (where no infinitive is used) and suggestion:

Do you think it right that people should be treated like that?

I am shocked that such a thing should have happened here.

It is inconceivable that they shouldn't have known about it.

She crept in lest her husband should wake up.

It is quite wrong that people should be forced to live in such squalor.

We are surprised that you should have been treated so rudely.

He gave orders that it should be done at once.

That he should have behaved like that astounds me.

EXERCISES

a. Put the verbs in brackets into the right form. Most of them are subjunctives.
1.   *It is shocking that people (have) to live in such overcrowded slums.*
2.   *If I (be) Prime Minister now I know exactly what I (do).*
3.   *I would really rather you (leave) it until next month.*
4.   *He left orders that nothing (be) touched until the police arrived.*
5.   *If you (live) in London for six months it is time you (know) where Trafalgar Square is.*
6.   *Long you (enjoy) the best of everything.*
7.   *He did it quickly lest he (repent) of it.*
8.   *Whatever (be) the outcome of the election, I (watch) it with interest.*
9.   *It is time he (make) a real effort to settle down.*
10. *It is scandalous that you (be) treated like that.*
11. *I suggest he (be) asked to tender his resignation.*
12. *If only I (behave) differently he might still be alive now.*
13. *Long you (cling) to your delightful illusions: you never (become) cynical.*
14. *If he (be) here now, what you (say) to him?*
15. *I wish I (know) what to say in cases like this.*

b. Explain the meaning of these nouns that are used as verbs.
1.   to *buttonhole* someone
2.   to *table* an amendment
3.   to *bed* down for the night (colloquial)
4.   to *axe* expenditure
5.   to *mirror* public opinion
6.   to *mouth* one's words
7.   to *ferret* something out
8.   to *toe* the line
9.   to *skewer* a fish
10. to *tax* someone's patience
11. to *pot* a plant
12. to *elbow* one's way through the crowd
13. to *inch* one's way along
14. to *corner* someone
15. to *foot* the bill
16. It *preys* on my mind
17. to *fork* out (colloquial)
18. to *line* a coat
19. to *fox* someone (colloquial)
20. to *lace* one's tea with whiskey
21. to *floor* someone in an argument (colloquial)
22. to *corner* the market
23. to *thumb* a lift (colloquial)
24. to *shoulder* responsibility

25. to *tiptoe* in
26. to *man* a ship
27. to *board* up a window
28. to *sponge* on someone (colloquial)
29. to *house* the survivors
30. to *referee* a match
31. to *vacuum* the carpet
32. to *coat* something with varnish
33. to *ship* goods abroad
34. to *outline* government policy
35. to *cotton* on (colloquial)
36. to *head* for somewhere
37. to *dwarf* something
38. to *dog* someone's footsteps
39. to *peter* out
40. to *guy* something (colloquial)
41. to *map out* a holiday
42. to *egg* someone on (colloquial)
43. to *loaf* about (colloquial)
44. to *beard* the lion in his den
45. to *cash* in on something

c. Choose the right idiomatic word from the three given at the end of the sentence.

1.   *That hideous power station is certainly a ...... on the landscape. (stain, blot, mark)*
2.   *I don't know him at all well; he's only a ...... acquaintance. (slight, slender, casual)*
3.   *Some clergymen agree to remarry the so-called innocent ...... in a divorce. (party, individual, partner)*
4.   *The firm prospered because the Directors ...... back a lot of money into it. (took, ploughed, invested)*
5.   *When he went bankrupt he had to start again from ...... (everything, nought, scratch)*
6.   *As none of the students who went out to lunch together had much money, they decided to go ...... (Dutch, independent, halves)* (colloquial)
7.   *It was realised that there was a lot of ...... money in circulation. (unreal, false, counterfeit)*
8.   *He refuted the accusations ...... against him. (done, levelled, given)*
9.   *He left when it was his turn to ...... a round of drinks. (proffer, pay, stand)*
10.   *She was such a chatterbox that no-one could get a word in ...... (sideways, edgeways, upside-down)*
11.   *Goodness knows whether this Cabinet ...... will lead to more efficient government. (rearrangement, shake-down, reshuffle)*

12. *I am afraid the result of the coming election is a ...... conclusion.* (foregone, foreseen, predictable)

13. *Charlie Chaplin's ...... comedies were a source of universal pleasure.* (funny, slapstick, maudlin)

14. *There was such a thin ...... wall between those two houses that every sound could be heard through it.* (barrier, party, weak)

15. *As Mr Pickwick thought that everyone was as kind and nice as himself he was in for a ...... awakening.* (crude, rough, rude)

16. *I bet he has earned a ...... penny since he has been with that firm.* (pretty, good, solid) (colloquial)

17. *He certainly has a ...... on his shoulder about being born in the lower classes.* (complex, chip, neurosis) (colloquial)

18. *The patient is much worse again today; she has had a ...... (collapse, breakthrough, relapse)*

19. *I can cook quite reasonably now, but it took me a long time to get the ...... of it.* (habit, art, hang) (colloquial)

20. *Some people have the ...... of putting you at your ease at once.* (flair, knack, ability)

21. *As long as I have known him he has always lived in the ...... of luxury.* (lap, middle, midst)

22. *He is so wealthy that, as far as buying a house is concerned, money is no ......* (object, consideration, preoccupation)

23. *A lot of people who have had a ...... deal in life will show surprising cheerfulness.* (bad, rough, raw)

24. *I think he is quite disinterested, though some people attribute a(n) ...... motive to him.* (secret, ulterior, subconscious)

25. *He is a ...... master at hiding his feelings.* (past, clear, true)

26. *That author's name is always ...... up in the most unlikely places.* (cropping, running, bobbing)

27. *I have only come to ...... you goodbye.* (say, tell, wish)

28. *He was such a ...... recruit that he did not even know how to make his boots shine.* (new, green, raw)

29. *Many people nowadays are too fond of their ..... comforts.* (animal, creature, brute)

30. *John is certainly a very ...... wire.* (vigorous, live, lively) (colloquial)

10: The constructions with basic verbs O-S

Order

1. *I ordered a meal immediately.* (No preposition before the direct object.)
2. *I ordered him to do it at once.* (The object and infinitive construction.)
3. *I ordered it to be done at once.*
4. *I gave orders that it should be done at once.* (A clause with a subjunctive as an alternative to 3.)
5. *It was done on the policeman's orders.*
6. *I don't take orders from him.*
7. *It was done by order of the Queen.*
8. *They are studied in order of importance.*
(Note the prepositions in the last four sentences.)

Verbs of perception

All verbs of perception *(see, hear, feel, smell, watch, notice, etc.)* are followed by the object and infinitive without *to* unless the action is definitely not finished. In that case, the present participle replaces the infinitive:
I heard you come in last night. (Finished)
I saw him shoot her dead. (Finished)
He noticed her go into that shop. (Finished)
Come and look at the soldiers walking down the street. (Not finished)
Could you smell anything burning? (Not finished)
I can feel something crawling along my arm. (Not finished)

Prefer

1. *I prefer tea to coffee* (Note the preposition)
2. *I prefer swimming to skiing.* (The same preposition as in 1 used with gerundive nouns. This indicates general taste.)
3. *I would prefer to leave at once.* (This refers only to one occasion. Where only one half of the comparison is put in and the other is understood—as here—*prefer* can be followed by the infinitive.)
4. *I would prefer you to stay at home tonight.* (The accusative and infinitive referring to one occasion, like 3.)

Remember

1. *I remember the man very well.* (No preposition before an ordinary noun.)
2. *I remember telling you that last week.* (No preposition before a gerundive noun. The gerund is used here to refer to a past action.)
3. *I remember your telling me that last week.* (The possessive adjective indicates a different person remembering and telling.)
4. *I hope I remember to post that letter.* (No preposition before an infinitive, as *to* is only a sign of the infinitive. The infinitive is used here to refer to a future action.)
5. *I hope I remember that I have to post that letter.* (The clause is an alternative to 4.)
6. *I remembered how to do it, etc.* (an infinitive phrase.)
7. *Please remember me to your parents.* (Note the preposition. This is an idiom meaning: *Please give your parents my kindest regards.*)

Say

1. *I came to say goodbye to you.* (Almost the only common example except *Say the word,* or, *say* followed by an ordinary noun object.)
2. *I came to say what I think.* (A noun clause as the object of the verb: a much commoner construction.)
3. *She said that she loved me.* (Another very common kind of clause.)
4. *She wouldn't say why she did so.* (Another kind of clause.)
5. *Surely I have some say in the matter?* (An idiom meaning: *Surely my opinion should be asked for and taken some notice of?*)

Speak

1. *He spoke his lines well.* (No preposition before an ordinary noun.)
2. *He spoke (to me) of/about politics.* (Note the prepositions.)
3. *He spoke (to me) of/about going into politics.* (The same prepositions as in 2 before a gerundive noun.)
4. *Speak for yourself.* (Note the preposition. The meaning is: *Don't include me in what you are saying.*)
5. *He spoke to calm down the crowd.* (The infinitive indicates purpose and means in order to. It is therefore not dependent on *spoke.*)
6. *Speak up!* (Note the preposition. The meaning is: *Speak more loudly.*)

Stop

1. *I stopped the car.* (No preposition before an ordinary noun.)

2. *I stopped driving the car to look at the map.* (No preposition before a gerundive noun. The action you are stopping is always in the gerund but the sentence can be shortened to read: *I stopped to look at the map.* Here the infinitive indicates purpose and the meaning is almost the opposite of: *I stopped looking at the map* – i.e. *I put the map away and drove on.*)

3. *Nothing would stop him (from) driving fast.* (Here *stop* means *prevent* and like *prevent* can have *from* before the gerund.)

4. *He soon put a stop to all that nonsense.* (An idiom.)

Succeed

1. *He succeeded in the examination.* (Note the preposition.)

2. *He succeeded in passing the examination.* (The same preposition before a gerundive noun.)

3. *He succeeded by working hard.* (*By* and the gerund always indicates the method used. See pages 87 and 88.)

4. *She has great success with the boys.* (Note the preposition after the noun *success*.)

5. *He did not make a success of that business.* (Note the preposition.)

6. *He did not make a success of running that business.* (The same preposition as in 5 before a gerund.)

In the meaning of *to inherit a position* the constructions are:

1. *Edward VI succeeded Henry VIII.* (No preposition.)

2. *Edward VI succeeded to the throne at the age of nine.* (Note the preposition.)

Suspect

1. *I suspect foul play.* (No preposition before an ordinary noun.)

2. *I suspect him of foul play.* (If a personal object is introduced *of* must follow it.)

3. *I suspect him of murdering her.* (The preposition as in 2 before a gerund.)

4. *I suspect him of murdering her.* (The object and infinitive construction is slightly literary and here the infinitive cannot be omitted.)

5. *I suspect that he is the murderer.* (The clause is a commoner alternative to 4.)

6. *I had no suspicion of his being the murderer.* (The same preposition as in 2 and 3 after the noun *suspicion*.)

EXERCISES

a. Do what is necessary to the words in brackets, adding prepositions if necessary.

1.   Who ordered (you do) such a ridiculous thing?
2.   Shush! I think I can hear someone (walk) about upstairs.
3.   Do you remember (go) to your first Commemoration Ball at Oxford?
4.   Many people nowadays prefer (ski) (do) any other kind of sport.
5.   Scarlett O'Hara generally succeeded (make) men (fall) in love with her, when she had set her heart on doing so.
6.   Did you actually see the man (take) the money?
7.   On my way to work I stopped (talk) to an old school-friend.
8.   He never spoke to me (want) to marry my sister.
9.   Why do you always ,suspect (I pull) your leg?
10. Stop (tell) me that you cannot do it and get (move)!
11. Most people do not make a great success (bring) up their children.
12   I would prefer (not come) out with you tonight. I am feeling very exhausted.
13. I saw your book (lie) on the hall table.
14. I looked at the people (sunbathe) on the terrace.
15. Do you remember (ask) him how his wife is?

b. Use the following words in sentences so as to bring out their meaning clearly.

counsel	diligent	fit	to twinkle
to counsel	indigent	feat	to tinkle
chancel	indignant	fist	to tickle
council	indulgent	feast	to trickle

a game
a play
some game

credible
credulous

c. The following is a list of thirty verbs ending in '-ate'. One of them could be used in each of the following sentences to replace the italicised part. Assign the right verb to the right sentence.

1. procrastinate	2. rejuvenate	3. perpetrate
4. incarcerate	5. gesticulate	6. proliferate
7. underrate	8. abominate	9. facilitate
10. litigate	11. exterminate	12. infuriate
13. deteriorate	14. vitiate	15. prevaricate
16. intimidate	17. expiate	18. prefabricate
19. incapacitate	20. alleviate	21. delegate
22. implicate	23. placate	24. fumigate
25. annihilate	26. expatiate	27. resuscitate
28. reiterate	29. rehabilitate	30. reverberate

1.   Most people feel very much younger when they come back from their holidays.
2.   When I asked him point-blank what he was doing on the premises he avoided giving a direct answer.

3. She *talked enthusiastically and at some length* on the joys of having a large family.

4. Everything they had built up together and made their lives around was *utterly destroyed* in that bloodthirsty revolution.

5. A very serious view is taken of any attempt to *bring pressure to bear on* witnesses.

6. He was *out of action* for some time after being badly injured in a car crash.

7. I did my best to *calm her down*, but she remained in a terrible temper.

8. Were you *involved* in that attempt to topple the Government?

9. The Director was grossly overworked because he refused to *hand over* any of his authority to his subordinates.

10. It is very dangerous to *think* the power of your enemies *less than* it really is.

11. It is very unwise to *take legal action* against someone unless it is absolutely necessary.

12. The political situation is *worsening* to such an extent that I doubt if war can be avoided.

13. It makes one ashamed if one thinks of how many crimes have been *committed* in the name of religion.

14. My friend is the kind of person who always *puts off doing anything* if it is at all possible.

15. I can only *repeat* what I have already said.

16. We are told that Lazarus was *brought back to life*.

17. The report of, the gun *echoed round and round* in the huge vaulted room.

18. There is nothing that *angers* some people more than being held up in a traffic jam.

19. He was *waving his arms about* so wildly that he fell overboard.

20. Unfortunately the impact of his words, which obviously came from the heart, was *marred* by his having a pronounced stutter.

21. The component parts of that house were *made in advance*: they only had to be assembled on the spot.

22. Christians believe that Christ *atoned for* the sins of the world on the Cross.

23. In cases of death from certain diseases it is necessary to *remove all traces of infection by means of smoke in* a house.

24. I *detest* beer and never drink it, even when I am taxed with being a snob because I do not do so.

25. One of the arguments against having the death penalty is that if someone has been wrongly found guilty and put to death he cannot be *restored to his former position* if fresh evidence comes to light to prove his innocence.

26. Modern drugs can considerably *lessen* the pain of people suffering from cancer and other dreadful diseases.

27. The authorities did everything possible to *make* his leaving the country *as easy as possible*.

28. One of the sons of the last Dowager Empress of China was *kept in prison* for a long time for some quite trivial offence.
29. Coffee bars have *multiplied enormously* in recent years in some parts of London.
30. Rigid restrictions on hunting have been imposed in Africa to prevent big-game hunters from *utterly destroying* certain species.

11: Inversion

1. A number of adverbial expressions can be put at the beginning of the sentence for greater emphasis. Any adverbial expression that is directly negative or which suggests a negative will be compulsorily followed by an inversion *with an auxiliary verb*. Some positive openings, however, also have this inversion, especially those beginning *to such*. This inversion is a useful way of breaking up the usual subject−verb−object word order, but, in general, its effect is rather literary and it should not be over-used. The following are the commonest expressions which, if placed at the beginning, must be followed by an inversion.

in no circumstances
least of all
hardly ...... when
hardly ever
not infrequently
in no way
not otherwise
not only (unless it qualifies the subject)
scarcely ...... when
scarcely ever
rarely
very rarely
seldom
very seldom
still less
much less
even less
only (unless it qualifies the subject)
under no roof

not a word (unless it is the subject of the sentence)
not a soul (unless it is the subject of the sentence)
not often
not as
not till
not until
neither, nor (when used quite separately)
not a single word (unless it is the subject of the sentence)
not one word (unless it is the subject of the sentence)
by no means
no longer
no sooner ... than
at no time
at no other time
in no country, town, etc.

little	*to such extremes*
in vain	*to such lengths*
never	*to such a degree*
nowhere	*to such an extent*
on no account	*in/to such a plight*
in none of	*in/to such straits*
such	*in such a desperate situation*
such	*to such a point*
so (unless it qualifies the subject)	*well/with good reason/with every*
so great	*justification*

Not a single word did he say for a whole hour.
Not often do you see snakes in England.
Never had she seen anything like it before.
No sooner had he said it than he wished he had not done so.
Not until a long time afterwards did I realise that he was mixed up with that gang.
In no way am I responsible for what has happened.
In no country will you be offered stranger coffee than in England.
To such straits was he reduced by his extravagance that he took to begging.
Well may you say that it is too late to do anything about it now.
Only on very rare occasions does he give you a word of praise.
He doesn't even like her; still less is it his intention to marry her.
She didn't like it and neither did I .
but: *Only a few people understood what he was saying.*
Not a soul came to that political meeting.
Not a single word that he said entitles you to make that accusation.

2. There is, however another type of inversion which does not use an auxiliary verb. This is even more literary than the first kind and is found after certain kinds of adverbial phrases. It must certainly not be used indiscriminately by foreign students. They are advised to use it only when they have seen it in an English book.
It is possible only with a verb of movement or position, and this verb is almost always in the simple present or simple past. The verb *to be* is also used with this kind of inversion, after a superlative:
Best of all was the Christmas pudding.
In front of me lay the whole valley like an untouched paradise on earth.
After the war came the problem of rehabilitation.
Through the fog loomed an eerie castle.
Most picturesque of all are the street vendors.
Away into the distance stretched ridge after ridge of snow-clad peaks.
Last but not least walked my grandfather bearing a large bird-cage.

3. Sometimes adverbs are put at the beginning to dramatise actions. In this case the verb must be a verb of movement in either the simple past, the

simple present or the imperative. There is an inversion (type 2) unless the subject is a pronoun:

Off you go!
Round we went.
In you get!
Away went coach and horses at full speed.
Down fell a clutter of cartons and boxes.
Up went a mountain of luggage on to the racks.

4. Inversion (type 2) may be used after direct speech if there is no qualifying adverb and no indirect object. It is more commonly used when the subject is a noun than when it is a pronoun:

'Any more fares, please?' asked the conductor.
'Any more fares, please?' the conductor shouted cheerfully.
'What a nuisance!' exclaimed my sister.
'This is how you do it,' my sister explained to me.
'Go ahead,' he said grumpily.
'I'm the King of the castle,' he told me.
'Well I never!' remarked my grandfather.
'What utter rubbish!' he whispered to his fiancée.

EXERCISES

a. Put the verb in brackets into the right form, using inversions (type 1).
1. *To such an extent her bad temper (get) on his nerves that he is filing a petition.*
2. *Hardly he (come) into the room when he saw someone disappearing through the French window.*
3. *Very seldom one (come) across snakes in England.*
4. *In none of his books Dickens (show) greater understanding of the human heart than in* Bleak House.
5. *Only after I had known him for some time I (begin) to appreciate his real worth.*
6. *On no account I ever (believe) a word he says.*
7. *Not as a critic but as a close friend I (urge) you to reconsider your decision.*
8. *In such a plight he (find) himself that he was at his wit's end what to do.*
9. *Not a soul I (meet) as I rambled over the Downs.*
10. *At no time in the history of mankind women (have) greater opportunities for following careers than they have now.*
11. *In none of his novels Hardy (give) vent to his pessimism so openly as in* Jude the Obscure.
12. *With every justification he (be) called an incompetent bungler.*

b. Put the italicised expressions at the beginning of the sentence. It may be necessary to make minor alterations to them and to the rest of the sentence to make the sentence grammatically correct. Many sentences require an inversion (either type 1 or type 2) but not all of them.

e.g. I didn't see *a soul* all day.
　　Not a soul did I see all day.

1. The pirate ship lay *far out to sea.*
2. That can happen to you *nowhere else in the world.*
3. He would go on working *in any circumstances.*
4. The car sped *round the bend.*
5. I have *very rarely* seen such a strikingly beautiful person.
6. He didn't say *a single word* all afternoon.
7. I don't think he would like it *anyway.*
8. I wouldn't offend you *on any account.*
9. You have seen it already *perhaps*?
10. The children scrambled *into the coach.*
11. The Flea Market was *the most fascinating part of the town.*
12. He *little* thought that he would one day see his name in all the headlines.
13. I haven't seen that kind of tree *anywhere else in England.*
14. John goes to the theatre only *on very rare occasions.*
15. Jane Austen is *undoubtedly* one of the foremost English novelists.
16. The tall figure of a man loomed *out of the swirling mist.*
17. Let us have your ideas *by all means.*
18. We found ourselves *in such a desperate situation* that we had to shoot our way out.
19. He is called a fool *with good reason.*
20. It is not *by any means* true that all English people know their own language well.
21. A pheasant rose *out of the brushwood ahead of me.*
22. He had not been treated so abominably *in any city he had previously visited.*
23. I have told him not to do that *on innumerable occasions.*
24. You shouldn't panic *in any circumstances.*
25. The throbbing beat of drums came *through the silence of the jungle.*
26. I have received complaints about you *on numerous occasions.*
27. A great pile of plates and dishes fell *down* with a resounding crash.
28. The director did not realise what was going on *until his attention was drawn to certain irregularities.*
29. The mass of luggage went *up on the backs of sturdy porters.*
30. The success of the scheme has been *such* that the same principle is to be applied in other cases.

c. Use the following words in sentences of your own.

seizure	*grudge*	*trudge*	*venomous*
cessation	*drudge*	*begrudge*	*venerable*
session	*judge*	*dregs*	*vulnerable*
sitting	*dredge*		

| opportunity | effort | to deduct |
| possibility | afford | to deduce |

d. Give the past simple form and the past participle of the following verbs.

e.g. *to do   did   done*

1. *to strew*   2. *to loose*   3. *to broadcast* 4. *to spill*
5. *to spit*   6. *to glide*   7. *to dwell*   8. *to shoe*
9. *to creep*   10. *to knit*   11. *to shear*   12. *to hew*
13. *to arouse*   14. *to bleed*   15. *to forbear* 16. *to sting*
17. *to slim*   18. *to withhold* 19. *to mow*   20. *to pay*
21. Explain the difference between *sped* and *speeded up.*
22. Explain the difference between *hung* and *hanged.*
23. Explain the difference between *seek* and *look for.*
24. Give the meaning in modern English of *abide.*
25. Give two examples of modern English in which *wrought* as the past tense of *work* is still used.

12: The constructions with basic verbs T—Z

Take

1. *I took him to be a student.* (Object and infinitive construction. No preposition before the object.)
2. *He took to opera late in life.* (Note the preposition.)
3. *He took up golf late in life.* (Note the preposition.)
4. *I took it that he was a student.* (The pleonastic *it* and a clause as an alternative to 1.)
5. *She took running the house in her stride.* (No preposition—as in 1—before a gerund. The meaning is: *She did it quickly and efficiently.*)
6. *She took my saying that in very bad part.* (A different person considering the words and saying them. The meaning is: *She was very offended at what I said.*)
7. *He took to going to operas late in life.* (The same preposition as in 2 before a gerund. This construction indicates the beginning of a habit.)
8. *He took up playing golf late in life.* (The same preposition as in 3 before a gerund. This construction indicates the beginning of a hobby.)
9. *He took it all for granted/as a matter of course.* (These idioms mean: *He considered it quite natural and ordinary, and did not appreciate how lucky he was to have it.*)

Talk

1. *He talked (to me) of/about exotic lands.* (Note the prepositions.)
2. *He talked (to me) of/about travelling in exotic lands.* (The same prepositions before a gerundive noun.)
3. *He gave a talk on the international situation.* (Note the different preposition. This indicates not a cosy chat but a formal speech.)
4. *He gave a talk on joining the Common Market.* (The same preposition as in 3 before a gerund, with the same formal connotation.)
5. *He talked me into that purchase.* (Note the preposition. The meaning is: *He persuaded me against my better judgement to make that purchase.*)
6. *He talked me into buying that.* (The same preposition as in 5 before a gerundive noun. *Into* and the gerund always indicates dishonest persuasion or dishonest forcing. See section 1, page 80.)
7. *He talked down to me.* (Note the preposition. The meaning is: *He talked simply because he thought me too stupid to understand otherwise.*)

Tell

1. *He told (me) the truth.* (The indirect object, though not essential here, always precedes the direct one after *tell* except in cases of special emphasis, e.g. *Hamlet told the truth to Horatio but not to Claudius.*)
2. *He told me to keep quiet about it.* (The indirect object is compulsory before the infinitive.)
3. *He told me that I should keep quiet about it.* (The indirect object is compulsory also before a clause that can be used as an alternative to the infinitive in 2.)
4. *He told me why he had kept quiet about it.* (Another clause construction.)
5. *He told me how to do it, etc.* (An infinitive phrase.)
6. *There is no telling him anything.* (An idiom meaning: *It is impossible to tell him anything because he thinks he knows it all.*)
7. *The producer made a telling use of colour.* (The adjective means: *effective, striking.*)
8. *Who can tell the difference between them?* (This is a common use of *tell* and means: *distinguish, know.*)

Think

Think has two principal meanings:
a. to have the opinion
b. to intend
The constructions in the meaning of *have the opinion* are:
1. *I think that he is clever.* (A clause.)

2. *I think him to be clever.* (The Latin accusative and infinitive construction which is rather literary. The infinitive is more commonly omitted.)
3. *I think so: I think not.* (See page 103.)
The construction in the meaning of *intend* is:
4. *He is thinking of suicide.* (Note the preposition and the fact that the verb is in the continuous form.)
5. *He is thinking of committing suicide.* (The same preposition before a gerundive noun.)
The following idiomatic uses of *think* should also be noted:
6. *Please think it over first.* (Note the preposition. The meaning is: *Don't make up your mind without really considering the matter.*)
7. *I must think up some excuse.* (Note the preposition. The meaning is: *I must invent some excuse.* For this use of *some* before a singular noun see page 130.)
8. *I can't think how to do it. etc.* (An infinitive phrase. The meaning is: *I can't imagine how to do it.*)
9. *I can't think how we can do it.* (A clause as an alternative to 8.)

Try

1. *He tried a new method.* (No preposition before the direct object.)
2. *He tried to use a new method.* (The infinitive indicates that he made an effort to use the new method.)
3. *He tried using a new method.* (The gerund indicates that he has chosen to experiment with a new method because he was not satisfied with the way the old one worked.)
4. *He tried his hand at devising a new method.* (The meaning is: *He tried to think of a new method in order to see if he could manage it.*)
5. *He tried out a new method of doing it.* (Note the preposition. The meaning is: *He experimented to see if the new method worked.*)

Understand

1. *I don't understand modern art.* (The direct object.)
2. *I understand him to be a painter.* (The object and infinitive construction. This is rather literary and the infinitive cannot be omitted.)
3. *I understand that he is a painter.* (The clause is a common substitute for 2.)
4. *I cannot understand his painting such weird subjects.* (A different person is understanding from the one painting.)
5. *I cannot understand why he paints such weird subjects.* (A commoner alternative to 4.)
6. *I do not understand how to do it, etc.* (An infinitive phrase.)
7. *I understand so: I understand not.*

8. *What do you understand by that?* (Note the preposition. The meaning is: *What do you deduce from that?*)

9. *He has no understanding of the real situation.* (Note the preposition after the noun *understanding*.)

10. *I will lend you the money on the understanding that it is paid back within a month.* (An idiom meaning:...*on condition that...*)

Use

1. *I use an ordinary razor to shave with.* (The direct object and the infinitive to indicate purpose. For a fuller consideration of this construction see page 93.)

2. *I use an ordinary razor for shaving with.* (A less common alternative to 1. Whereas 1 is a common construction, 2 is possible only after the verb *use*.)

3. *I used to work hard.* (This means: *In the past I worked hard*, and it implies: *but now I don't*. Therefore it does not exist in the present tense.)

4. *I am used to hard work.* (Note the preposition.)

5. *I am used to working hard.* (The same preposition as in 4 before a gerundive noun. This means: *I work hard now and I am accustomed to doing so*. It must not be confused with 3.)

6. *I got used to working hard.* (This is similar to 5, but whereas 5 indicates a habit, this indicates the beginning of something that became a habit later.)

7. *It is no use saying that now.* (Note the use of the gerund after *it is no use*.)

8. *Did you make good use of your time in France?* (Note the preposition after the noun *use*.)

9. *Did you make good use of living in France for a year?* (The same preposition before a gerund.)

Want

1. *He wants a house of his own.* (Direct object.)

2. *He wants to have a house of his own.* (The infinitive construction is an alternative to 1.)

3. *He wants his son to have a house of his own.* (The object and infinitive construction. Never use a clause beginning with *that* after *want*.)

4. *This room wants painting.* (The gerund after *want* only replaces the passive infinitive. See page 43.)

5. *A rich person is seldom in want of a friend.* (An idiom meaning: ...*seldom lacks a friend*.)

6. *He does not want for money.* (Note the preposition. The meaning is: *He is not short of money*.)

Would rather/sooner

1. *I would rather/sooner stay in than go out.* (Note the use of the infinitives without *to* and the comparative word *than*. Compare this with the construction with *prefer* on page 58.)
2. *I would rather/sooner you stayed in than went out.* (Here *stayed* and *went* are subjunctives. See page 54.)

EXERCISES

a. Do what is necessary to the words in brackets, adding prepositions if necessary.
1. *I am not used (be) called a liar!*
2. *I cannot understand (he get) engaged to such an empty-headed girl.*
3. *She would rather (not discuss) the matter.*
4. *She would sooner (dance) (study).*
5. *She prefers (dance) (study).*
6. *I do not enjoy (play) football or cricket.*
7. *He has now got used (be) a hen-pecked husband.*
8. *My sister's fiancé is thinking (buy) a sports car.*
9. *I thought I heard a bomb (go) off in the middle of the night.*
10. *You will never talk me (invest) any money in such a risky speculation.*
11. *She has no intention (forgive) him for making her (look) so small.*
12. *If wine has gone a little sour, have you ever tried (heat) it and (add) a little sugar?*
13. *Why do you suspect (I pull) your leg?*
14. *It is no use (cry) over spilt milk.*
15. *He was talking (apply) for a job as a private secretary.*
16. *He will not consider (leave) London, whatever inducements you may offer him.*
17. *Some people like (tramp) about the world better than (settle) down in one place.*
18. *Why do you let him (behave) like that to you?*
19. *I do not want (she know) anything about it.*
20. *Fancy (he be) married all these years without (I know) it.*
21. *I mean (you have) my money when I die.*
22. *When did you take (go) such long solitary walks?*
23. *I can't help (be) silly; stop (be) unkind.*
24. *I am surprised to find you (study) philosophy.*
25. *I saw the two cars (collide) head-on.*
26. *Can't I make you (understand) how serious this is?*
27. *I don't see the use (mope) about all day.*
28. *My tennis shoes certainly need (clean).*
29. *I never use an electric razor (shave) with.*
30. *I don't believe (pull) down so many interesting old buildings.*
31. *She would rather (die) (be) thought 'fast'.*

32. *How can I ever forget (spend) that wonderful holiday with you in Venice?*
33. *You had better (be) careful what you say to her.*
34. *Who would suspect him (be) a gigolo?*
35. *Of course I expect (you apologise) (put) me in such an embarrassing situation.*

b.   Insert the missing idiomatic words.
1. *That is a ...... distinction; only a subtle mind could appreciate it.*
2. *She is sitting ......; her husband left her £60,000. (colloquial)*
3. *Because of the thundery weather the milk has ......*
4. *I don't want to ...... a leaf out of your notebook.*
5. *I'm so cold that my teeth are ......*
6. *Sit down by the fire; you'll soon be as warm as ...... (colloquial)*
7. *Everything was strewn around in confusion. During his absence the flat had been ......*
8. *The night was as black as ......*
9. *He went white as a ...... when he read that letter.*
10. *Quick as ...... he vanished behind the curtain.*
11. *Mary has been as good as ...... all day.*
12. *Those twins are as like as two ......*
13. *I am already ...... with quite enough responsibilities.*
14. *I'm afraid you must just take ...... luck.*
15. *Your money will be as safe as ...... with us!*
16. *She has arrived back safe and ...... from her world tour.*
17. *He committed suicide by taking an ...... of sleeping pills.*
18. *It is often better to let sleeping dogs ......*
19. *His mother gave him a resounding ...... on the ears for being impertinent to her.*
20. *It is no good going to see him now; he is in a ...... rage.*

c. Use the following idiomatic expressions in sentences of your own. (The teacher may think it advisable to explain the meaning of these expressions first.)

1. *cock and bull*	2. *stuff and nonsense*	3. *heart and soul*
4. *off and on*	5. *so-and-so*	6. *skimp and scrape*
7. *pros and cons*	8. *sick and tired of*	9. *down-and-out*
10. *give-and-take*	11. *up and about*	12. *once and for all*
13. *up-and-coming*	14. *over and done with*	15. *dead and alive*
16. *high and mighty*	17. *by and large*	18. *rack and ruin*
19. *a free-for-all*	20. *head over heels*	21. *there and then*
22. *life and soul of*	23. *far and away*	24. *long and short*
25. *touch and go*		

d. Form as many words as possible from the following by adding prefixes or suffixes.

1. *encourage*	2. *press*	3. *help*	4. *light*

5. *circle*	6. *respect*	7. *sense*	8. *most*
9. *custom*	10. *act*	11. *like*	12. *trust*
13. *comfort*	14. *spirit*	15. *treat*	16. *head*
17. *able*	18. *serve*	19. *just*	20. *state*

13: The pleonastic 'it' (the extra 'it')

a. In certain kinds of sentence *it* is used as a kind of preparatory object before the real object which is either an infinitive phrase or a clause. This has already been observed in considering some of the basic verbs. Notice the following examples:
Some people find it difficult to understand English construction.
That makes it hard for you to bear.
I put it to you that you need to make more effort.
I leave it to you to make up your own mind.
I don't think he would like it if you said that to him.
I owe it to you to tell you the truth.
I take it that you know what I am talking about.
I imagine it to be hard work, learning the violin.
Don't take it amiss if I say that you are allowing your ambition to run riot.
She hates it if I touch her things.
I dislike it when people make me look small.

b. It also appears as a kind of preparatory subject, if the real subject begins with an infinitive or gerund. In general this is considered better style if the real subject is a long one, as it enables the longest part of the sentence to stand at the end:
It must be difficult teaching mentally handicapped children.
It is fun going abroad for the first time.
It is amusing to watch children playing.
It is funny running into you again after so many years.
It is heart-rending to see them since the loss of their only child.
It is embarrassing not being able to understand what people say to you.

14: The gerund

It is important to realise what a gerund is and not to imagine that all verb forms in *-ing* are gerunds. If I say *'running water'*, *running* is merely an adjective. If I say *'He was running down the road'*, *running* is merely a present participle used in the continuous tense. But if I say *'Please forgive my smoking a cigar in here'*, *smoking* is a gerund; that is to say it is both a noun and a verb in the same sentence. Here *smoking* is a noun, the object of *forgive*. *My* is an adjective agreeing with the noun *smoking*. *A cigar* is the direct object of the verb *smoking*.

In modern English it is more usual to put a verb that forms the subject of a sentence into the gerund (although Shakespeare said: *'To be or not to be: that is the question'* and a well-known proverb says: *'To err is human: to forgive divine.'*)

Learning to ride a bicycle is not easy as it looks.
Making people look fools is not the job of a teacher.
Understanding English is easier than writing it.
Being young has its drawbacks.
Collecting old playbills is a harmless craze.

The gerund can also be used as the object of a sentence:

I don't understand filling in football coupons.
She enjoys flirting with men.
Don't mention seeing me there, will you?

It will have been noticed that the gerund can be preceded by a possessive adjective. It can also be preceded by a noun in the Saxon genitive. One or other of these is necessary:
1. to limit the gerund to the action of one particular person.
2. to indicate who is doing the action of the gerund when it is not the same as the subject of the sentence.

Understanding English is easy.
Your understanding that so quickly surprised me.
Smoking is not allowed in class.
His smoking in church shocked me.
I wouldn't recommend staying there.
I wouldn't recommend your staying there.
Flying abroad is very common nowadays.
My aunt's flying off to Africa took the whole family by surprise.
Her deciding to do it at the age of 93 shows she is still full of spirit.
Would you mind opening the window?
Would you mind my opening the window?
Would you mind if I opened the window?
Anything that involves working hard is deprecated nowadays.
If that involves my staying indoors on such a lovely day, I am not prepared to do it.

Behaving like that is quite inexcusable.
John's behaving like that was a great shock to us.

The following are some of the commonest verbs that are always
followed by a gerund without any preposition before it.

to abandon	*to admit*	*to advocate*
to anticipate	*to appreciate*	*to avoid*
to begrudge	*to be busy*	*can't face*
can't help	*can't stand*	*can't stick*
to catch someone	*to celebrate*	*to comprehend*
to contemplate	*to defer*	*to delay*
to deny	*to detest*	*to dislike*
to enjoy	*to entail*	*to envisage*
to escape	*to evade*	*to excuse*
to feel like	*to finish*	*to forgive*
to grudge	*to involve*	*it is no good*
it is no use	*it is worth*	*to loathe*
it looks like	*to mean* (meaning:	*to mention*
to mind	necessitate)	*to miss*
to necessitate	*to overlook* (meaning:	*to postpone*
to pardon	pardon)	*to practise* (unless the
to regret (if it refers	*to relish*	meaning is *in order*
to the past)	*to renounce*	*to do something* in
to resent	*to resist*	which case the
to resume	*to risk*	infinitive is used)
to shirk	*to spend one's life*	*to spend one's time*
to stop (but see	*to suggest* (this verb	*there is no*
page 60)	can be used also	*to tolerate*
to waste time	with 'that' and a clause)	

I miss seeing you so frequently.
He admitted stealing the money.
Don't mention seeing me there.
Please forgive my harping on the subject.
I couldn't resist teasing him.
It is worth going to Hampton Court.
I resent your taking such liberties.

It can automatically be assumed that the gerund will be used after all
prepositions, whether or not used after verbs:
He put off going there too long.
They have done away with using trams.
He is worried about getting into debt.
Many more verbs are followed by the gerund preceded by a preposition.
As foreign students have the greatest difficulty in deciding which
preposition to use in this case, lists of some of the commonest expres-
sions with different prepositions are given here so that the student can

refer to them in case of doubt. This 'government of verbs' is perhaps the most difficult thing in the whole of English construction. The principle stated at the beginning of section 1 should be borne in mind throughout this section.

Followed by *on* and gerund.

to be bent on	*to be intent on*
to be keen on	*to calculate on*
to compliment someone on	*to concentrate on*
to condole with someone on	*to congratulate someone on*
to count on	*to depend on*
to embark on	*to focus attention on*
to gamble on	*to harp on*
to insist on	*to make a start on*
to pride oneself on	*to reckon on*
to rely on	*to set one's heart on*
to spend money on	*to sympathise with someone on*
to theorise on	

N.B. At the beginning of a sentence *on* and the gerund is used to mean *as soon as:*
On coming to England he got arrested.
As soon as he came to England…
On stepping out of the station my brother found himself face to face with an old friend of his.

Followed by *for* and gerund.
(In most cases these will be seen to be the result of some previous action or someone's reaction to such an action. The meaning, therefore, is usually *because he had.*)
I criticised him for saying that/because he had said that.
I admired her for showing such courage/because she had shown such courage.
He told me off for making such a noise/because I was making such a noise.

to account for	*to admire someone for*
to answer for	*to apologise for*
to arrest someone for	*to atone for*
to be celebrated for	*to be famous*
to be in the mood for	*to be notorious for*
to be renowned for	*to be responsible for*
to be sorry for (generally referring to the past. If it refers to the present the infinitive can be used.)	*to be well known for*
	to blame someone for
	to care for (meaning: *to like*)
	to chide someone for
to claim damages for	*to commend someone for*

to compensate for
to criticise someone for
to expiate (for)
to forgive someone for
to get one's revenge on someone for
to give someone credit for
to have a gift for
to have a weakness for
to have many opportunities for
to justify oneself for
to make allowances for
to make up for
to pardon someone for
to praise someone for
to punish someone for
to reprimand someone for
to reward someone for
to stand for
to suffer for
to take revenge on someone for
to thank someone for

to condemn someone for
to despise someone for
to find an excuse for
to get one's own back on someone for
to have a flair for
to have a talent for
to have much opportunity for
to have someone up for
to let oneself in for
to make reparation for
one reason for
to pay for
to prosecute someone for
to rebuke someone for
to reproach someone for
to scold someone for
to sue someone for
to take someone to task for
to tell someone off for

Followed by *from* and gerund.
(In general this is used logically because most of these expressions have the meaning of preventing someone from doing something or of taking something from something else.)
I discouraged him from doing it. (It was his intention but I turned him away from the idea.)
He benefited from attending those lectures. (He took some knowledge away from them afterwards.)

to abstain from
to be far from
to deduce something from
to desist from
to discourage someone from
to draw an inference from
to exempt someone from
to free someone from
to get pleasure from
to infer something from
to prohibit someone from
to refrain from
to restrain someone from
to shrink from
to suffer from (meaning: *be unhappy because of*)
to turn someone aside from

to ban someone from
to benefit from
to defend someone from
to deter someone from
to dissuade someone from
to draw back from
to flinch from
to get benefit from
to hinder someone from
to prevent someone from
to protect someone from
to rescue someone from
to save someone from
to stop someone (from)

EXERCISES

Put the verbs in brackets into the gerund, adding *on*, *for* or *from* if necessary.
1. *Petrarch is given credit (perfect) the sonnet.*
2. *I appreciate (you be) so patient with me.*
3. *I abstained (vote) in the election.*
4. *He claimed damages (lose) the use of his right arm in that accident.*
5. *During his lifetime Shakespeare was well-known (be) a brilliant conversationalist.*
6. *She prides herself (be) a really good driver.*
7. *He counted (get) home before his wife.*
8. *Does the death penalty really deter people (commit) murder?*
9. *He spent his time (hang) around street corners.*
10. *Some people shrink (do) what they know to be their duty.*
11. *Some people have a flair (make) a room look homely.*
12. *My friend was banned (drive) for three years.*
13. *It looks like (be) fine for our picnic tomorrow.*
14. *She never envisaged (find) herself faced with such poverty.*
15. *Florence Nightingale had set her heart (become) a nurse and no-one was able to dissuade her (put) her ambition into practice. She found an excuse (make) herself useful in the Crimean War.*
16. *What do you deduce (look) over these figures?*
17. *Don't delay (get) that bad tooth seen to.*
18. *The Prime Minister focused attention (improve) the standard of living in the country.*
19. *Most people enjoy (hear) a good bit of gossip.*
20. *He was exempted (do) military service on compassionate grounds.*
21. *He could not account (be) found in possession of the stolen articles.*
22. *He abandoned (teach) and set up in business.*
23. *Why do you insist (treat) me like an idiot?*
24. *As soon as you have finished (read) that book, please lend it to me.*
25. *I am not in the mood (play) tennis today.*
26. *How I detest (have) my teeth drilled!*
27. *I sympathised with him (have) such a shrewish wife.*
28. *Most people attempt to justify themselves (do) what they really want to do.*
29. *She needs (reprimand) (treat) her daughter so unfeelingly.*
30. *When are you going to make a start (construct) shelves for this alcove?*
31. *The magistrate commended him (risk) his life in an attempt to save the drowning man.*
32. *You must make allowances (he be) very young and silly.*
33. *She spends a great deal of money (buy) clothes.*
34. *Why did you suggest (come) to this cinema?*
35. *Thank you (give) me such a wonderful weekend.*
36. *He is contemplating (become) a Buddhist.*

37. *That newspaper was had up (libel) my friend last week.*
38. *I have not much opportunity (play) the piano these days.*
39. *Her children hindered her (hurry).*
40. *He was arrested (be) drunk and disorderly in the street.*
41. *Why do you waste so much time (daydream)?*
42. *I wish everyone would renounce (manufacture) nuclear weapons.*
43. *I am depending (get) a cheque very soon.*
44. *I do not blame you (ask) for more time to consider the offer.*
45. *Kindly refrain (smoke) in the auditorium.*

Followed by *of* and gerund.
(It will be noticed that this list contains a large proportion of nouns and predicative adjectives.)

to accuse someone of
to approve of
to be apprehensive of
to be capable of
to be confident of
to be doubtful of
to be fond of
to be guilty of
to be in charge of
to be on the point of
to be proud of
to be risk of
to be terrified of
to be thinking of (meaning: *it is your intention in the future*)
to be wary of
to boast of
to consist of
to despair of
to dream of
to find a means/method/way of
to have a sense of
to have no intention of
instead of
it is a matter of/question of
I will not hear of
to make a pretence of
to make a success of
to make no secret of
to show no sign of
to take the liberty of
the advantage of
the chance of
the danger of

to acquit someone of
to be afraid of
to be ashamed of
to be chary of
to be desirous of
to be fearful of
to be frightened of
to be horrified of
to be in favour of
to be on the verge of
to be scared of
to be sure of (in a subjective sense: in an objective sense use the infinitive)
to be tired of
to be worthy of
to complain of (or *about*)
to deprive someone of
to disapprove of
to fight shy of
to have a dread of
to have enough of
in spite of
it is a case of
in the event of
to make a habit of
to make a show of
to make no mention of
to repent of
to suspect someone of
the act of
the anxiety of
the choice of
the difficulty of

the disadvantage of   *the drawback of*
the feeling of   *the fun of*
the hope of   *the idea of*
the impression of   *the insinuation of*
the job of   *the likelihood of*
the opportunity of   *the object of*
the notion of   *the pain of*
the pleasure of   *the point of*
the possibility of (Do not use   *the probability of*
    the word *possibility* after the   *the problem of*
    verbs *have or get*. Use *chance*   *the prospect of*
    instead.)   *the responsibility of*
the risk of   *the satisfaction of*
the shock of   *the system of*
the task of   *the thought of*
the temptation of   *the worry of*
What is the good/use of ?

Followed by *into* and gerund.
(These are all verbs of dishonest persuasion or dishonest forcing.)
to beguile someone into   *to be betrayed into*
to blackmail someone into   *to browbeat someone into*
to bully someone into   *to cajole someone into*
to coerce someone into   *to delude someone into*
to force someone into (if the meaning *to inveigle someone into*
    is not that such forcing is   *to lure someone into*
dishonest, use the infinitive)   *to mislead someone into*
to persuade someone into (use the   *to shame someone into*
infinitive if it is not dishonest)   *to talk someone into*
to tempt someone into (the infinitive   *to terrify someone into*
    is an alternative here)   *to wheedle someone into*
to trick someone into

Followed by *about* and gerund.
(This, in general, is used quite logically as *about* usually means *on the subject of*.)
to be angry about   *to be anxious about*
to be blasé about   *to be concerned about*
to be cut up about (or *at*) (colloquial) *to be enthusiastic about*
to be excited about (or *over*)   *to be explicit about* (with gerund
to be grieved about (or *at*)   or *how* and infinitive
to be lazy about   *to be mean about*
to be modest about   *to be optimistic about* (or *in*)
to be pessimistic about (or *in*)   *to be sorry about* (Referring to
to be serious about (or *in*)   the past. If it refers to the
to be unhappy about (or *at*)   present or future use the
to be upset about (or *at*)   infinitive.)

to bother about (Except in the imperative where the infinitive is used.)
to make a scene about
to make no bones about (colloquial)
to set about
to talk about (or *of*)
to worry, to be worried about

to give someone advice about
to give someone instructions about
to have no scruples about
to make a fuss about
to reach an agreement about
to speak about (or *of*)
to think about (or *of*)

EXERCISE

Put the verbs in brackets into the gerund, adding *of*, *into* or *about* if necessary.

1. *He has been deceived so often that now he is chary (trust) anyone.*
2. *Few women these days will tolerate (be) bossed about.*
3. *The miser was shamed (give) something to the collection.*
4. *Naturally she is proud (win) that competition.*
5. *Anything that involves (concentrate) on what he is doing is anathema to him*
6. *She never really got over the shock (hear) that her son had been killed in a mining accident.*
7. *Sometimes criminals are betrayed (give) the police information by a clever form of bluff.*
8. *She was so busy (argue) with her husband that she did not hear me knock.*
9. *Do you deny (work) for the Communist Party?*
10. *The likelihood (you win) a football pool is extremely remote.*
11. *The doctor swore to find a means (cure) his patient.*
12. *She was very upset (fail) in that examination.*
13. *You must not risk (offend) her by talking (vote) socialist. You know she is an out-and-out Tory.*
14. *Why do you disapprove (I go) out with Mary? It's only a 'Platonic friendship' you know, though Plato never envisaged (have) his theory of love so distorted.*
15. *That document has no validity at all because I was browbeaten (sign) it.*
16. *Do you make a habit (snap) people's head off?* (colloquial)
17. *At least he is sincere; he makes no bones (sponge) on the kinderhearted of his friends.*
18. *Coming face to face with her in the street like that, I couldn't very well avoid (say) a few words to her.*
19. *There is no (know) what may happen if a woman becomes Prime Minister.*
20. *Most children are afraid (be) left alone in the dark.*
21. *It is a case (do) as you are told or (be) sacked.*
22. *Would you mind (light) the candles? Dinner is ready.*

23. *I will overlook (you be) so rude to my sister this time but don't let it happen again.*
24. *He blackmailed her (hand) over a considerable sum of money.*
25. *He made no secret (be) in love with her.*
26. *I won't hear (you go) home alone at this time of night.*
27. *I really cannot postpone (write) that letter any longer.*
28 *The thought (commit) murder even in wartime is abhorrent to some people.*
29. *Why do you make such a fuss (do) such a simple thing?*
30. *When he went to prison Mr Pickwick had no intention (pay) a penny of the fine imposed on him for breach of promise.*
31. *The Government concerned failed to reach agreement (partition) the country.*
32. *It is easy for a 'gilded youth' to become blasé (do) everything.*
33. *Mary wheedled her mother (buy) that doll.*
34. *The prospect (spend) some of the best years of his life in prison appalled him*
35. *It is not easy for a playwright to coerce people (accept) his philosophy of life: if he wishes to proselytise, it is a question (make) people think that the idea was their own.*
36. *If you want me to look after your cat while you are on holiday please be more explicit (feed) it.*
37. *Profiteers have no scruples (take) advantage of shortages.*
38. *Why did you mislead me (think) you were rich?*
39. *She is optimistic (get) the part after her audition.*
40. *What is the use (make) yourself miserable about it now?*
41. *Haven't I had the pleasure (meet) you before?*
42. *He escaped (be) punished by resorting to cunning.*
43. *I tricked him (admit) his guilt.*
44. *'If a thing is worth (do) at all, it is worth (do) well.'*

Followed by *with* and gerund.

not to agree with	*not to hold with*
to be bored with	*to be charged with*
to be entrusted with	*to be fed up with* (colloquial)
to be preoccupied with	*to be satisfied with*
to content oneself with	*to credit someone with*
to disagree with	*to have an obsession with*
to have one's attention taken up with	*to interfere with*
	to put up with
to reproach someone with	*to taunt someone with*
to threaten someone with	

Followed by *against* and gerund.
(Quite logically there is an idea of opposition in these.)

to defend oneself against	*to guard against*
to protest against	*to react against*

to rebel against
to advise someone against
to warn someone against

to set one's face against
to decide against (the same as
  decide not to)

Followed by *in* and gerund.
(The large number of predicative adjectives in this list will be noted.)

there is no harm in
there is some merit in
there is a certain satisfaction in
to be absorbed in
to be barking up the wrong tree in
  (colloquial)
to be correct in
to be diligent in (or *about*)
to be engaged in
to be experienced in
to be implicated in
to be inefficient in (or *at*)
to be instrumental in
to be involved in
to be lazy in (or *about*)
to be mistaken in
to be obstinate in
to be pessimistic in (or *about*)
to be prompt in
to be right in* (meaning: *to think*
  correctly)
to be steadfast in
to be thwarted in
to believe in
to come a long way in (or *towards*)
to delay (*in*)
to have (*no*) *difficulty in* (If there
  is no gerund but an ordinary
  noun, *in* is replaced by *with*.)
to have no hesitation in
to lose no time in
to make progress in
to persevere in
to revel in
to sink capital in
to succeed in
to take pleasure in

there is no merit in
there is some satisfaction in
to acquiesce in
to be active in
to be concerned in
to be conscientious in (or *about*)
to be dignified in
to be efficient in (or *at*)
to be engrossed in
to be frustrated in
to be indefatigable in
to be inexperienced in
to be interested in
to be justified in
to be long (*in*)
to be nimble in
to be optimistic in (or *about*)
to be pig-headed in (colloquial)
to be quick in
to be wrong in* (meaning: *to think*
  incorrectly)
to be stubborn in
to be useful in
to collaborate (*with someone*) *in*
to co-operate in
to delight in
to have (*no*) *trouble in* (If there
  is no gerund but an ordinary
  noun, *in* is replaced by *with*.)
to join in
to make headway in
to participate in
to persist in
to see some point/object/purpose in
to specialise in
to take part in
to take the initiative in

---

to be wrong/to be right are followed by an infinitive, if used in a moral sense: *Mary was wrong* (i.e. naughty) *to disobey her mother.*

Followed by *at* and gerund.

to aim at	*to be all right at*
to be clever at	*to be dense at*
to be dismayed at	*to be (an) expert at*
to be frightened at (or *of*)	*to be good at*
to be impressed at (*by* or *with* before a noun)	*to be plunged into despair at*
	to be skilful at
to be smart at	*to be stupid at*
to chafe at	*to draw the line at*
to frown at	*to have a go at*
to have a shot at	*to laugh at* (If it is in retrospect *about* replaces *at*.)
to play at (*with* before a noun)	
to scowl at	*to smile at*
to try one's hand at	*to work at* (The infinitive is used after *work* to convey purpose.)

EXERCISE

Put the verbs in brackets into the gerund, adding *with*, *against*, *in* or *at* if necessary.

1.   *She is quite clever (knit) rather shapeless things.*

2.   *There is no harm (drink) in moderation.*

3.   *I advised him to guard (be) too sure of succeeding in the examination.*

4.   *It is no good (make) yourself miserable and hankering after the impossible. Content yourself (make) life as pleasant for yourself and others as possible.*

5.   *I have always been incredibly dense (do) mathematics.*

6.   *He celebrated (get) married by getting drunk.*

7.   *Why don't you try your hand (write) a play instead of criticising what others have attempted?*

8.   *I really credited her (have) a little more common sense.*

9.   *Boys love playing (be) cowboys and Indians; girls prefer to play (be) mother.*

10.   *She frowned (be) asked such a personal question.*

11.   *Some animals chafe (live) in captivity.*

12.   *I do not hold (give) children too much pocket money.*

13.   *Do you think I was justified (intervene) in that dispute?*

14.   *I am so sorry; I was engrossed (read) this novel and did not hear you come in.*

15.   *She did not feel that she was making any progress (learn) to cook.*

16.   *There is no merit (not do) something if you have no temptation to do it.*

17.   *He was charged (embezzle) money from his employers.*

18.   *Young people have always rebelled (be) expected to follow convention.*

19.   *He persists (deny) (have) anything to do with that bank raid.*

20. *You are quite mistaken (think) that I had no difficulty (learn) French.*
21. *Some film stars delight (have) their photographs in the newspapers.*
22. *I draw the line (be) expected to polish the floors after office hours.*
23. *I have always regretted (not spend) longer abroad when I was young.*
24. *She was put off (go) to Greece by her friend who had been upset by the rich food there.*
25. *Stop (play) (be) so naïve and try to understand.*
26. *It is difficult to find time to practise (play) the piano.*
27. *I recollect (be) introduced to you in India some years ago.*
28. *The police are barking up the wrong tree (think) that the crime was committed by an outsider.*
29. *She will not put up (be) treated like that much longer.*
30. *I do not see any point (apologise) now; it is too late.*
31. *They aimed (raise) the standard of living of all classes.*
32. *The Prime Minister took the initiative (open) negotiations.*
33. *Unfortunately intelligent children are indefatigable (ask) questions.*
34. *Aren't you being rather optimistic (take) that examination?*
35. *Do you believe (educate) everyone in state schools?*
36. *I appreciate (be) allowed to do it in my own way.*
37. *He was plunged into despair (have) to start all over again.*
38. *You are quite right (think) him a fool: he is!*
39. *Lady Dedlock was very bored (do) nothing all day at Chesney Wold.*
40. *Few people joined (sing) 'God Save the Queen'.*

Followed by either *at* and gerund or infinitive.

(In general *at* and gerund is commoner if you are referring to the past and the infinitive is commoner if you are referring to the present or future. As usual, however, usage defies firm rules. It should also be observed that almost the entire list consists of predicative adjectives indicating various degrees of surprise, anger, happiness or unhappiness.)

I was surprised at not having received an invitation. (This refers to the past.)
I am surprised to see you here. (This refers to the present.)
I am annoyed at being turned out of that pub. (It refers to the past: the ejection has taken place.)
I am annoyed to see that pub closed. (This refers to the present.)

to be amazed at
to be annoyed at or *about* (with before an ordinary noun.)
to be astounded at
to be delighted at or *about* (with before an ordinary noun.)
to be disgruntled at or *about*
to be disgusted at or *about* (with before an ordinary noun.)

to be angry at or *about* (with before an ordinary noun.)
to be astonished at
to be cross at or *about* (with before an ordinary noun.)
to be disappointed at (followed by with, in, or by before a noun.)
to be dumbfounded at
to be excited at or *about*

to be flabbergasted at
to be grieved at
to be happy at or about
to be nonplussed at
to be pleased at (with before a
   noun.)
to be puzzled at or about
to be shocked at
to be taken aback at
to be unhappy at or about
to be vexed at or about

to be furious at or about (with
   before an ordinary noun.)
to be miserable at or about
to be offended at (with before a
   noun.)
to be put out at or about
to be sad at
to be surprised at
to be thrilled at or about
to be upset at or about
to rejoice at

Followed by *to* and gerund.
(This is a very common construction and is used whenever *to* has a
prepositional force; that is, when it could be followed by an ordinary
noun instead of a gerundive noun):
He is looking forward to a holiday/to having a holiday.
She is quite used to English life/to living in England.
He was reduced to extreme poverty/to begging in the streets.
The thief confessed to the crime/to having stolen the money.
I am not accustomed to this work/to doing this kind of work.

that is no obstacle to
there is more to
to adjust oneself to
to amount to
as to
owing to
to attend to
to be accustomed to
to be attached to (meaning: *to like*
   something very much)
to be committed to
to be equivalent to
to be impervious to
to be near to
to be opposed to
to be tantamount to
to be used to
to bear witness to
to become addicted to
to certify to
to come close to
to come round to (meaning: *to be*
   persuaded)
to contribute to
to descend to

the evidence points to
to adapt oneself to
to allude to
to apply oneself to
to attach importance to
to attribute something to
to be addicted to
to be averse to
to be close to
to be conducive to
to be given to (meaning: *to be*
   inclined to)
to be on the way to
to be reduced to
to be up to (meaning: *to be well*
   or clever enough to)
to become acclimatized to
to bring someone round to
   (meaning: *persuade*)
to come near to
to confess to
to confine oneself to
to dedicate oneself to
to devote oneself to
to fall to (meaning: *to begin*)

to expose oneself to
to feel up to
to get accustomed to
to get down to (only in a moral sense)
to get used to
to give one's attention to
to give one's life to
it is due to
to lay oneself open to
to look forward to
to make allusion to
to object to
to plead guilty to
to react to
to refer to
to resort to
to see one's way to (meaning: to be in a position to)
to stoop to (only in a moral sense. In a physical sense the infinitive is used.)
to take exception to
to take to (meaning: to begin something that becomes a habit: used in a general sense.)
What do you say to...?
when it comes to
with a view to

to get acclimatized to
to get attached to
to get round to (meaning: find an opportunity to)
to give a little thought to
to give one's mind to
in addition to
it is thanks to
to limit oneself to
to lower oneself to
to make reference to
to own up to
to put someone up to
to reconcile oneself to
to resign oneself to
to restrict oneself to
to see to (or about)
to settle down to (meaning: to concentrate on)
to submit to
to swear to (only if it refers to the past)
to testify to
to turn to (meaning: to begin something that becomes a habit, especially an artistic habit of some kind.)

The following are followed either by to and the gerund or by to and the infinitive.

to agree to
to be driven to

to be condemned to
to consent to

to lead someone on to (in the passive the infinitive is preferred with this verb.)

It should also be noted that there are two exceptions to the general principle, in which the infinitive is used instead of the gerund.

He is inclined to laziness/to be lazy.

He is prone to laziness/to be lazy.

By and the gerund.

No list of these can be given because no expressions are completed with by, but it is always used to indicate the method used to achieve something:

He succeeded by working hard.

I annoyed her by saying I didn't like her new hair style.

He laid himself open to a heavy fine by driving without a licence.
He asked for trouble by marrying someone after only knowing her a week.
She risked her life by dashing into the road to save her child.
She angered her father by refusing to continue her university studies.
Sometimes *through* and the gerund are used for a similar reason, though rather less directly:
He made progress through persevering with his studies.
Many a man has been led to a life of crime through developing complexes in his childhood.
Enlightenment came to him through studying the ancient writings of his ancestors.

EXERCISES

a. Replace the italicised noun with a gerundive phrase of basically the same meaning, though possibly of greater precision.
1. He testified to *my qualifications*.
2. Dr Schweitzer devoted himself to *the Africans*.
3. What do you say to *an aperitif?*
4. He made no reference *to the affair*.
5. The evidence points to *his guilt*.
6. He soon got acclimatized to *the tropics*.
7. She easily adapts herself to *life abroad*.
8. In addition to *wealth* she has beauty.
9. Even thieves do not stoop to *theft* from their friends.
10. Please confine yourself to *the subject* set.
11. I soon brought him round to *my point of view*.
12. She attaches a lot of importance to *elegance*.
13. Your wit contributed to *the success of the party*.
14. I am naturally opposed to *unnecessary violence*.
15. She came here with a view to *marriage*.
16. Excuse me: I must see to *the dinner*.
17. He pleaded guilty to *manslaughter*.
18. Most people resign themselves to *a humdrum life*.
19. He is given to *violent fits of temper*.
20. That is tantamount to *insubordination*.

b. Put the verbs in brackets into the gerund adding any prepositions that may be necessary.
1. *You are capable (do) much better than that.*
2. *Try to get the maximum benefit (live) in England.*
3. *Don't despair (meet) the right girl some day.*
4. *The job (clear) away the slums in London is a hard one.*
5. *He came near (die) of pneumonia.*
6. *Most people are scared (get) up in public and (make) a speech.*

7. *I am by no means averse (have) drink, but I prefer (drink) with a meal (pub crawl).*

8. *One learns a language (make) mistakes and (be) corrected.*

9. *It takes courage to own up (steal money.*

10. *The Government is committed (help) a number of under-developed countries.*

11. *My wife does not approve (I be) out late at night.*

12. *He is a nice person but he is rather given (moralise).*

13. *The old lady was nonplussed (be) spoken to so rudely.*

14. *She beguiled me (buy) her the brooch.*

15. *Why are you thinking (emigrate) to South Africa?*

16. *When I was a child I was far (think) that I should now be living in London.*

17. *Most women enjoy (furnish) their first house, though only a small proportion make a real success (do) so.*

18. *(Be) married is not all beer and skittles—or even love-making and nappies. There is more (make) a success of it than this.*

19. *He tried to make an impression (wear) outrageous clothes.*

20. *She made a great show (be) quite indifferent to him.*

21. *Did you have any difficulty (find) the house?*

22. *He certainly lost no time (ask) for a loan!*

23. *The girls fell (discuss) their boyfriends.*

24. *I attribute Dickens' sympathy for the poorer classes (he work) and (live) among them in his youth.*

25. *(Say) that the Minister laid himself open (be) attacked.*

26. *She was very annoyed (not receive) an invitation.*

27. *Are you in favour (lower) the age at which people can vote?*

28. *Am I right (think) that I have met you before?*

29. *She is very excited (go) home to Italy next week.*

30. *Her parents dissuaded her (accept) his proposal.*

c. Use the following words in sentences so as to bring out their meaning clearly.

deposit	gargoyle	to ramble	to flood
to depose	to gargle	to rumble	to inundate
to dispose of	to gurgle	to rumple	
disposal	to goggle at	to crumple	
disposition	to bungle	to crumble	to clinch
		to grumble	to clench
inexhaustible	monarchy		
indefatigable	kingdom		

d. Correct the mistakes in the following sentences. This is a revision exercise. All the constructions needed have already been studied under basic verbs, tenses, passives, inversions, subjunctives and gerunds.

1. *Have you your house decorated every year?*

2. *It is love that makes the world going round.*
3. *That money gave them the possibility to go to a university.*
4. *He uses to get up early in the morning.*
5. *If you prefer to mess about rather than to work hard I cannot prevent you to waste your time.*
6. *I have come to say you goodbye.*
7. *Naturally I like that people tell me I am clever.*
8. *Is it worth to instal such expensive equipment?*
9. *It would be easier to decide if my wife would be here.*
10. *If you are living here since 1956 it is time you look for somewhere nicer to live.*
11. *Have you got used to live in a flat yet?*
12. *What would you do if he was to propose to you?*
13. *As soon as he saw the policeman, he flew.*
14. *Please excuse that I am so late.*
15. *He was let to play in the streets.*
16. *If you already saw the film, tell me about it.*
17. *The funny-looking girl was glanced by all the passers-by.*
18. *My friend was acquitted to commit that crime.*
19. *Only after I had threatened to sue him he sent me back the money he owed me.*
20. *Please forgive me being so rude to you last time we have met.*
21. *A new dance-hall is opened there soon.*
22. *On no account you should believe such a ridiculous story.*
23. *The meeting was presided by my grandfather.*
24. *I am waiting to meet you for a very long time.*
25. *He thinks to go to Greece for his holiday next year.*
26. *Need you to go there really?*
27. *He has some hope to pass the examination.*
28. *I would like visiting that house very much.*
29. *Nelson ordered to nail the flag to the mast.*
30. *So great the success of the Exhibition has been that all records have been broken.*

15: The infinitive

Although most verbs in English that govern other verbs are followed by the gerund (with or without a preposition preceding) there are some verbs that are always followed by the infinitive. The following are some of the commonest:

1. Governing the direct infinitive only:
He deserves to be severely punished.
You omitted to tell me some important facts.
She threatened to sue him for breach of promise.
John is prone to resent criticism.
I would hesitate to recommend that film.
The train is due to leave in five minutes.
Would you care to join me for a drink?
He hastened to add that he excluded present company from his generalisation.

to appear to	to arrange to	to attempt to
to be able to	to be apt to	to be bound to
to be due to	to be eager to	(meaning: *it will*
(meaning: *it is*	to be entitled to	*certainly happen*
the right time for	to be inclined to	to be liable to
it to)	to be prepared to	to be prone to
to be ready to	to be relieved to	to be reluctant to
to be unwilling to	to bother to	to care to
to dash to	to decline to	to deign to
to deserve to	to determine to	to endeavour to
to fail to	to feel impelled to	to happen to
to hasten to	to have the right to	to hesitate to
to hurry to	to guarantee to	to learn to
to long to	to make up one's	to manage to
to offer to	mind to	to omit to
to pause to	to plan to	to pretend to
to promise to	to refuse to	to resolve to
to rush to	to scorn to	to seem to
to take pains to	to take the trouble to	to take time to
to tend to	to threaten to	to trouble to
to try to (unless there	to undertake to	to volunteer to
is an idea of	to yearn to	
experimentation:		
see page 69).		

2. Governing the accusative and infinitive only:
I implored her to keep calm.

What induced you to say such a thing?
He forbade me to mention it.
The blackmailer instructed her to meet him at 11 p.m.
She persuaded me to reconsider my decision.

to beseech	*to bride*	*to command*
to compel	*to counsel*	*to encourage*
to exhort	*to forbid*	*to force* (unless
to implore	*to induce*	dishonestly)
to instruct (or *how to*)	*to invite*	*to oblige*
to persuade	*to press*	*to prompt*
to sentence	*to teach* (or *how to*)	*to tell* (or *how to*)
to tempt	*to urge*	

3.   Governing the direct infinitive or the accusative and infinitive:
He chose to resign.
He chose me to succeed him.
I want to go shopping.
I want you to go shopping for me.
She requested to leave early.
She requested me to leave the room.
She begged to be allowed to help.
She begged me not to do it.
I desire to know the truth.
I desire you to tell me the truth.

to beg	*to choose*	*to desire*
to entreat	*to request*	*to want* (except with
to wish		passive meaning)

4. Governing the accusative and infinitive or a clause with *that:*
I realise the problem to be difficult.
I realise that the problem is difficult.
I assume him to be out of town.
I assume that he is out of town.
She guesses me to be married.
She guesses that I am married.

to assume	*to deduce*	*to gather*
to guess	*to realise*	*to suppose*

5. Governing *how, when, who(m), what, where, whether* or *which* and
infinitive (Noun infinitive phrases):
I do not remember how to cook that dish.
Try and think how to outwit the police.
I decided where to go for my holidays.

I wondered whether to tell her about it or not.
I can't think what to give him for a present.
I guessed who(m) to speak to.
I forgot when to use that form of address.
He explained what to do if the car broke down.

to agree on	to arrange	to ask
to consider	to decide	to demonstrate
to discover	to divulge	to explain
to find out	to forget	to guess
to imagine	to inquire	to know
to learn	to recall	to recollect
to remember	to settle	to think
to understand	to wonder	

6. Governing the accusative and *how, when, who, what, where* or *which* and infinitive:
I told them who(m) to look out for.
I showed him where to find the best specimens.
I will show you how to do it.
Please inform me how to get my passport renewed.
I instructed them whom to address as 'Your Honour'.
I taught them how to dance.
I told him what to say.

to inform	to instruct	to show
to teach	to tell	

7. Followed indifferently by the infinitive or gerund;
She can't bear to be/being criticised.
When did you start to learn/learning English?

to begin	to cease	to continue
can't bear	to start	

In addition to being used after certain verbs, as in the above lists, the infinitive is mainly used:

1. to indicate purpose
You came to England to get away from the restrictions of family life, but you told your parents it was to learn English.
He hid in the woods to escape capture.
She went into the shop to buy some sausages.
He put several things at the bottom of his suitcase to smuggle into England.
I employed a very good man to re-upholster my settee.
He wore outrageous clothes to show his contempt for convention.

2. to replace a conditional

To speak frankly/If I may speak frankly, I don't like your attitude.
To get back to what I was saying/If I am to get back to what I was saying, women should make up their minds what they want in life.
Strange to say/Even if it is strange that I should say it, I really enjoyed it.
To put it mildly/If I may express it in the most moderate terms, he is not above suspicion.

3. to indicate an unwelcome and unexpected result or state of affairs.

I tried the door, only to find it locked.
He opened a conversation, only to be rebuffed.
He returned home to find his wife gone.
I refuted the suggestion only to be accused of hypocrisy.
She arrived at the flat to find the police already there.
They fought on only to be overwhelmed in the end.
N.B. The use of *only* here is to avoid any possible ambiguity with the infinitive for purpose.

4. as an alternative to the gerund (though less commonly used) as the subject of a sentence.

To know defeat is to know humiliation.
To stand out against common beliefs requires more courage than to accept them.
To find happiness through marriage is most people's aim in life.
To serve God and Mammon is not easy.
To make people feel uncomfortable about exploiting the poor was one of Dicken's aims.

EXERCISES

a. Do what is necessary to the verb in brackets. It will be either in the infinitive or the gerund. Add any prepositions that may be necessary.
1. *She omitted (tell) me that she was already married.*
2. *You had better (leave) now before my wife gets home.*
3. *Can you blame anyone (want) (make) a success of his career?*
4. *I forbid (you say) such things.*
5. *He said he would rather (beg) than (starve).*
6. *He was made (publish) an official apology.*
7. *I wasted the whole afternoon (go) through piles of old letters.*
8. *The captain exhorted everyone (keep) calm.*
9. *Let me (show) you how (do) it properly.*
10. *He is bound (put) in an appearance sooner or later.*
11. *Are you serious (want) (marry) my aunt?*
12. *He intends (his son become) a doctor.*
13. *I pressed him (tell) me the latest news.*

14. *Can you forgive (he treat) you like that?*
15. *He has no idea (attempt) (make) himself agreeable.*
16. *She was understandably annoyed (not receive) an invitation to that party.*
17. *(Speak) bluntly: will you pay or shall I hand the matter over to my solicitors?*
18. *I will not have you (use) language like that.*
19. *If you persist (treat) your friends so casually, you risk (lose) them altogether.*
20. *He is prone (be) lazy and rather given (moralise), but one can't help (like) him all the same.*
21. *Some people are very stupid (do) practical things.*
22. *I cannot give my mind (read) with all that noise (go) on.*
23. *I was taken aback (be) asked (make) an extempore speech.*
24. *I promise (make) no mention (see) you there.*
25. *He owned up (make) the prisoner (scrub) the floor on his hands and knees.*
26. *The man guaranteed (finish) (repair) the roof that afternoon.*
27. *She endeavoured (maintain) that it was all my fault.*
28. *They compelled (I give) them the names of the people concerned.*
29. *I resent (be) talked to like a child.*
30. *Whatever induced (you take) him into your confidence?*
31. *I feel like (go) for a long walk today.*
32. *I disapprove (join) a union just because everyone else does so.*
33. *I absolutely refuse (allow) myself (be) browbeaten (agree) (you marry) such a creature as that.*
34. *I arranged (meet) her here but so far she has failed (turn) up.*
35. *I helped (she put) on her coat.*
36. *I will not consider (you live) by yourself at your age.*
37. *Let me (give) you some advice (buy) houses.*
38. *Why do you disagree (I try) to get into Parliament?*
39. *He testified (I be) a graduate of Oxford.*
40. *What prompted (you take) such a drastic step?*
41. *Dr Schweitzer spent his life (help) the Africans.*
42. *I did not make allowances (he be) so hot-headed as to get himself into such a scrape*
43. *(They leave) all their money to that hospital rather surprised the family.*
44. *Everyone urged (he show) a little more flexibility.*
45. *The police ought to be ashamed (stoop) (use) such methods. I would hesitate (use) them myself.*

b. Put the right prepositions into these sentences.
1. *The police connived ...... the criminal's escape.*
2. *If you continue to live ...... your means, as you are doing ...... present, you will soon find yourself ...... serious trouble.*

3.   *She objected ...... doing any housework ...... the grounds that it was ...... her dignity.*

4.   *The driver was absolved ...... all blame.*

5.   *Be careful ...... those books: they are only ...... loan ...... us.*

6.   *I have been feeling rather ...... the weather recently; I do not know what is wrong ...... me.*

7.   *...... my dismay, I found that I could not remember a word ...... the speech I had so painstakingly learnt ...... heart.*

8.   *The trouble ...... you is that you are always hankering ...... the impossible.*

9.   *The man was handed .... the chief of police ...... further questioning.*

10. *She is now ...... arrest ...... having been found ...... possession ...... certain stolen articles.*

11. *...... boarding schools boys do preparation ...... supervision.*

12. *You have been ...... trouble ...... speeding ...... several occasions already. If you are caught again you risk being deprived ...... your driving licence.*

13. *Any book can be obtained ...... you ...... demand.*

14. *The examination should be ...... the capabilities ...... any intelligent child ...... that age.*

15. *...... the time you are twenty-one you will have come round ...... accepting my point ...... view.*

c.   Use the following words in sentences so as to bring out their meaning clearly.

insolent	reminder	adversity	subsistence
insolvent	remainder	adversary	subsidence
dissolve	remains	adverse	subsidy
dissolute	remnants	averse	subsidiary
irresolute		aversion	sustenance
	stationery	avert	
executor	stationer		
executioner	stationary		

d.   Give the opposite(s) of:

1. to *interrupt* someone	2. a *peace-loving* nation
3. to *take up* an idea	4. economical
5. out-of-date	6. an atheist
7. a drunkard	8. impassioned
9. accidentally	10. bad-tempered
11. to impoverish	12. self-satisfied
13. to look forward to	14. *forelegs*
15. voluntary	16. permanent
17. concise	18. dissolute
19. comfort	20. to catch hold of
21. to hope	22. invaluable

23. idle
24. to assault
25. *the ebbing* tide
26. dawn
27. mealy-mouthed
28. shabby
29. a *well kept-up* garden
30. a *hen* party
31. facetious
32. momentous

16: Compound or phrasal verbs B

Compound verbs (such expressions as *put up with, do away with, make do with, cut down on*) are an integral part of English, though foreign students, not generally encountering them until they have been doing English for some time, have a natural tendency to think of them as bothersome luxuries. The plain fact is that what distinguishes the writing and, above all, the speech of a good foreign student from those of an Englishman is that what an Englishman writes or says is full of these expressions, whereas most foreigners are frightened of them, carefully avoid them, and sound stilted in consequence. Foreign students who enjoy being flattered on their English can best achieve this by correctly using masses of these compound verbs.

There are at least seven hundred of these in ordinary, everyday use in English. Some of them have a certain logic about them. For example, when an aeroplane *takes off* (leaves the ground) there is the same idea of *separation* as when you *take off* a coat. To *do away with* trams (abolish them) suggests that they are no longer there but *away* somewhere else (probably in a scrap merchant's yard). In general, however, I think that, though such rather childish associations of ideas may help some people to remember particular phrasal verbs, they are not much use with the majority of these expressions, which lack even such elementary principles of logic. They just have to be learnt, like any other kind of vocabulary.

In order to avoid giving the students mental indigestion, I have cut up this section into shortish sections (arranged alphabetically for easy reference) which punctuate the rest of the book.

Compound verbs B

Back

1. to back someone *up* (To support someone morally.)

2. to back *out of* something (To try to avoid doing something when you have promised to do it.)
3. to back *on to*
The house backs *on to* a factory (Overlooks it from the back windows.)
4. to back *away from* (To shrink back in fear from)
5. to back *down* (To apologise)

Be

1. to be *around* (To be still in the same place and so be able to be contacted.)
2. to be *out to* (To be aiming very seriously to do something.)
3. to be *over* (To be finished or ended.)
4. to be *through with* (To want no more to do with something or someone.)
5. to be *off*
a. (To leave)
b. (To be cancelled.)
c. (To finish work.)
d. (To go bad, of meat, butter etc.)
6. to be *up to something/no good* (To be doing something mischievous or dishonest.)
7. to be *up to*
I am not *up to* it (I am not well/intelligent enough to do it.)
8. to be *behind with* (one's work) (To have allowed more and more (work) to accumulate.)
9. to be *in for* (To be going to get—usually something unpleasant.)
10. to be *back* (To have returned.)
11. to be *on* (To take place—of concerts, theatrical performances, exhibitions, sports fixtures, arrangements etc.)
12. to be *up to*
It is *up to* you (It is your responsibility.)
13. to be all *over between.*
It is all *over between* us (*I don't want anything more to do with you.*)
14. to be *over at* (a friend's) (To be on a visit to a friend's house.)
15. to be *behind* it all (To be really responsible for it.)
16. to be *on to* someone about something (To be continually criticising someone about something.)
17. to be *on to a good thing* (To be concerned with something that is very profitable.)
18. to be *well up on* something (To know a lot about something.)

EXERCISES

Replace the italicised parts of the sentence with expressions with *back* or *be*.

1. He is *very anxious* to make a career for himself in Parliament.
2. I do not trust him at all; I am sure he is *engaged in something dishonest*.
3. I hope you will *second my suggestion* when I raise the matter at the next Board meeting.
4. The police never discovered who was really *responsible for* that carefully planned robbery.
5. It is too late to *change your mind* now; you are commited to doing it.
6. My wife is always *nagging* me about my untidiness.
7. *I want nothing whatever to do with* it in future.
8. If you cling to those illusions I am afraid you *will* get a nasty shock.
9. When he invested his money he found that he was *able to make a lot of money out of it*.
10. The concert will *finish* at about ten o'clock.

Break

1. to break *up*
a. (To begin the school holidays.)
b. *a fight* (To interrupt and stop it.)
c. (To disintegrate.)
d. a car etc. (To knock it into pieces.)
e. of weather
The weather is breaking *up* (The good weather is coming to an end.)
2. to break *down*
a. (To lose one's self-control and start crying.)
b. *into its component parts* (To analyse.)
c. (To go wrong and stop working; used of things like cars, trains etc.)
d. *someone's resistance* (To overcome it.)
3. to break *out*
a. (To start—of bad things.)
b. *in spots* (To develop a rash.)
c. (To escape from prison.)
d. (To explode with anger.)
4. the *outbreak* (The beginning of something bad, like wars, epidemics, fires etc.)
5. to break *in/into*
To break into a house (To force an entry into it in order to steal from it.)
6. to break *in* a horse (To get it used to being controlled by men.)
7. to break *oneself of* a habit (To force oneself to give it up.)
8. to break *into*

a.   *a run* (To start running.)
b.   *a laugh* (To start laughing.)
c.   *a note* (To offer it in payment for quite a small thing.)
9.   to break *off*
a.   (To stop suddenly.)
b.   (To become detached, of branches, etc.)
c.   (To cause to become detached.)
10.   to break *with* someone (To stop having anything to do with someone.)
11.   to break *with tradition* (To do something quite different or new.)
12.   to break *the news to* someone (To tell someone some bad news as gently as possible.)
13.   to break *the back of* something
I have broken *the back of* it now. (I have done most of it and all the hardest part.)
14.   to break *away from* someone (To escape with difficulty.)
15.   to break *through*
The sun has broken *through* (It has appeared through the clouds.)
16.   *a break-through* (A major discovery in research etc.)
17.   *a lucky break* (A stroke of luck, generally for a criminal.)
18.   to drive *at breakneck speed* (To drive dangerously fast.)

Bring

1.   to bring *up* a child (To teach it manners, speech etc.)
2.   *upbringing* (Education by the parents.)
3.   to bring *up* a subject (To raise it, start talking about it.)
4.   to bring *up* one's food (To be sick, vomit.)
5.   to bring *the house down* (To be a great success in a theatre.)
6.   to bring something *off* (To succeed in something.)
7.   to bring something *about* (To cause something to happen.)
8.   to bring something *on* (To cause something to happen precipitately, generally used of illnesses.)
9.   to bring *out*
a.   a book (To publish it.)
b.   someone (To make someone less retiring and more sophisticated.)
c.   *the best* or *worst in* someone (To cause the best or worst side of someone's nature to react to your stimulus.)
10.   to bring something *upon* oneself (To be the cause of one's own troubles.)
11.   to bring *in* legislation (To introduce new laws and pass them.)
12.   to bring someone *round*
a.   (To invite someone to accompany you on a visit.)
b.   (To help someone to recover consciousness after he has fainted.)
c.   *to one's way of thinking* (To persuade someone to accept the rightness of your ideas.)
13.   to bring someone *through* an illness (To cure someone of an illness.)

EXERCISES

a. Replace the italicised parts of the sentence with expressions with *break* or *bring*.

1. I am very sorry that you are in trouble but really you *are the cause of your own misfortunes.*
2. When did your son *develop this rash*?
3. I should like to know what *caused* this heart attack.
4. In that terrible storm a large number of branches were *torn from the trees.*
5. When the man was being escorted to the police-station by two burly policemen, he managed to *escape by punching them both violently and running away.*
6. I soon *convinced her that my ideas were not so silly as she had at first supposed.*
7. Now that I have painted the ceiling and three walls of the room I have *nearly finished it.*
8. A few years ago he was an alcoholic, but he has managed to *give up drinking* now.
9. We are still hoping for *some important discovery* that will tell us the real cause of cancer.
10. Every time that actor appears he *has tremendous success.*
11. I believe that next year they are *publishing* a new edition of that work.
12. What a nuisance that my car *went wrong* just as I was taking Mary for her first drive with me!

b. Fill in the blank space with a word formed from, or related to, the word given in brackets at the end of the sentence.

e.g *Although he was no longer young his face was ...... (boy)—boyish*

1. *He was living in the old ...... palace. (bishop)*
2. *You know very well that most jobs become ...... after a while (repeat)*
3. *Let me give you a little ...... advice. (uncle)*
4. *Mary Queen of Scots was ...... (head)*
5. *I think that child had better be removed from the class; he is very ...... and is making a nuisance of himself. (quarrel)*
6. *That was a ...... thing to say. (despise)*
7. *...... remarks are sometimes out of place. (joke)*
8. *I refuse to pay so such money to sit in such ......, however good the spectacle may be. (uncomfortable)*
9. *She brought some ...... in a large shop and made them into cushions. (remain)*
10. *That does not seem a very ...... arrangement. (business)*
11. *There was a call for an immediate ...... of hostilities. (cease)*
12. *In general the English like to have some ...... (private)*
13. *It is important to see that criminals get their just ...... (deserve)*

14. *The ...... of the Moors from Spain led to a sharp decrease in trade.* (expel)
15. *I was amazed at the ...... of his observations.* (profound)
16. *I was surprised at seeing him drunk because I had always thought of him as an ...... person.* (abstain)
17. *He fell into a ...... quarry and lay for some hours before he was found.* (use)
18. *You are not ...... for that post.* (elect)
19. *As there was no ...... transport of any kind, we had to walk.* (vehicle)
20. *It would be ...... of me to correct you in your own language.* (presume)
21. *Appearances are sometimes ......* (deceive)
22. *Eagles are some of the most ...... of birds.* (prey)
23. *He was very ...... about keeping me waiting so long.* (apologise)
24. *He told me quite ...... that he had no intention of paying me back any of the money he owed me.* (brass)
25. *Actors must have ...... memories.* (retain)
26. *I wonder if there is really more ...... in England than in other countries.* (snob)
27. *I would not trust him an inch; he has shown himself a ...... friend on far too many occasions.* (traitor)
28. *Most churches in England are ......* (cross)
29. *'...... is the soul of wit.'* (brief)
30. *If you are going to tell lies, you might at least give them a ...... of truth.* (seem)
31. *Mr Pickwick was tried for ...... of promise.* (break)
32. *Waiters are normally charged for ....* (break)
33. *I thanked him for the ...... of the book.* (lend)
34. *The ...... of work after the strike has been delayed by further disagreements.* (resume)
35. *Such ...... surprised even his worst enemies.* (infamous)

c. Put the verbs in brackets into the right tense.
1. *How can you make such dreadful mistakes when you (learn) English for so many years?*
2. *I (die) but a clever doctor (manage) to save my life.*
3. *That girl infuriates me. She constantly (interrupt) to ask some idiotic question or other.*
4. *His housekeeper (work) for him for fifteen years before he decided to ask her to marry him.*
5. *In old age everyone (like) to look back to see what he (achieve) in life.*
6. *Only after several serious accidents (take) place on that dangerous corner the Minister of Transport (agree) to a road-widening scheme.*
7. *Don't you think it shocking that people still (be) forced to live in shanty towns?*

8. *It is a long time since I (go) to Covent Garden.*

9. *If he (start) to abuse the Government yesterday what your reaction (be)?*

10. *I wonder how much progress (be) made on constructing those flats.*

11. *Inquiries (be) made in several parts of the country and you must just wait until the results of them (be) known.*

12. *How long you (know) my sister?*

13. *He (kill) his victim easily, (remove) his wallet, (wipe) away all fingerprints and just (make) for the front door to make his escape when he (hear) a key turning in the lock. Someone (come) in! What he (do) if he (be) seen?*

14. *In such a desperate situation he (find) himself that he decided to shoot his way out.*

15. *I suggest that something (be) done about it at once.*

16. *So great the success of this exhibition (be) that I (decide) to extend it for another month.*

17. *It is inconceivable that she (not see) me.*

18. *What a pity that he gave orders that all those lovely trees (be) cut down!*

19. *That programme (finish) anyway long before I need to get ready to go out.*

20. *Not only he (murder) his wife but he (try) to lay the blame on someone else.*

17: 'So' and prepositions at the end of sentences

Verbs followed by *so* in the positive can take a direct negative (i.e. one not using *do*).

positive	negative
I think so	*I don't think so*
	I think not
I believe so	*I don't believe so*
	I believe not
I imagine so	*I don't imagine so*
	I imagine not
I fancy so	*I don't fancy so*
	I fancy not
I expect so	*I don't expect so*
	I expect not
I hope so	*I hope not* (only one negative form)

I am afraid so	*I am afraid not* (only one negative form)
I'm telling you so	*I'm not telling you so*
	I'm telling you not
I said so	*I didn't say so*
	I said not
I understand so	*I don't understand so* (uncommon)
	I understand not

Where two negative forms are possible the one with the direct negative is much stronger.

'Are they going to get married?'
'I don't think so'. (I doubt it; I have not heard anything about it)
'I think not.'(I definitely think they will not; I have heard that the engagement has been broken off.)

Where the sentence really ends with *to do so*, the *do so* is often omitted, leaving the sentence ending with *to*.

'Why didn't you go in?' 'I didn't like to.'
'Call me sir!' 'I refuse to.'
'Why don't you ask her?' 'I don't wish to.'
I offered to give him private lessons but he didn't want me to.
I asked him to tell me the truth but he seemed unwilling to/was reluctant to.
'Will you read to me?' 'I am not in the mood to.'
'Why haven't you bought any butter?' 'I meant to but I forgot about it.'
'Why have you hidden the whiskey?' 'Mother told me to.'
I didn't object because I had been ordered not to.

In this connection it should be noted that there is no objection whatever in English to ending sentences with prepositions. Any prejudice against doing so must be overcome because many very natural English sentences can only sound artificial if the preposition is moved forward or if the whole phrase is replaced by something Latinized.

Here are some common examples.

What do you take me for?
Kindly tell me where you took this from.
That is something I will not put up with.
That is nothing to go by.
As he was coming into the room, he fell down.
What are razors for? To shave with.
What are beds for? To sleep on.
What an extraordinary thing to accuse me of!
As he walked past, she looked up.
That's a nice thing to waste money on!
Your car is very difficult to get into or out of.
What on earth are you talking about?
It's something you must learn to do without.
My coat button has come off.
What scrapes you do get yourself into!
What are you getting at?

EXERCISES

a. Answer the following questions, beginning your answer with an infinitive and ending it with a preposition.
1. *What is a lawn-mower for?*
2. *What is a tin-opener for?*
3. *What is a stamp album for?*
4. *What is a doorhandle for?*
5. *What is a swimming pool for?*
6. *What is a diving-board for?*
7. *What is a breadboard for?*
8. *What is a vacuum cleaner for?*
9. *What is a bathmat for*
10. *What is a ball for?*
11. *What is a tennis court for?*
12. *What is a spade for?*
13. *What is a gun for?*
14. *What is an armchair for?*
15. *What is a path for?*
16. *What is a sink for?*
17. *What are scissors for?*
18. *What are the straps on the Underground for?*
19. *What is a window-box for?*
20. *What is a suitcase for*
21. *What is a comb for?*
22. *What is a well for?*
23. *What is a screw-driver for?*
24. *What is a door-mat for?*
25. *What was an executioner's axe for?*

b. Insert the right verb in these sentences.
1. *The fox tried hard to ...... his pursuers off the scent.*
2. *I tore up an old shirt to ...... the flow of blood from the gaping wound.*
3. *Why don't you ask Mary to ...... some ballet steps to ...... up the proceedings?*
4. *I left John to ...... up with the landlord.*
5. *An acquaintance of mine ...... in his lot with a troupe of gipsies for several months.*
6. *I wish you would stop ...... on the subject of your girlfriend.*
7. *She ...... open house for all her friends and relatives.*
8. *It is strange how great men can still ...... an influence over people, even in this century.*
9. *I was ...... my neck to see over the heads of the crowd in front of me.*
10. *The pomposity of his writing ...... on the ludicrous.*
11. *The fact that one day she would inherit a lot of money just ...... the scales in favour of his marrying her.*

12. *'You look very relaxed.' 'Yes, I am ...... my energy for the tennis tournament this afternoon.'*
13. *On the strength of that small win on the football pools he ...... all his colleagues a drink.*
14. *Insolvents generally ...... up in prison.*
15. *He ...... his knowledge of languages to good account.*
16. *Always ...... up the facts before ...... to a decision.*
17. *Political agitators are always ...... up trouble.*
18. *The workmen were so angry that they ...... tools on the spot.*
19. *All that praise certainly ...... his ego.*
20. *Scandals ...... dull reading after a time. One's interest soon ......*
21. *I cannot imagine why you should ...... to the whims of an old crank like him.*
22. *I decided to ...... to his better feelings.*
23. *They have ...... up production at that factory by introducing some new machinery.*
24. *He found that his telephone was being ...... because he was suspected of being a spy.*
25. *Love affairs that cannot come to fruition are like cancer; they are better ...... in the bud.*

18: Interrogative sentences

1.   *Who* is used in enquiring about people unless the choice is limited. If it is limited use *which*.
In practice, though not in theory, *who* is generally used for subject and object, though in formal writing *whom* is preferred for the object.
Who is coming to the party?
Who was speaking?
Who(m) do you think you are talking to?
Who(m) are you holding responsible?
Which of those brothers are you in love with?
Which son is his father's favourite?
Those twins are very alike. Do you know which is which?
Which of your boyfriends gave you that?

2.   *What* is used in enquiring about things unless the choice is limited. If it is limited use *which*.
If *what* is the subject of the sentence it is followed by a verb in the normal form. If *what* is the object of the sentence the inversion

form—with *do* or *did* if necessary—is used.
What happened then?
What has been built there?
What went wrong in that experiment?
What is your name?
Which of the names on this list is yours?
Which day of your holiday did you enjoy most?
Which of the books I lent you did you like best?
What did he say to that?
What play does 'Frailty, thy name is woman,' come from?

3.   *Whose* is used when you are enquiring about whom something belongs to.
Whose book is this?
Whose daughter is he proposing to?
Whose dictation did you crib from?
Whose house was the party held at?

4.   *Ever* or *on earth* may be added to interrogative pronouns to make them more emphatic.
Whatever are you talking about?
Who on earth told you that?
Whoever would believe such a silly story?
Wherever did you pick up that lovely candelabra?
Whichever of her friends said that to her is to blame for her suicide, don't you think?
N.B. *On earth* is not normally used with *which*. Such interrogative words as *how, where, why* etc. are also used like this.
How on earth did you find that out?
Where on earth did I put my umbrella?
Why ever did you do that?

5.   *Else* can be added to any of these interrogative words to mean *other*. It can also be added to words like *someone, no-one, nothing* etc.
What else did you notice about the flat?
Who else would have got out of that scrape so cleverly?
How else could I behave?
If this coat isn't yours who else's can it be?
Someone else paid for you, didn't he?
Why don't you go and pick someone else's pocket?
N.B. It will be noted that because *which* indicates limited choice it is not used with *else*.

6.   Only auxiliary verbs can come before the subject in interrogative sentences. If the subject is a long one this may lead to a wide separation of auxiliary and principal verbs.

What did those people who came to tea yesterday say about my father?
What can such an intricate piece of machinery be used for?
Who do people who show such utter disregard for the feelings of others think they are?
Why should people who can very well afford to pay an economic rent be subsidised out of local rates?

7.   In connection with *else* it should be remembered that its use is not limited to interrogative sentences.
I wish you would find someone else to pester!
Nothing else worth mentioning took place at that meeting.
He wants to marry a rich woman and no-one else will do.
I wouldn't mind living somewhere else if I could find a nice flat.

EXERCISES

a.   Rewrite the following sentences using the form with *else*.
1.   *For what other reason would he fear the police?*
2.   *What other person asked you to marry him?*
3.   *In what other way could I make him understand?*
4.   *If this isn't yours what other person's can it be?*
5.   *If he isn't in this room I do not know in what other place he can be.*
6.   *Some other person must have told you that.*
7.   *For what other purpose could I use this?*
8.   *What other place could I have gone to?*
9.   *Didn't you see any other person on the platform?*
10.   *Haven't I told you to go and play in some other place?*
11.   *At what other time could I do it?*
12.   *In what other way could the crime have been committed?*

b.   Write questions to which these could be the answers.
1.   *I was in a very daredevil mood.*
2.   *Someone whose information is usually reliable.*
3.   *One means that you intend to burn the building down, and the other that you want to get warm in winter.*
4.   *One is for transporting goods and the other is for transporting people.*
5.   *He told me he was planning the perfect murder.*
6.   *Oh, it's mine; I left it here yesterday.*
7.   *A pack of cards, a penknife, some string and a very ripe apple.*
8.   *I've had it dyed. Do you like it?*
9.   *Some people are silly enough to believe anything.*
10.   *The last one on the list.*
11.   *She's rather plump and a bottle-blonde.*
12.   *It's for keeping tea in.*
13.   *But I did tell you; you were not listening.*
14.   *The Conservatives, of course.*

15. *It's about two hundred yards further on on the left-hand side of the road.*
16. *To stick my press cuttings in with.*
17. *By pretending that I was laid up with a chill.*
18. *Oh, it belonged to my grandfather.*
19. *I have my own methods of getting information.*
20. *A large, ugly block of flats which completely ruins the view.*
21. *Don't be silly; of course he won't.*
22. *One has a motor and the other hasn't.*
23. *Yes, but you must remember that it isn't in perfect condition.*
24. *I got it for five pounds in a sale.*
25. *Columbus, I think.*

c. Insert the missing idiomatic words.
1. *He was born with a silver ...... in his mouth.*
2. *To everyone's relief the Government ...... the storm.*
3. *As a newspaper reporter he must know the ...... story of many interesting scandals.*
4. *There was no suspicion of ...... play, so the jury brought in a verdict of death by ......*
5. *They are as different as ...... and cheese.* (colloquial)
6. *They have to share the bathroom with one other person, so their flat is not really self ......*
7. *Mary is unusually brilliant and if you don't want to lose your place at the head of the class you must look to your ......*
8. *A ...... for your thoughts.* (colloquial)
9. *You cannot play fast and ...... with people like that without getting into trouble.*
10. *He is lonely because he is shy and the longer he puts off overcoming the shyness the lonelier he becomes: it is a ...... circle.*
11. *When John offered to do that he did not realise that he would get more than he ...... for.*
12. *We are all ...... with the same brush, so you needn't look so self-righteous.*
13. *She was a very fine actress in her ......*
14. *He is a very ...... customer and has escaped from no ...... of prisons.* (colloquial)
15. *It goes without saying that I will ...... the job through.*
16. *The roof was ...... in and looked as if it might collapse at any moment.*
17. *In spite of all the confusion and panic around her Margaret never ...... an eyelid.*
18. *If only she realised that if you show people that you want to be friends with them, most of them are quite ready to meet you ......*
19. *A lot of people pay ...... service to the idea of the United Nations.*
20. *There has been such a ...... of strawberries this year that many have been left to rot.*

21. *As he made no mention of repaying the money I decided to say something to ...... his memory.*
22. *He stood there, ... in the beauty of the scene before him.*
23. *They have ...... up their quarrel for the moment but I don't think the reconciliation will last.*
24. *You should never look a ...... horse in the mouth.*
25. *A ...... crop of wheat has led to an unexpected surplus.*

19: Relative pronouns

1. Use *who* for people when the pronoun is the subject of the clause.
The man who said that was a fool.

2. Use *whom* for people when the pronoun is the object of the clause. It can, however, normally be omitted.
The man (whom) you saw was a fool.
The woman (whom) he married was rich.

3. Use *whose* for the possessive case of people. This is, however, a bit heavy in style and should be avoided wherever possible. The commonest way of avoiding it is by using *with*.
The boy whose hair is red/with the red hair is very clever.
The man whose property adjoins mine/with the property adjoining mine is a pilot.
The man whose sports car that is/with that sports car happens to be a millionaire.

4. Use *which* for things, subject or object of the clause. If it is object it can be omitted.
The book which is lying there is the one (which) you borrowed from me.
The village (which) you see down there is mentioned in the Domesday Book.

5. If you omit *whom* or *which* any preposition that would have stood before them goes to the end of the clause.
The house in which we were staying/we were staying in was said to be haunted.
The man by whom he was cheated/he was cheated by was a card sharper.
The village in which he lives/he lives in is a beauty-spot.
The woman to whom I was talking/I was talking to was a poetess.

6. Use *that* for people and things, subject or object, after a superlative. It can be omitted if it is the object.
That is the nicest thing that has happened to me for a long time.
That is the wittiest speaker that has yet addressed this Society.
It is the best book (that) I have read for ages.
The last person that said that to me got a black eye.
N.B. With *first* and *last* an alternative construction with an infinitive can be used.
The last person to say that to me got a black eye.

7. Always use *that* instead of *which* after indefinite pronouns (i.e. *something, all, everything, anywhere* etc.). *Who* and *whom* are also generally replaced by *that* after indefinite pronouns (i.e. *someone, everyone, nobody* etc.) This is not, however, compulsory.
Everything that happened then was like a nightmare.
I did not hear all that was said at the meeting.
We couldn't find anywhere that suited us.
Nobody that/who spoke said anything interesting.
Someone (that)/(whom) you know must have sent it.

8. *What* can be used only when there is no antecedent (i.e. noun or pronoun to which it refers).
I did not hear all that he said.
I did not hear what he said.
Goodness knows what will happen now.
I did not understand what he wanted.

9. *Which* is used as a relative pronoun when it refers to a complete part of a sentence, not just to one word. It must have a comma before it in this case.
He usually speaks very fast, which makes it hard to understand him.
The habit of giving dowries has been discontinued in many countries, which is a great pity.

10. It will have been noticed that in all the relative clauses so far dealt with—except those in point nine—no commas have been used and relative pronouns which were objects of the clause could be omitted. This was because in every case the relative clause was an integral part of the sentence (e.g. in a sentence like *People who behave like that should't be allowed in the school*, the sentence would be meaningless without the relative clause).
On comparatively rare occasions, however, the sentence is absolutely complete without the relative clause. If it is complete without it, even without considering the context of the sentence, the relative clause is rather like a parenthesis. In this case it must be surrounded by commas and all relative pronouns must be inserted.
The parts in italics form complete sentences on their own.

The Pope, whom I had never seen before, *spoke to the crowd while I was there.*

My sister Mary, who is now living in the harem of an Arabian chief, *is a sweet girl.*

If, in the first of these sentences, the relative pronouns and commas were omitted (i.e. *The Pope I had never seen before spoke to the crowd while I was there*) the meaning would be different. It would imply that I had seen the other Pope or Popes but not that particular one.

EXERCISES

a.   Insert the correct relative pronoun where necessary.
1. *Everything ...... happened after that seemed unreal.*
2. *I am going out to buy some food, ... will take me about half an hour.*
3. *Did you understand all ...... you read in that book?*
4. *Maupassant, ... you have no doubt heard of, went mad in the end.*
5. *The man ...... daughter jilted you has just died.*
6. *Nothing ...... Shakespeare wrote is entirely without merit.*
7. *Ford is one of the best-known firms ...... turns out cars.*
8. *Did you hear ...... he said to me just now?*
9. *The man ...... called round this morning had a funny face.*
10. *The Government is trying to do something about it, ... is praiseworthy if somewhat tardy.*
11. *All ...... glitters is not gold.*
12. *It is the most heart-rending story ...... I have read for a long time.*

b.   Put into more natural English.
1. *The boy whose eyes are vivid blue wants to be an actor.*
2. *The policeman from whom we are running away is too old to catch us.*
3. *The pond into which he fell was quite deep.*
4. *Am I the person for whom you are looking?*
5. *The man whose large house you can see down there is very miserly.*
6. *The delusion under which you are labouring is quite a common one.*
7. *Alexander, than whom perhaps no greater general has ever existed, was an ambitious man.*
8. *The train by which I was coming was cancelled.*
9. *That is the woman whose son is in prison.*
10. *The map at which I was looking was rather torn.*

c.   Put the verbs in brackets into the infinitive or gerund, adding prepositions if necessary.
1. *The caretaker collaborated with the burglars (rob) the warehouse.*
2. *She was really upset (lose) her only sister.*
3. *I do not deny (sign) that document but I was coerced (do) so.*
4. *She is very excited (go) to Greece next month.*

5. *You are only playing (be) ill just (annoy) me.*
6. *Are you accusing me (mislead) you (think) that I was a qualified practitioner?*
7. *He is mean (spend) money on other people.*
8. *She complained (feel) ill and left the room.*
9. *Sadists get pleasure (hurt) others.*
10. *They were disgusted (be) treated so rudely.*
11. *It was thanks (I miss) that aeroplane that I arrived safely.*
12. *Why don't you try your hand (design) a bungalow for yourself?*
13. *Listen to that man (sing) in the house over the road.*
14. *I did not refer (see) you there because I thought you might be furious (have) people's attention drawn to your movements.*
15. *Did you take part (quell) that riot?*
16. *(Know) nothing about a subject is sometimes no obstacle (get) up and (speak) about it in public.*
17. *Are you in favour (abolish) the death penalty?*
18. *I am not responsible (he make) a nuisance of himself.*
19. *The boy soon got bored (play) by himself.*
20. *I attributed his failure (he be) so lazy.*
21. *I would scorn (take) part (play) such a dirty trick on him.*
22. *She gave me the impression (want) (I fall) in love with her.*
23. *How do you account (be) found in possession of the stolen articles?*
24. *(Do) crossword puzzles easily is mainly a question (get) used to the way the creator's mind works.*
25. *It is often claimed that women are better (adapt) themselves (live) in different surroundings than men are.*

d. Below are twenty verbs ending in *-ise* or *-ify*. The italicised part of the sentences following can be replaced by one of these verbs. Assign the right verb to each sentence.

to ostracise	to proselytise	to crystallise
to improvise	to stylise	to tantalise
to jeopardise	to bowdlerise	to cauterise
to lionise	to plagiarise	to temporise
to rectify	to mollify	to clarify
to ratify	to petrify	to nullify
to specify	to vilify	

1. Over the last few years his point of view has *become more definite*.
2. That agreement has not yet been *approved and sanctioned*.
3. Plato admired Egyptian art because it had remained *stereotyped* for so many centuries.
4. No-one thought anything of *rehandling other people's work* in Shakespeare's day.
5. As we had some unexpected guests we had to *rustle up* some kind of lunch for them.
6. The tramp was *tormented* by seeing such delicious food in the shop-window.

7. She didn't go *into details about* what kind of scarf I was to get her.
8. Perhaps Mexico is the best place for getting marriages *dissolved*.
9. I disapprove of *expurgated* editions of Shakespeare.
10. I found it very difficult to *placate* her after I had so deeply offended her.
11. In ancient Greece it was not uncommon to *banish* people *from* society as a legal punishment.
12. When he was brought face to face with the problem, the Minister tried to *gain time*.
13. The wound was *burned with hot metal* to prevent infection.
14. Nowadays it is common to *disparage* previously admired characters.
15. In *The Ideal Husband* one piece of past dishonesty *endangers* the whole career of a public figure.
16. When I felt a ghostly presence in the room I was so *transfixed* with fear that I sat absolutely still.
17. If one is *fêted* too much it is bad for one's character.
18. The Government is doing its best to *put right* certain glaring injustices.
19. It annoys me when Christians *try to convert others*.
20. The Prime Minister was asked to *explain more precisely* his attitude to that conflict.

20: Compound verbs C—D

Call

1. to call *on* someone (To visit someone.)
2. to call *on/upon* someone to do something (To ask someone officially to do something.)
3. to call *for* someone (To meet someone at his house before you go out together.)
4. to call *for* something.
a. (To require or need something.)
b. (To call somewhere to get something.)
5. to call *at* (To visit for a short time for a specific purpose.)
6. to call something *off* (To cancel something.)
7. to call someone *up* (To conscript someone for military service.) (To telephone someone.)
8. to call someone *in* (To request someone's professional help.)
9. to call workers *out on strike* (To order them to stop work and go on strike.)

10. a *roll-call* (The calling out of a list of names so that those present can answer.)
11. to be *on call* (To be liable to be asked to give one's services.)
12. a *calling* (A vocation: job done from internal compulsion.)

Cast

1. to be cast *away* (To be marooned on an island.)
2. to cast *off* (To weigh anchor or unmoor a boat.)
3. *cast-offs* (Old clothes that have been discarded.)
4. to be cast *down/downcast* (To be very miserable.)
5. to be cast *up* on an island (To reach it after being shipwrecked.)
6. to cast *about* in one's mind (To think very hard.)
7. an *outcast* (Someone rejected by respectable society, as from the Hindu religion, for example.)
8. *overcast* (Cloudy.)

Catch

1. to catch *up with*.
a. (To draw level with someone.)
b. (To work hard on accumulated work. Alternatively 'to catch *up on*': the opposite is 'to get *behind with*'.)
2. to catch someone *out* (To find someone in the wrong.)
3. to catch *sight of* (To glimpse; get one's first sight of.)
4. to catch *fire* (To start to burn; to burst into flames.)
5. to catch *on*.
a. (To understand: colloquial.)
b. (To become popular—of fashions etc.)
6. to catch *at* the slightest hope (To try to persuade oneself that there are grounds for hoping.)
7. to catch *it* (To get into trouble, to get punished: slang.)
8. a *catch* (A snag.)
There must be a catch in it. (There must be something wrong with it or dishonest about it.)

EXERCISES

Replace the italicised parts of the sentence with expressions with *call*, *cast* or *catch*.
1. John was *conscripted* last week, so he is a very raw recruit.
2. Naturally a war *demands* sacrifices from everyone.
3. *Robinson Crusoe* is probably the most famous book about someone who was *shipwrecked* on an uninhabited island.

4. Widespread and severe frost has led to many football matches being *cancelled*.
5. When the chimney caught fire he *asked* the Fire Brigade *to come round* to be on the safe side.
6. Fashion designers often try to introduce styles that do not *appeal to the public*.
7. Sometimes even the police are unable to *draw level with* their quarry.
8. I do not like students who are always trying to *prove that* their tutors *are wrong*.
9. Mr Jones was *required* to read his paper to the assembled company.
10. I must just *pop into* the post office to buy some stamps. (colloquial)

Come

1. to come *to* (To recover consciousness after fainting.)
2. to come *round*.
a. (To recover consciousness.)
b. (To visit.)
3. to come *round to* accepting a certain point of view (To be persuaded that it is reasonable.)
4. to come *upon/across* something (To find something unexpectedly.)
5. to come *about* (To happen.)
6. to come *by* something (To obtain something surprisingly or suspiciously.)
7. to come *between* two people (To break up their love or friendship.)
8. to come *down in the world* (To lose one's wealth, power or prestige.)
9. to come *into* money (To inherit it.)
10. to come *into it*.
That does not come into it. (That is not relevant to it.)
11. to come *into one's own* (To obtain recognition as a genius or very talented person.)
12. to come *off* (To become detached, of buttons etc.)
13. to come *off well* or *badly* in something (To be successful or unsuccessful in something—a fight, an examination etc.)
14. to come *out with* (To say very unexpectedly.)
15. to come *out*.
a. (To be published.)
b. (To be discovered eventually.)
c. (To be presented to society as a debutante.)
d. (To open fully, of flowers.)
e. (To appear, of stars.)
f. well or badly (To be successful or unsuccessful, of a photograph.)
g. (To be removed, of stains etc.)
16. to come *over*.
a. (To visit.)
b. faint (Suddenly to feel faint.)

17. to come *over* someone.
What has come over him? (Why is he behaving so strangely?)
18. to come *through* (To survive a war, an illness etc.)
19. to come *under* someone's influence (To be influenced by someone.)
20. to come *up to.*
It did not come up to my expectations. (It was not as good as I had expected.)
21. Come *on! (Hurry up!)*
22. *oncoming.*
The *oncoming* traffic (Traffic approaching in the opposite direction.)
23. to *overcome* (To surmount, of obstacles etc.)
24. *income* (Total amount of money a person gets in the course of a year.)
25. the *outcome (*The consequence, generally used if it is not entirely within one's own control.)
26. a *come-back.*
to stage one's *come-back* (To return to the public eye with brilliant success, generally used of performers, actors, etc.)
27. to be *overcome* with (To be full of emotion, e.g. remorse.)

EXERCISE

Replace the italicised part of the sentence with an expression with *come.*
1.   When his grandfather died, John *was bequeathed £10,000.*
2.   It is remarkable how that family has *lost all its power and fortune.*
3.   In the course of conversation *I discovered* that he had been to school with my cousin.
4.   It is sad that someone like Emily Brontë should only *be recognised as a genius* after her death.
5.   Children often *say* outrageous things *quite unexpectedly.*
6.   One day you will *realise that there is some sense in* my point of view.
7.   That is the kind of stain that *cannot be removed* easily.
8.   I *found* this quaint old book *quite by chance* in the attic.
9.   I am not at all photogenic; I never *look at all presentable* in photos.
10. How on earth did you *obtain possession of* that mink coat?
11. A button *is missing on* your coat-sleeve.
12. It took him a long time to *recover consciousness* after his anaesthetic.
13. That film *was a great disappointment to me.*
14. I cannot imagine how it *happened* that my brother was picked up in that disreputable nightclub.
15. He *was not very successful* in that fight.

Cut

1.   to be cut *off* (To be isolated.)

2. to cut *off* (To disconnect electricity etc. because the bill has not been paid.)

3. to be cut *off* with a shilling (To be disinherited.)

4. to cut something *out* (To do without something, to stop it completely.)

5. to cut *down on* something (To reduce expenditure on, and consumption of, something.)

6. to be cut *out for*.

He is not cut out for that job. (He is not temperamentally suited for it.)

7. to cut *school* (To play truant from school: colloquial.)

8. to be cut *up about* something (To be very upset about something: colloquial.)

9. to cut *right across*.

That cuts right across our plans. (That quite prevents us from putting our plans into practice.)

10. to cut *in*.

a. (To interrupt a conversation.)

b. (To swerve too quickly in front of a car that you are overtaking so that it has to slow down.)

11. to cut *down* (To fell, e.g. trees.)

12. cut *along! (Run off now:* colloquial.)

13. to *undercut* someone (To offer goods at a lower price than someone else.)

14. to cut *someone* (To pretend not to see someone.)

15. to be *a cut above the rest* (To be superior to the others: colloquial.)

16. a *short cut* (A direct path, avoiding a detour.)

17. a *cutting*.

a. (An article cut out of a newspaper.)

b. (A way through a hill, but not roofed in like a tunnel.)

c. (Small branch or stem of a bush or flower that can be put in water and then in the ground to propagate it.)

18. a *cutting remark* (A sarcastic remark, designed to hurt.)

EXERCISES

Replace the italicised part of the sentence with an expression with *cut*.

1. I do not feel that he is altogether *fitted* for that post.

2. It is far from easy to *stop* smoking.

3. The village was *inaccessible* for a time because of the severe floods.

4. She was *exceedingly unhappy* when she learned of her husband's death.

5. You really should *eat less* sugar; it's so fattening.

6. My friend's illness *completely disrupted* our plans to spend that holiday together.

7. He *really fancies his chances*.

8. Bad drivers *never leave enough room when overtaking*.

9. What a pity it seems to *fell* those trees.

Do

1. to do *away with* (To abolish.)
2. to do someone *down* (To cheat someone, especially financially: colloquial.)
3. *It won't do* (It is not good enough or suitable.)
4. to do *for* someone.
a. (To do the housework for someone.)
b. (To ruin someone completely.)
c. (To kill someone: colloquial.)
5. to be done *up* (To be very tired, exhausted: colloquial.)
6. to do *up*
a. (To tie up.)
b. a room (To decorate it: colloquial.)
c. a button (To fasten it.)
d. a parcel (To wrap it and tie it up.)
7. to do *out* a room (To clear it thoroughly and put it in order.)
8. to do *without* something (To manage without having something.)
9. to be *hard done by* (To be unfairly and cruelly treated.)
10. to have to do *with* someone (To have dealings with someone.)
11. to do *with*.
a. I can't do *with* it (I can't stand it, bear it, put up with it.)
b. I could do *with* (I would like to have, I need.)
12. to make do *with* something (To make oneself satisfied with something, usually because one cannot afford anything better.)
13. to *outdo* someone (To do more or better than someone else).

Draw

1. to draw *up*.
a. A car drew *up* (A car stopped by the kerb: this expression is only used of vehicular transport.)
b. *plans* (To make detailed plans.)
c. *a chair* (To bring it nearer.)
2. to draw *in*.
The evenings are drawing in. (It is getting dark earlier every evening—i.e. June to December.)
3. to draw *out*.
a. *The evenings are drawing out.* (It is getting dark later and later every evening—i.e. December to June.) ,
b. someone (To induce someone to talk more freely.)
4. to draw *upon*. (To use for material.)
5. to draw *back from* doing something (To shrink from doing something.)
6. to draw *off* water (To let water flow from a tap so as to empty the tank.)

7. to draw someone *aside* (To lead someone away from other people so as to talk to him privately.)

8. to draw *off* (To move away.)

9. to *withdraw* (To retire from a position.)

10. to *withdraw one's consent* (To change one's mind after one has agreed to something.)

11. to be drawn *down in* something (To be pulled under and killed by something—quicksands, a whirlpool etc.)

12. to draw *on*

Night is drawing on. (It is already getting dark.)

EXERCISES

a. Replace the italicised part of the sentence with an expression with *do* or *draw*.

1. If I were you I should not *concern yourself at all with him in future.*

2. She spent the afternoon *sorting out and cleaning* that cupboard.

3. He knew what his duty was, but *was reluctant to do* it.

4. During wartime Governments have to *make* detailed plans to cope with air raids.

5. You had better *button up* your coat; *it is getting dark* and a chilly wind is getting up.

6. We simply have not enough money to replace this carpet: we shall have to *manage* with it for another year.

7. A lot of out-of-date laws ought to be *rescinded.*

8. We had to *manage without* a lot of luxuries at that time.

9. He has a chip on his shoulder and always thinks himself *ill-treated.*

10. If people are shy it is often difficult to *make them talk.*

b. Put in the missing prepositions or particles in these sentences.

1. *I have had enough of her tantrums I'm .... her.*

2. *Desperately he cast ...... for something to say.*

3. *It's drizzling now; I'm ringing to see whether our game of tennis this afternoon is ...... or ......*

4. *A suspicious character has been lurking about in those bushes all day; I'm sure he is .... no good.*

5. *You are getting too fat; you had better cut .... sugar, cream, butter and stodgy foods.*

6. *Many people in politics are .... make a name for themselves.*

7. *Little by little he brought her .... accepting his view of life.*

8. *Napoleon referred to the English as 'a nation of shopkeepers'. Furthermore not all of them are honest; some will try to do you ......*

9. *Even nowadays people are sometimes cast .... desert islands.*

10. *To understand grammar you must break the sentence .... its component parts.*

11. *I wonder what brought ...... this headache.*
12. *I have decided not to apply for that job. Really I do not feel that I am .... it.*
13. *I was arrested but managed to break .... my captors.*
14. *He is very cut .... not getting promotion.*
15. *He caught ...... the slightest hope of saving himself.*
16. *Many people bring their own ruin ...... themselves.*
17. *It is a long time since they did .... trams in England.*
18. *The child backed .... him in terror.*
19. *I wish you would stop galloping; how can I possibly catch .... you?*
20. *Seeing the lights of the coastguardsmen, the smugglers cast ...... with all speed.*
21. *I should like to know how he came ...... such an expensive car; perhaps he came ...... some money when his uncle died.*
22. *I suddenly came ...... dizzy and had to sit down.*
23. *I cannot do ...... background noise of any kind.*
24. *A large limousine drew ...... and out stepped a rather flashily dressed girl.*
25. *A woman comes in once a week to do ...... him.*

c. Insert the right verbs in these sentences.
1. *That decision ...... disaster for us.*
2. *A lot of people are only concerned with ...... their own nests.*
3. *I do hope I am not ...... on your privacy.*
4. *I wonder of it is a good thing or a bad one for people to ...... their wild oats when they are young.*
5. *Vercingetorix' army ...... in wait for Caesar's soldiers and suddenly set on them.*
6. *Why do you ...... exception to a remark that was said without any malicious intention?*
7. *Those heavy rains have ...... havoc with the wheat crop.*
8. *When one is first introduced to someone it is natural to try to ...... him up.*
9. *No quarter was ...... in that battle; all prisoners were ...... to death.*
10. *A number of Members of Parliament are ...... amendments to that new bill.*
11. *It would be interesting to know how many people really ...... what they preach.*
12. *What inference do you ...... from looking at these figures?*
13. *You certainly ...... a surprise on me by telling me that.*
14. *A friend of mine ...... host to a number of Russian students.*
15. *The Trade Unions ...... an ultimatum to the Government, threatening to ...... on strike if their demands were not ...... within a week.*
16. *Wars ...... sacrifices from everyone and a great many things have to ...... by the board.*

17. *As far as we can ...... the murder was ...... some time between 9 and 10 p.m. on the 5th June last.*
18. *Sooner or later most favourites of kings have ...... to grief.*
19. *It must be a shattering experience for a judge to ...... sentence of death on anyone for the first time.*

d. Use the following words in sentences so as to bring out their meaning

to thresh	exposure	supercilious	to conceal
to thrash	exposition	superficial	to congeal
trash	exhibition	superfluous	congenial
to truss	expedition		
to trust		to besiege	
to thrust	ostensible	to beseech	
thrush	ostentatious		

21: Uncountable nouns

1. All substances can be assumed to be uncountable: china, coal, gold, mud, butter, grass, wheat, wool, salt, milk, tobacco, flour, alcohol, sugar, smoke, soil, cloth etc.
2. The majority of uncountable nouns are either collective or generic nouns or are abstract qualities. In either case it would be illogical to attach a number to them. If they cannot be used with a number, they cannot be used with *a* or *an*, because these mean *one*—a number. They cannot either be used with any other singular word, such as *each, every* or *either*. They cannot furthermore be used in the plural, or with any plural word, such as *both*.

The following is a list of some of the most common uncountable nouns*:

accommodation	*admiration*	advice
aggression	agitation	agriculture
air (atmosphere)	*amazement*	*ammunition*
anarchy	anger	anguish
anxiety	applause	approval
architecture	*arrogance*	assistance
astonishment	attention	automation

*N.B. Students should check the words in a dictionary as several of them have other meanings which can be used with *a* or *an* or in the plural (e.g. an *air* of wisdom/ musical *airs*. For words in italics see note 7, page 125.

awe
behaviour
blackmail
boredom
capital (money)
chaos
commerce
compassion
confusion
constancy
countryside
craftsmanship
damage (except in the
  legal sense of
  damages, meaning
  compensation)
dismay
distress
earthenware
elegance
employment
encouragement
enthusiasm
evidence
filth
flux
fodder
foresight
fuel
gaiety
give-and-take
gratitude
greed
gunfire
harness
heat
hesitation
honesty
hostility
humility
ignorance
imprisonment
initiative
invective (this has a
  plural
junk (meaning *trash*)
lassitude

baggage
bewilderment
bloodshed
bravery
caviare
clothing
common sense
conduct
conscription
cordiality
courage
cruelty
debris
despair
dirt
discouragement
disorder (except in a
  medical sense)
education (unless
  qualified by an
  adjectuve)
endurance
equipment
excitement
fish (if dead)
food
fog
freedom
fun
garbage
gossip (the thing, not
  the person)
guidance
handwriting
headway
help (the thing, not the
  person)
hope (generally)
humanity
hunger
illiteracy
impudence
innocence
jealousy
jewellery
jurisprudence
laughter

bait
bigamy
booty
calligraphy
censorship
comfort (except
  in the
  meaning of
  consolation)
counsel
cowardice
cutlery
demur
dessert
discomfort
disillusionment
dissent
drudgery
effeminacy
electricity
enchantment
energy
espionage
fiction (in the
  sense of
  literature)
folly
freight
furniture
generosity
grammar (the
  thing, not the
  book)
harm
health
heroism
hilarity
hospitality
humidity
hysteria
immorality
information
insolence
jeopardy
joviality
justice
legislation

leisure

lightning

litter (*rubbish*)

luck

lumber

magnificence

merriment

mist

money

negligence

normality

obstinacy

permission

photography

poetry

poverty

privacy

produce

progress

propaganda

publicity

refuse

resentment

romanticism

sabotage

sarcasm

sculpture (generally)

shame (except in the
  idiom: *what a shame*)

sorcery

strength

sunlight

suspense

thunder

trash

treatment

upholstery

vegetation

vermin

wealth

wisdom (except in the
  idiom: *a wealth
  of wisdom*)

work (except for *works
  of art, road works*, and
  works meaning *factory*
  or *mechanism*)

lethargy

literacy

loot

luggage

machinery

mail

mirth

modesty

morality

news

notoriety

penitence

perplexity

pity (except in the
  idiom: *what a pity*)

practice (except
  in the meaning
  of *a doctor's
  practice*)

prudence

recognition

remorse

rivalry

rubbish

safety

scaffolding

seaweed

shrapnel

snuff

stamina

strife

sunshine

tact

traffic (meaning
  vehicles)

uncertainty

valour

vengeance (except in the
  expression: *with a
  vengeance*, meaning
  *more than is right or
  proper*)

witchcraft

worry

wrath

liberty (except
  in the idiom:
  *to take
  liberties*)

magic

merchandise

mischief

moisture

music

nonsense

oblivion

permanence

phlegm

plunder

poultry

price (except in
  the idiom:
  *take a pride
  in something*)

psychology

refreshment

research (this
  has a plural)

rubble

sagacity

scenery

servitude

slavery

sobriety

stationery

stupidity

supervision

tension

transport
  (except in the
  meaning
  *transports of
  delight*)

wartime

weather (except
  in the idiom:
  *to go out in
  all weathers*)

worth

zeal

3.   In addition all abstract nouns ending in *-ness* are uncountable: happiness, cleverness, usefulness, mildness, gladness etc.

4.   All illnesses are uncountable, except colds, coughs and headaches: influenza, rheumatism, polio, cancer etc.

5.   All sports are uncountable: hockey, cricket, tennis, golf etc.
6.   Most nouns ending in *-ing* are uncountable:
hunting, fighting, swimming, shopping, boxing, sightseeing, quarrelling, timing, striving etc.
Some common exceptions are:
soft furnishings, a blessing, a parting, meetings, comings and goings, babblings, murmurings, savings.

7.   Some uncountable nouns (those in italics in the list given) can be used in the singular if they are followed by a relative clause or any other expression indicating *of the kind that:*
An education that did not include a foreign language would be incomplete.
A humility like that of Uriah Heep is detestable.
A modesty that verges on prudery is excessive.
Mayan architecture was an architecture incapable of roofing large areas.
A morality that condones such bloodshed is totally unacceptable to me.
A merriment that is forced is ghoulish.

8. In a general sense most uncountable nouns can be used without any article at all. *The* can be used before them to make them precise (i.e. referring to a particular example at a particular time.) *Some* (or *any* in a negative sentence) can also be used with most of them to limit them:
Furniture is expensive.
The furniture in that room was hideous.
He has some nice furniture.
Advice is not always welcome.
The advice he gave me was very silly.
I asked him for some advice about investing my money.
He did not give me any advice that I found useful.
Luggage can be a nuisance.
The luggage I had sent on in advance got lost.
He had not any luggage with him.

9.   All adjectives, verbs and pronouns referring to uncountable nouns are singular (but see note 2):
He had so much luggage that I helped him to carry it.
Cheap accommodation is hard to find in London.
The traffic was noisy but he did not notice it.
How much butter is left?
The magic has worn off.

10. Most uncountable nouns can be used with *a good deal of*, *a great deal of*, *a fair amount of* and *a great amount of* as alternatives to *a lot of*. No other nouns can be used with these alternatives:

There is a fair amount of influenza about at present.
He has a great deal of money.
She gave me a good deal of useful information.
There was a great deal of tension at the time.

It should be noted that when *a lot of* is used before an uncountable noun the verb following is singular. When *a lot of* is used before plural nouns the verb following is, of course, plural:

A lot of modern furniture is ugly.
A lot of money is spent on defence.
A lot of people are fond of sport.
A lot of shops sell shoddy goods.

11. The majority of uncountable nouns can be made singular by adding *a bit of* or *a piece of*, and can be made plural by adding *bits of* or *pieces of*:

That is a subtle bit of propaganda.
A bit of debris was left there.
That is my favourite piece of poetry.
Some complicated pieces of equipment were installed.
Show a bit of compassion for once.
The flat was cluttered up with bits of trash.
Some pieces of sculpture were tastefully disposed about the park.
That piece of scaffolding looks dangerous.

12. Quite a lot of uncountable nouns that are not normally used with *a bit of* or *a piece of* have special words to make them singular or plural. Here are some of the commonest:

a spell of good weather
a peal/clap of thunder (overhead)
a flash of lightning
a fit of anger/madness
a cloud/pall of smoke (large)
a lump of coal/sugar
a stroke of luck
a spot of work (used in positive sentences)
a loaf of bread (complete, uncut or pre-cut by the manufacturers)
a state of chaos/emergency/ lethargy/listlessness/anarchy/ tension/apathy/confusion health/ hiatus/disorder/uncertainty/ poverty/perplexity/agitation/flux

a round of ammunition
a rumble of thunder (in the distance)
a means of transport
a puff/wisp of smoke (small)
a suit of armour
a stroke of work (only used in negative sentences)
a slice of bread/toast/meat
a ray of sunshine (used figuratively as well)
a shaft of sunlight (literally)
a moment of leisure/happiness
a stretch of scenery/countryside (*a piece/bit of scenery* is used only of scenery in a theatre)
a scrap/morsel of food

a ripple of girlish laughter
an expression/a feeling of gratitude
a specimen of handwriting
an article of clothing
a chorus of dissent
a feat of endurance
a roar of laughter
a peal of laughter (rather romantic)
a rasher of bacon (slice)
a burst of applause/cheering
a method/course of treatment
a flood/volley/stream of abuse/invective(s)
a blade of grass
a patch of fog/mist
a pane of glass
a pitch of excitement (more extreme than a state of excitement)
a source of anxiety/worry/pleasure
a drop of water

a token of gratitude (a gift, as a tangible expression of it)
an item of news
a splinter of wood/glass
an act of cowardice/courage/bravery
a wave of enthusiasm/hysteria
a flitch/side of bacon (large uncut piece)
a term of imprisonment
a volley of gunfire
a pattern of behaviour (generally used by psychologists)
a gust of wind
a pang of anxiety
a pat of butter
a breath of air
a string of invective(s)
a term of abuse (one word only)
a grain of sand
a speck of dust

N.B. Many words are sometimes used as uncountable nouns and sometimes as ordinary nouns and detailed usage varies from writer to writer. The lists and rules given above are solely designed to prevent the foreign student making grammatical mistakes.

EXERCISES

a. Put in the missing words where necessary.

1. ...... antique furniture is expensive, but you can find it cheaply in England.
2. ...... education is compulsory in most countries of the western world.
3. I wanted to give him ...... assistance, but was forcibly restrained from doing so.
4. A loud ...... of thunder woke me up last night.
5. He put on a ...... of armour for my benefit and very silly he looked in it, I thought.
6. He had ...... luggage with him which I helped him to carry.
7. I gave him ...... excellent advice about looking after the canary but of course he didn't take ......
8. What is your favourite ...... of transport?
9. Do you really suspect ...... sabotage?
10. What ...... awful weather we are having!
11. Most psychiatrists look for certain ...... of behaviour in their patients.

12. *Burglars had ransacked the flat which was in a ...... of absolute chaos.*
13. *How many ...... of bacon do you want for breakfast?*
14. *We went into the pub for ...... light refreshment.*
15. *...... traffic is throttling the centres of most modern towns.*
16. *There was ...... dismay at the Prime Minister's announcement.*
17. *In wartime ...... espionage is usually punishable by death.*
18. *A ...... of abuse greeted me as I opened the door.*
19. *Put another ...... of coal on the fire, will you?*
20. *...... machinery has enabled production to be increased.*
21. *A ...... of hysteria swept through the assembled crowd.*
22. *'...... vengeance is mine', said the Lord.*
23. *...... scaffolding collapsed recently; fortunately ...... did not kill anyone.*
24. *A ...... of smoke hung over the industrial town.*
25. *It is refreshing to find such an unspoilt ...... of countryside. I hope ...... will be preserved.*
26. *A great ...... of drudgery had been done away with through labour-saving devices.*
27. *...... rank vegetation grew at the water's edge.*
28. *I have not done ...... research into the matter.*
29. *Unfortunately we soon ran into a ...... of mist.*
30. *There is a fair ...... of wisdom in that philosophy.*
31. *The little girl was like a ...... of sunshine in the house.*
32. *One expects ...... comfort in one's friends' flats.*
33. *The cricket ball broke a ...... of glass.*
34. *...... slavery was abolished in England in 1833.*
35. *Some people never do a ...... of work in their lives.*
36. *...... capital is normally ...... money invested.*
37. *...... shrapnel embedded itself in his arm.*
38. *The explorers of the Antarctic inspired many by their ...... of endurance.*
39. *What a nuisance! I haven't ...... stationery left.*
40. *The garden was immaculate: not a ...... of grass was out of place.*

b.   Put the verbs in brackets into the right tense.
1.   *I wish my wife (be) here to advise me.*
2.   *Only after a lot of persuasion she (agree) to carrying out my plans.*
3.   *As he (swim) across that river he (get) cramp and (certainly drown) if John (not dive) in and (pull) him out.*
4.   *We sat entranced. Swirls of fog (curl) round the lower part of the house which little by little (disappear) and (be) swallowed up.*
5.   *I assure you that everything possible (be) done to put out the fire.*
6.   *It is quite time that child (learn) how to use a knife and fork.*
7.   *Not infrequently one (hear) reports of robberies in London.*
8.   *I (leave) the house and (walk) half way to the bus before I (remem-*

ber) that I (leave) my umbrella behind. So I (go) back to fetch it.
9. *If you (be) born in England in the 16th century what you (like) to do with your life?*
10. *I (try) to mend this lawn-mower for the last half-hour, but I still (not succeed).*
11. *Try not to leave anything behind as you (do) last time we (go) to Aunt Jemima's.*
12. *I should like to know how long you (study) English before you (come) here three months ago.*
13. *You (avoid) me all day. What I (do)?*
14. *When you (make) up your mind to apologise you may have some lunch, but not before.*
15. *He (not sell) ice-cream on the beach if his father (not die) last year, leaving nothing but debts.*

c. Use these words in sentences of your own so as to bring out the meaning clearly.

to jilt	to flaunt	to decrease	epitaph
guild	to flout	decrease	epithet
guilt		disease	epigram
to gild			
gilt	momentary		
	momentous	decent	to insure
		descent	to ensure
deep	to prolong	dissent	to assure
profound	to lengthen		

22: The uses of 'some', 'other', 'any', 'none', 'neither', 'one' and 'ones'

1. The uses of *some*.
a. Before plural and uncountable nouns as a kind of limiting article in positive sentences.
Some men were standing about drinking tea.
Some hostility was shown to him on account of his political affiliations.
I want some information about how to get to Loch Ness.
b. In questions when the answer expected is *yes*.
Surely you have some money on you?
If she works at the Embassy don't you think she may know some useful people?
Aren't there some vegetables in the larder?

c. Before singular nouns to imply a studied indifference to the exact identity of the person or thing. In this case it means *some ...... or other.*
Some tax form or something arrived for you this morning. Of course I threw it on the fire.
I read that in some book or other; does it matter which it was?
She has some ridiculous idea about having been a friend of Marie Antoinette in some previous existence.
I got it in some shop or other in Soho; I don't remember its name.

2. The uses of *any.*
a. In negatives and ordinary questions before plural and uncountable nouns, even if the negative is only implied.
Is there any news of your brother?
I haven't any money on me at the moment.
Hardly any information has been received about the fate of the hostages.
b. Before singular nouns to mean *it does not matter which.*
Any fool can do that!
Oh! Any book will do; I just want something to read on the train.
Make it any day you like; it is all the same to me.

3. The rules about the use of *some* and *any* apply to all compounds of them. Pronouns, adjectives and verbs referring to these compounds are singular.
Someone has been using my razor.
Someone has left his glasses on the table.
I can't hear anyone cleaning his teeth.
Anyone that promises to do that must be an idiot.
Anyone who really sets his mind to it can do it.

4. *None* means *not one* and is therefore singular. It is used to mean *not one out of three or more. Neither* is also singular. It means *not one out of the two.*
None of the reasons given was really convincing.
Neither he nor his sister was at the wedding.

5. *One* and its plural *ones* are used with countable nouns to avoid having an adjective standing by itself or to reinforce an adjective.
'Would you like the red apples or the green ones?' 'The red ones, please.'
'Do have some strawberries: I have some lovely ones here.'
I thought that film was a very poor one.
He has some lovely dogs, but the little black one over there is my favourite.
Aren't those delphiniums splendid? Those mauvish ones are some of the loveliest I have ever seen.

6.   *One* as an indefinite pronoun exists in all cases, which is why its use is not to be recommended: it is rather heavy and pedantic.
When someone suggests to one that one might like something delicious to eat, it makes one's mouth water.
It makes one think, doesn't it?

EXERCISES

a.   Put in *some, other, any, none, neither, one* or *ones* as required.
1.   *This apple is a really juicy ...... Would you like it?*
2.   *...... idiot or ...... has put this advertisement through the letter-box.*
3.   *It is a pity that ...... of her two husbands has been capable of really understanding her.*
4.   *Have you got ...... thing that I can read on the way home?*
5.   *Surely ...... thing can be done to curb such vandalism?*
6.   *He thought up ...... ridiculous pretext for being there.*
7.   *Hardly ...... thing can yet be seen of the new cathedral.*
8.   *...... drunken fool started abusing me on the train.*
9.   *He left without leaving ...... message.*
10. *You will love that film: it's a very amusing ......*
11. *...... of the proposals put forward by various members of the committee was adopted unanimously.*
12. *You are a funny ......; I never know what you are thinking.*
13. *Have you ...... idea what I am talking about?*
14   *...... wag or ...... once said: 'The emancipation of women has led to the emaciation of men'.*
15. *...... of the twins was arrested, because I saw them both at a party last night.*

b.   Explain the difference in meaning between:
1.   *out of work*
     out of order
2.   *long-sighted*
     far-sighted
3.   *There is nothing to do.*
     There is nothing to be done.
4.   *to set fire to something*
     to light a fire
     to put on a fire
5.   *He is good to do that.*
     He is good at doing that.
6.   *Only I spoke to his sister.*
     I only spoke to his sister.
     I spoke only to his sister.
     I spoke to his only sister.

7. *to attend a lecture*
    to attend to a lecture.
8. *He stooped to do it.*
    He stooped to doing it
    He stopped to do it.
    He stopped doing it.
9. *to do work*
    to make work
    to make it do
    to make it work
10. *to overhear a conversation*
    to eavesdrop on a conversation
11. *to do good*
    to make good
    to make good a loss
12. *He is sure to pass the examination.*
    He is sure of passing the examination.
13. *He used to teach English.*
    He is used to teaching English.
14. *to make a fuss of*
    to make a fuss about
15. *I am not afraid.*
    I am afraid not.

c. Give one word for the following.
1. *a man who never drinks alcohol*
2. *a man who hates everyone*
3. *a man who loves everyone*
4. *a man who hates women*
5. *a man who hates marriage*
6. *a man who illegally takes a second wife*
7. *a man who is always putting off doing things*
8. *a man who pretends to be quite different from what he really is*
9. *a man who collects stamps*
10. *a man who accepts a particular religion*
11. *a man who believes in God but does not accept the interpretation of him of any religion*
12. *a man who does not know if God exists or not*
13. *a man who denies the existence of God*
14. *a man who remains with the enemy as a prisoner as a pledge of good faith*
15. *a man who enjoys suffering*
16. *a man who enjoys making others suffer*
17. *a man who goes to church to pray*
18. *a man who is in charge of a court of enquiry into someone's death*
19. *a man who writes something defamatory about someone*
20. *a man who publicly says something defamatory about someone*

21. *a man who moves herds of animals from place to place*
22. *a man who owes money*
23. *a man to whom money is owed*
24. *a man who designs and lays out new gardens*
25. *a man who betrays his country*
26. *which cannot be taken by storm*
27. *which cannot be rubbed out or forgotten*
28. *which cannot be beaten*
29. *which cannot be reached physically*
30. *which cannot be reached morally*
31. *which cannot be destroyed*
32. *which cannot be done without*
33. *which cannot be perceived*
34. *which cannot be permitted*
35. *which cannot be touched*
36. *which cannot be used up*
37. *which cannot be read because of the bad handwriting*
38. *which cannot be read because it is so boring or ineptly done*
39. *which cannot be corrected*
40. *which cannot be easily noticed*

23: Plurals

1. The *s* added in normal plurals derives from the accusative case Latin plural (*mensas, dominos*) and normally replaced the old Anglo-Saxon plurals with the Norman Conquest of England in 1066. Some Anglo-Saxon plurals, however, remain:

man	*men*
woman	*women*
foot	*feet*
mouse	*mice*
ox	*oxen*
child	*children*
goose	*geese*
tooth	*teeth* etc.

2. *Es* is added where the plural could not otherwise be pronounced.

glass	*glasses*
church	*churches*
brush	*brushes*

branch	branches
fox	foxes
splash	splashes
bus	buses etc.

3.   Words ending in a consonant and *y* change the *y* to *i* before adding *es* to form the plural. Words ending in a vowel and *y* simply add *s* in the plural.

lady	ladies	boy	boys
poppy	poppies	valley	valleys
party	parties	day	days
pony	ponies	monkey	monkeys etc.

(The only exceptions are: *the two Germanys* (i.e. East and West Germany) and *monies*, used in legal jargon.)

4.   A lot of words ending in *f* or *fe* change to *ves* in the plural. A lot, however, do not change but just add *s*. Words ending in *ff* always just add *s*. Occasionally there is a choice.

Changing		Not changing		Choice	
life	lives	reef	reefs		wharf
shelf	shelves	chief	chiefs	wharfs	wharves
thief	thieves	chef	chefs		
sheaf	sheaves	handkerchief	handkerchiefs		
loaf	loaves	roof	roofs		hoof
half	halves	proof	proofs	hoofs	hooves
self	selves	fife	fifes		
knife	knives	cliff	cliffs		turf
wife	wives	ruff	ruffs	turfs	turves
wolf	wolves	dwarf	dwarfs		
calf	calves	safe	safes		
leaf	leaves	serf	serfs		
scarf	scarves	cuff	cuffs		
		belief	beliefs etc.		

5.   Words ending in *o* generally form their plurals in *oes*. Those which do not, have still kept something of their foreign characteristics and mostly came into English later.

torpedo	torpedoes	curio	curios
tornado	tornadoes	concerto	concertos
cargo	cargoes	torso	torsos
hero	heroes	piano	pianos
potato	potatoes	solo	solos
tomato	tomatoes	canto	cantos
Negro	Negroes	halo	halos
volcano	volcanoes	tremolo	tremolos
echo	echoes	inferno	infernos
mango	mangoes etc.	banjo	banjos etc.

6.   Some words do not change in the plural. They include game-birds, some wild animals and most kinds of fish: also some words ending in *s*.

sheep	*deer*	*buffalo*
herring	*trout*	*brace* (=pair)
giraffe	*swine*	*partridge*
species	*mews*	*barracks*
grouse	*pheasant*	*salmon*
gallows	*means*	*series* etc.

7.   Uncountable nouns have neither singular nor plural. (See page 122.)

8.   Some words have no singular. They include:

annals	*bellows*	*trousers*
pincers	*scissors*	*shears*
tongs	*pliers*	*shorts*
politics	*goings-on*	*cattle*
economics	*aesthetics*	*mathematics*
winnings	*belongings*	*police*
takings	*statistics*	*dregs*
tweezers	*braces* (for trousers)	*suds*
travels	*thanks*	*victuals*
binoculars	*outskirts*	*pants*
makings	*surroundings*	

9.   The majority of irregular plurals are words from foreign languages which have not been fully assimilated into English. Some of the commonest are:

from Greek

phenomenon	*phenomena*
criterion	*criteria*
analysis	*analyses*
crisis	*crises*
basis	*bases*
axis	*axes* etc.

from Latin

agendum	*agenda*
erratum	*errata*
datum	*data*
addendum	*addenda*
memorandum	*memoranda*
stratum	*strata*
appendix	*appendices*
formula	*formulae* or *formulas*
person	*people*
(L. persona)	*(L. populus)*
terminus	*termini*
radius	*radii*

genus	*genera*
index	*indices* (in mathematics)
	indexes (lists of contents)

from Hebrew

cherub	*cherubim* or *cherubs*
seraph	*seraphim* or *seraphs*

from Italian

dilettante	*dilettanti*
concerto	*concerti* (only for Italian ones: otherwise *concertos)*
	spaghetti (uncountable noun)

from French

bureau	*bureaux*
château	*châteaux*
Mr	*Messieurs (Messrs.)*
Mrs	*Mesdames*

from Arabic (owing to a misunderstanding)

djinn
genie }   *genii*
(Arabic: singular *Jinnee* and plural *Jinn)*

10. Some collective nouns in English can be counted as either singular or plural. If their essential unity is stressed, they are followed by singular verbs, pronouns and adjectives. If the different people forming them are stressed, they are followed by plural verbs, pronouns and adjectives. The plural form seems to be becoming more commonly used, even if it is less 'tidy' grammatically.
The Government is/are hoping to make its/their findings known soon.
The team is playing well this year.
The team are scattered all over Europe during their holidays.
The B.B.C. is/are starting a new television channel.
The School is/are hoping to remedy the matter soon.
The Royal Navy is a very powerful factor in defence.
The Royal Navy are putting on a series of public displays soon.

11. Compound words form their plurals as follows:
a. with men or women both parts take the plural

manservant	*manservants*
woman-teacher	*women-teachers*

b. with nouns and adjectives only the noun takes the plural

knight-errant	*knights-errant*
court-martial	*courts-martial*

c. with two titles both take the plural

Lord Justice	*Lords Justices*
Knight Templar	*Knights Templars*

d. with nouns and phrases only the first noun takes the plural

mother-in-law	*mothers-in-law*

brother-at-arms	*brothers-at-arms*
bride-to-be	*brides-to-be*
an Inn of Court	*Inns of Court*

e.   most hyphenated nouns change only the second half in the plural

cat-burglar	*cat-burglars*
licence-holder	*licence-holders*
barrow-boy	*barrow-boys*
pipe-cleaner	*pipe-cleaners*
ice-cream	*ice-creams*

EXERCISES

Put into the plural where possible.
1.   *I bought a loaf of bread this morning.*
2.   *I asked you for information, not advice.*
3.   *He has a piano you can play on.*
4.   *Come and look at the pony walking down the lane.*
5.   *Thunder often frightens a child.*
6.   *He takes a pride in his garden.*
7.   *There was a poppy growing among the wheat.*
8.   *He was looking for employment.*
9.   *Antique furniture costs less in London than in Paris.*
10.   *By what criterion are you judging this man's work?*
11.   *How much luggage did that person bring with him?*
12.   *The man seems to enjoy shooting grouse.*
13.   *That is a genus of flower I have never seen before.*
14.   *The woman-teacher is not making much headway with her Italian studies.*
15.   *He has a château in Provence which I have stayed at.*
16.   *More nonsense has been talked about education in this century than in any other.*
17.   *A bus leaves the terminus at 11.50 p.m.: that is the last one.*
18.   *What is the basis of such a belief?*
19.   *A wife who cannot cook is a great liability.*
20.   *Good accommodation is scarce in London.*
21.   *Work that is done grudgingly is done badly.*
22.   *A border clash led to some excitement in the Government.*
23.   *The robber made off with his booty.*
24.   *A dilettante is not necessarily to be looked down on.*
25.   *Damage to property can be claimed for.*
26.   *A herd of giraffe came into view.*
27.   *The very latest equipment has been installed.*
28.   *A person convicted of espionage can be heavily punished.*
29.   *A sheaf of wheat was stolen yesterday.*
30.   *No harm came of it.*
31.   *The valley was veiled in mist.*

32. *An ox is a useful animal.*
33. *Such ignorance is beyond belief.*
34. *The potato was brought to Europe from America.*
35. *The enemy ship fired a torpedo at us.*
36. *News travelled fast within the Inca Empire.*
37. *One international crisis follows another these days.*
38. *Wealth does not always bring happiness.*
39. *A manservant is an expensive luxury nowadays.*
40. *It is sometimes difficult to distinguish fact from propaganda.*

24: Collective nouns

a *gang* of robbers
a *bunch* of grapes/bananas/cherries, etc/keys/flowers (to put in a vase)
a *flock* of birds/sheep
a *herd* of cows/buffalo/deer/moose/giraffe/elephant, etc.
a *pack* of hounds/wolves/cards/lies
a *litter* of puppies/kittens/piglets, etc.
a *shoal* of fish
a *swarm* of bees and all other insects
a *clump* of bushes/flowers (when still growing in a garden)
a *bouquet* of flowers (for carrying)
a *bundle* of laundry/firewood or faggots
a *medley/selection* of tunes
a *block* of flats
a *suite* of rooms
a *cluster* of houses/grapes (which are still growing)
a *team* of footballers/oxen
a *bevy* of beautiful girls
a *board* of directors
a *panel/team* of experts
a *sheaf* of wheat
an *assembly* of Churchmen
a *fleet* of ships
a *nest* of tables (i.e. a group that will fit under each other neatly)
a *set* of teacups
a news *bulletin*
a *crowd* of people
a *hum* of conversation
hordes/droves of tourists/sightseers

a *batch* of samples/loaves/letters
a *chain* of shops
a *tuft* of hair/grass
a *range* of mountains
a *wad* of notes
a *consensus* of opinion
a *pile* of books/magazines/newspapers (that could be carried)
a *heap* of books/magazines/newspapers (lying about)
a *confederation* of states
a *bed* of flowers (an area where they grow)

EXERCISES

a. Put in the missing words in these sentences
1. *He never felt the slightest ...... of anxiety on that score.*
2. *Did you hear a distant ...... of thunder?*
3. *Needless to say I had not been digging for long before a large ......
of wood pierced my thumb.*
4. *...... of robbers were prowling about in that part of the country.*
5. *I saw a tiny ...... of smoke far away on the horizon.*
6. *A ...... of rooms at the Hilton will not cost more than about £50 a
night.*
7. *For many people a Wagner opera is a ...... of endurance rather
than a ...... of pleasure.*
8. *Don't believe a word he is saying; it's all a ...... of lies.*
9. *The whole situation is in a ...... of flux.*
10. *The man hid in a convenient ...... of bushes.*
11. *The housekeeper jangled an imposing ...... of keys.*
.12. *A ...... of sunlight lit up one corner of the cell.*
13. *A violent ...... of wind blew his hat off.*
14. *The orchestra was playing a ...... of tunes by Cole Porter.*
15. *To some, the word 'intellectual' is a ...... of abuse: to others, an
inspiring hope.*
16. *Do ...... of gnats really indicate a ...... of fine weather to come?*
17. *Landed proprietors often keep ...... of deer on their estates.*
18. *Any discarded ...... of clothing will be gratefully accepted for
distribution among refugee families.*
19. *Will two ...... of toast be enough for you?*
20. *In mediaeval times a village was often little more than a ...... of
cottages clinging to the walls of a castle.*
21. *Would you mind collecting that ...... of laundry on your way back
from work?*
22. *Please accept this as a slight ...... of my gratitude.*
23. *The soldiers were halted by a fierce ...... of gunfire.*
24. *What an adorable ...... of puppies!*
25. *Was there any ...... of particular interest in that news ....?*

26. A ...... of beautiful girls high-kicked their way on to the stage.
27. ...... of oxen pulled the heavy wagons into the interior of North America.
28. Please count your ...... of ammunition.
29. He is now sitting on the ...... of Directors.
30. Several great ...... of bacon were hanging from the roof in the cavernous farmhouse kitchen.
31. A blinding ...... of lightning rent the murky air.
32. In that restaurant they charge ten pence for a ...... of butter.
33. The trawler ran into a ...... of herring.
34. The bank clerk asked for a ...... of my handwriting.
35. Medals sometimes reward outstanding ...... of bravery.
36. Mary bought a useful ..... of tables.
37. The U.S.A. is really a ...... of semi-independent states.
38. The commercial traveller needed a new ...... of samples.
39. The man ostentatiously took a ...... of notes from his wallet.
40. We could talk privately there: the ...... of conversation in the restaurant completely drowned our words.

b. Use the following words in sentences so as to bring out their meaning clearly.

vacuum	appearance	inheritance	adopt
vacancy	aspect	heritage	adapt
vacation	apparition	heredity	adept
vocation			addict
invocation	discomfiture	to linger	
evocation	discomfort	to loiter	

c.   Choose the right word(s) from those in brackets and use those that are wrong here in sentences of your own.
1.   I'm afraid that problem is (insolvent, insoluble, unanswerable).
2.   Your stealing the money was most (reprehensible, comprehensible, culpable).
3.   I will not put up any longer with his (childlike, childish) tantrums.
4.   I did not like the (decorum, decor, decoration) of that ballet.
5.   She was surprised at your (concerting, consorting with, conniving at) such people.
6.   In certain circles it is now fashionable to (whitewash, distemper, ameliorate, rectify) some famous villains in history.
7.   His (frivolity, facetiousness, giddiness, lightness) shocked some people.
8.   Trespassers will be (persecuted, prosecuted).
9.   Few things are more (pernicious, promiscuous, perspicacious) than brain-washing.
10. That is one of the (proscribed, inscribed, prescribed) books for the examination.

d. Give other words or phrases meaning the same as the words itali-cised in the following passage.

There is no *gainsaying* the fact that *brinkmanship* is a dangerous game. If we could *eavesdrop* on the private conversations of politicians, it would be interesting to see how their public *pontificating belies* their real thoughts. When they *flaunt* their latest weapons of *large-scale* destruction and *earmark* enormous sums of money for their produc-tion, can we *credit* what they say when they *vouchsafe* us *snippets* of information about their intentions? I, *for one,* should not like to *vouch* for their *integrity,* though I must admit that my interest in *current affairs* soon *flags.* I wonder if they will ever *knuckle down* to solving world problems, and stop getting *tied up* with their own affairs and concerns. I do not want to *belittle* their efforts in general, though there are some ministers I would like to *oust* from their positions, but I do feel that they often *flout* the wishes of the public in an attempt to avoid *losing face.* Those who *hold sway* must not *shrink from climbing down* when *expediency* demands it. If they go ahead and try to *do things off their own bat,* they may get more than they *bargained for.* One can *bluff* some people sometimes, but not everyone all the time and perhaps in matters of such *moment* as world peace such bluffings should be *frowned upon.* It is hard to *envisage* a world in which *disinterested* working for the good of humanity—however much *drudgery* is involved—will *override* considerations of personal gain and *face-saving,* but that should be the *Utopia* that our politicians are *striving* to achieve.

25: Compound verbs F−H

Fall

1. to fall *for*
a. a trick (To be deceived, taken in by it.)
b. someone (To fall in love with someone)
2. to fall *out with* someone (To have a quarrel with someone: colloquial.)
3. to fall *upon* someone (To attack someone, in a group.)
4. to fall *in with*.
a. someone (To meet someone by accident, when travelling.)
b. someone's plans (To agree with them.)
5. to fall *off*
a. (To tumble off—a ladder etc.)
b. (To diminish in numbers, grow fewer.)

6.   to fall *in* (To form up in threes—used of soldiers.)
7.   to fall *out* (To dismiss and rest—used of soldiers.)
8.   *fall-out* (As a noun means 'radioactivity'.)
9.   to fall *through*.
Our plans fell through. (Our plans came to nothing, could not be put into practice.)
10. to fall *away*
The ground falls away beyond the castle. (The ground slopes down.)
11. to fall *on one's feet* (To be lucky: colloquial.)
12. to fall *to* (To begin to eat a meal: colloquial.)
13. to fall *flat*.
a. *He fell flat.* (He tumbled over so that his nose hit the ground.)
b. *That joke fell flat.* (It failed dismally.)
14. *downfall* (As a noun means 'collapse' or 'ruin'.)
15. to fall *out of favour / into disgrace* (To lose one's popularity with some patron etc.)
16. to fall *down* (To collapse.)

Get

1.   to get *out of* something (To avoid doing something without getting punished.)
2.   to get someone *down*
It is getting me down (It is depressing me.)
3.   to get *down from table* (To leave the table after a meal.)
4.   to get *into bad ways* (To develop bad habits.)
5.   to get *at*
a. (To reach.)
b. (To mean, to try to say.)
c. (To attack morally: colloquial.)
6.   to get *away with* a crime (Not to be punished for it.)
7.   to get *off scot-free* (Not to get punished for doing something wrong.)
8.   to get *off lightly* (To receive a very slight punishment.)
9.   to get *off with* someone (To begin a relationship with someone.)
10. to get *on one's high horse* (To get angry and try to behave with great dignity: colloquial.)
11. to get *through*
a. an examination (To pass.)
b. money (To spend it very quickly.)
12. to get *up to mischief* (To do something naughty or forbidden.)
13. a *get-up*
What a get-up! (What extraordinarily odd clothes!—slang.)
14. to get *over*
a. an illness (To recover from it.)
b. a loss (To recover from it.)
c. a difficulty (To find the solution to it.)

15. to get *by* in an examination (To pass it rather unexpectedly.)
16. to get *by as...* (To succeed in being mistaken for ...)
17. to get *round* someone (To charm someone into doing what you want.)
18. to get *on well with* someone (To live in harmony with someone or have a pleasant relationship with him.)
19. to get *on in life* (To make a success of it from a commercial point of view.)
20. to get *on*
He is getting on. (He is no longer young.)
21. to get *on someone's nerves* (To make someone irritable, to annoy him very much.)
22. to get *behind with* something (To allow work etc. to accumulate and so to get behind schedule with it.)
23. to get *down to* work (To settle down to it, to begin it seriously.)
24. to get *away* (To make one's escape.)
25. to get *on with* something (To work as it and make progress in it.)

EXERCISE

Replace the italicised part of the sentence with an expression with *fall* or *get*.
1. Quite a number of crimes are *not satisfactorily solved so that no-one is punished for them.*
2. I hope you will *not make any difficulties about accepting* my plans to improve the efficiency of the department.
3. I am surprised that you should have *been deceived by* such a simple trick.
4. The numbers of students have *decreased* sharply.
5. If you persist in behaving like that I shall soon *pick a quarrel* with you.
6. A gang of robbers suddenly *attacked* the unsuspecting traveller.
7. 'Bonnie Prince Charlie' managed to *disguise himself successfully* as a servant maid and so *made his escape* to France.
8. The sergeant ordered the recruits to *disperse* and rest for ten minutes.
9. How easy it is to *let* one's correspondence *pile up*.
10. I always have the feeling that he is *putting me in a position where I have to try to justify myself.*
11. Beyond that ridge over there the ground *slopes down steeply* to the sea.
12. It is a formidable obstacle but I am sure that we can *overcome* it with a little thought.
13. John *struck up a friendship* with a very pretty girl at my party last week.
14. You have been wasting time for long enough: it is high time you *gave your mind to* some serious work.
15. All our plans *collapsed* because of my sudden illness

Give

1. to give *back* something (To return something borrowed.)
2. to give *off* a smell (To emit, to exhale.)
3. to give *in*
a. (To surrender.)
b. homework (To hand it to the teacher.)
4. to give *up* (To stop trying, to acknowledge oneself beaten.)
5. to give *out*
a. a smell (To emit it.)
b. (To be finished or all used up.)
c. (To announce publicly.)
d. (To distribute.)
e. (To pretend.)
6. to give *over*
a. *The rain has given over.* (The rain has stopped.)
b. *Give over playing the fool.* (Stop being silly.)
7. to give *away*
a. something (Not to charge money for it.)
b. someone (To betray someone.)
c. a bride (To give her to her husband at the marriage service.)
8. to give *way*
a. (To collapse.)
b. to someone (To agree to allow someone to do what he wants, to cease resistance to him.)
c. to one's feelings (To make no attempt to control them.)
9. *give-and-take* (A compromise on both sides.)

Go

1. to go *in for*
a. an examination (To sit for it, take it.)
b. sport (To practise it a lot.)
2. to go *down*
a. (To become cheaper.)
b. (To become worse.)
c. *for the vacation* (To begin the academic holiday.)
3. to go *down well*
That speech did not go down well. (It was not well received.)
4. to go *up*
a. (To become dearer.)
b. (To be built.)
5. to go *with* something (to look nice with, to blend with in colour.)
6. to go *into*
a. a crime (To investigate it.)

b.   a subject fully (To deal with it at some length.)
c.   *detail* (To consider something very closely and fully.)
7.   to go *over*
a.   a lesson (To revise it quickly.)
b.   a house etc. (To have a look at it before buying or renting it.)
c.   a road (To cross it.)
d.   *time* (To exceed the allotted time.)
e.   *to the enemy* (To change one's allegiance in mid-stream.)
f.   a problem (To think deeply about it.)
g.   *to see someone* (To visit someone.)
h.   the edge (To fall over the edge in an accident.)
8.   to go *on*
a.   *My shoe will not go on.* (I cannot get my foot into it.)
b.   with something (To continue to do something.)
c.   *duty* (To start work, especially shift-work.)
d.   *leave* or *holiday* (To begin a holiday.)
9.   *go on!*
a.   *(Hurry up!)*
b.   *(Really? Are you joking?*—slang.)
10.   *goings-on*
What goings-on! (*What scandalous behaviour!*—colloquial.)
11.   to go *off*
a.   (To explode—of bombs, guns, fireworks etc.)
b.   (To leave someone where he is; abandon him temporarily*.)
c.   (To deteriorate, get worse.)
d.   *someone* (To like someone less than you used to.)
e.   *duty (*To finish work, especially shift-work.)
f.   *How did the examination / interview go off?* (How do you think you did in it?)
12.   to go *round*
a.   *to see someone* (To visit someone.)
b.   *Is there enough sherry to go round?* (For everyone to have some.)
13.   a *go-between* (An intermediary.)
14.   to *undergo* (To suffer, to endure.)
15.   to *let go of* someone (To loose, to take your hands off someone.)
16.   to go *for*
a.   someone (To attack someone.)
b.   something (To like something: colloquial.)
17.   to *have a go at* doing something (To attempt to do something: colloquial.)
18.   *at one go* (At one attempt: without pausing or interrupting oneself.)
19.   to go *through* something
a.(To revise it.)
b.   (To explain it.)
c.   (To suffer it.)
20.   to be *on the go* (To be busy or active: colloquial.)

* 'to go off and leave someone' means to abandon him permanently, desert him

21. *The story goes that* ... (There are rumours that...)
22. to *make a go of* something (To make a success of something: colloquial.)
23. to go *by* what someone says
I never go by what he says. (I never believe it.)
24. to go *for nothing*
Carlyle's work went for nothing when his manuscript was burnt. (It was wasted, was completely lost.)
25. *It's all the go.* (It's very fashionable at the moment: colloquial.)
26. to go *by the board* (To be sacrificed to something else: colloquial.)
27. to go *back on one's word* (Not to keep one's promise.)
28. to go *to pieces* (To collapse morally: colloquial.)
29. to go *up* to someone (To approach someone.)
30. to *forgo* something (To manage without something, to renounce it.)

EXERCISE

Replace the italicised part of the sentence with an expression with *give* or *go*.
1. A lot of *compromise* is necessary to make a success of marriage.
2. *I have no confidence whatever in* what my sister says.
3. Sugar *is cheaper that it used to be.*
4. Why don't you *see if you can write* a play?
5. Quite often the police are enabled to make further arrests because one of the accused *betrays* his accomplices.
6. I hope there are enough glasses *for each guest to have one.*
7. He made a brilliant speech but it *was not at all liked by* his audience.
8. The first theatre to have its balconies suspended from the ceiling (to avoid pillars) *collapsed* the first time it was filled with people.
9. A hen-pecked husband is one who always *agrees to do what* his wife *wants*.
10. The restaurant has *deteriorated* a lot.
11. How many people are *taking* the test?
12. Everyone landing in England may have to *put up with* a search to make sure he is not smuggling anything in.
13. I will *examine* the matter as soon as possible.
14. The invigilator *distributed* the papers to the candidates.
15. I shall have to borrow some money until my next cheque arrives, because my supplies *are finished*.
16. We spent the afternoon *looking at* a house that we were thinking of buying.
17. For months the beleaguered garrison refused to *surrender*.
18. When you are sconced at Oxford you have to drink a flagon of beer *without taking the cup from your lips*.
19. What a pity all that hard work has *been wasted*.

20. It is too late to *back out of* the agreement now.
21. When you consider what he *endured* during the war it is amazing that he survived at all.
22. A lot of houses are *being constructed* all over the place.
23. His disguise was clever but his voice *betrayed* him.
24. The English are generally taught not to *let themselves be overpowered by* their feelings.
25. *Loose* me at once.
26. The date of the wedding has not yet been *announced*.
27. Don't you like this coat? It is *considered very smart* at the moment.
28. She is *bustling about* from dawn to dusk.
29. I got a shock when a firework *exploded* right under my feet.
30. The saucepan *emitted* such an appetising smell that my mouth began to water.

Have

1. to have *it out with* someone (To demand a full explanation for his strange or rude behaviour: colloquial.)
2. to have *a go at* something (To try to do something to see if you can: colloquial.)
3. to have someone *on* (To tease someone, to pull his leg: colloquial.)
4. to have *done with* it (To finish with it, get it over.)
5. to have *to do with* someone (To have dealings with someone.)
6. to have it *from* someone
I had it from him. (He told me it.)
7. to have *it in for* someone (To dislike someone and feel resentful towards him: colloquial.)
8. to have someone *up for* something (To sue or prosecute someone for something.)
9. to have *on*
What did she have on? (What was she wearing?)

Hold

1. to hold *up*
a. (To delay.)
b. someone as a model (To point to someone as an ideal.)
c. (To support.)
d. (To raise.)
e. someone (to point a gun at someone and demand money etc.)
2. to hold someone *up to ridicule* (To make fun of someone.)
3. to *uphold* a principle (To support it.)
4. to hold *out on* someone (Not to tell someone the whole truth: colloquial.)
5. to hold *on to* something (To cling to something physically or morally.)

6.   to hold *in* a horse (To restrain it, not to give it its head.)
7.   to hold someone *up to ransom* (To announce that someone will be set free on payment of a certain sum of money.)
8.   to *withhold* information or one's consent (Not to give them when they are asked for.)
9.   to hold *out* (To continue to resist, refuse to surrender.)
10. to hold *out hope*
I cannot hold out much hope of your doing that. (I do not think it likely that you will do it successfully.)
11. to hold *with* something
I don't hold with it. (I don't approve of/agree with it on principle.)
12. to hold *off*
a.   someone (To keep someone at a distance.)
b.   *The rain has held off so far.* (It has not started to rain yet.)
13. to hold *down*
a.   a nation (To oppress it.)
b.   a job (To keep it for some time.)
14. to hold *together*
That speech did not hold together very well. (It was not logically planned: it was not coherent.)
15. to hold oneself *in readiness* (To be prepared to do something immediately.)
16. to hold *one's own with the others* (To be as good as they are, especially at work.)
17. to hold *water*
That argument does not hold water. (It is not logically convincing: colloquial.)
18. to hold *one's breath* (Not to breathe for a few seconds, either under water or with fear or in suspense.)
19. to hold *one's tongue* (To keep quiet: a little old-fashioned.)
20. *Hold on!* (*Wait a minute!* This is particularly used if you do not want someone to put down the telephone receiver until you have fetched the person he wants to talk to: colloquial.)
21. to hold it *against* someone (Not to forgive someone.)
22. to hold something *over* (To leave something to be dealt with later.)
23. to hold something *over someone's head* (To threaten someone with something.)
24. to hold *good for*
That holds good for you to. (That applies to you too: colloquial)
25. to have a *hold on* someone (To know something about someone that could be used against him if he didn't do what you wanted.)

EXERCISES

a.   Replace the italicised part of the sentence with an expression with *have* or *hold*.

1. I do not *approve of* giving children too much pocket money.
2. You can be punished for *keeping back* information from the police.
3. I'm sorry I am late; I was *delayed* in a traffic jam.
4. Don't worry about your son; he is *as good as* the others in the class.
5. I do hope the rain will *not start* until the ceremony is over.
6. I don't understand her behaviour at all, but I intend to *ask her for a full explanation* next time I see her.
7. He has been *prosecuted* for driving under the influence of drink.
8. If people reject religion they will find something else to *cling to*.
9. Why do you *dislike me and treat me so unkindly?*
10. I am disappointed in you; you have been *keeping something back from me*.
11. Some people never realise that people are *making fun of them*.
12. How long can we *continue to fight* without reinforcements?
13. Feckless people cannot *keep* jobs.
14. I think it is right; *John told me of it*, and he is usually right.
15. If parents *do not give* their consent to their daughter's marriage, she can always elope to Scotland.
16. Your ideas are quite interesting but the essay *is not very well constructed*.
17. Why don't you *see if you can mend* the clock yourself?
18. Do you *support* the principle of the indissolubility of marriage? Personally I do not *agree* with an idea that is so lacking in simple, basic humanity.
19. Ever since I told you that you are not sincere with yourself, you have *felt resentful towards* me.
20. The rule that smoking is forbidden in class *applies to* you just as much as *to* the other students.
21. Blackmail stems from one person *knowing some shocking secret about* someone else.
22. I must go to the dentist's so I had better go soon and *get it over*.
23. The Duke of Austria *offered the English their King back in return for a considerable sum of money*.
24. It is impossible nowadays to *keep nations in subjection* if they are striving for freedom.
25. You have behaved disgracefully and I *want no further dealings* with you.

b. Put in the missing prepositions or particles in these sentences.
1. *I should not hold him ...... as a model to any child.*
2. *People who go .... their word are never respected.*
3. *The soldiers were ordered to fall .... threes*
4. *The boy gets .... mischief the moment you turn your back on him.*
5. *Dogs and cats kept together as pets in the same house sometimes get ...... very well ...... each other.*

6.   *I went .... see my great-aunt yesterday; I wonder if I shall come ...... any money on her death!*

7.   *If parents give .... their children too often, they have no control over them later.*

8.   *The most common thing that women are had .... is shoplifting.*

9.   *I went .... a policeman to ask him the way to the Stock Exchange.*

10. *Many decent ideas go ...... the board in wartime.*

11. *I gave that pullover .... an old tramp.*

12. *Mary never goes ...... what I say.*

13. *Byron got ...... a considerable fortune in his not very long life.*

14. *He has such charm that he could get .... murder.*

15. *Children soon learn how to get ...... their parents.*

c.   Complete the following sentences.

(Revision exercise on conditionals, subjunctives and inversions.)

1.   *Only on very rare occasions . . .*

2.   *If he had seen you, I am sure he . . .*

3.   *No sooner . . .*

4.   *He would marry her at once . . .*

5.   *To such an extent . . .*

6.   *The general gave orders that . . .*

7.   *I will clear away the tea things if . . .*

8.   *Should it rain . . .*

9.   *Mightn't he have seen it if . . .*

10. *Not a soul . . .*

11. *In such a desperate situation . . .*

12. *She crept in lest . . .*

13. *I should be grateful if . . .*

14. *In no circumstances . . .*

15. *On no account . . .*

16. *I agreed to lend it to him on condition that . . .*

17. *It is not right that . . .*

18. *Little . . .*

19. *I wish I . . .*

20. *It is inconceivable that . . .*

21. *Hardly had he finished . . .*

22. *If only he . . .*

23. *Couldn't you have done it if . . .*

24. *However noble his motives. . .*

25. *So great . . .*

26. *To such a point of despair . . .*

27. *It is high time you . . .*

28. *Were he to turn awkward . . .*

29. *Naturally I am very shocked that . . .*

30. *With good reason . . .*

26: Some points to note about the use of auxiliary verbs

1. The past tense of auxiliaries

Many auxiliary verbs form their past tense by changing the infinitive following them into the perfect infinitive. This is because the auxiliary verb itself is defective and has only one form. In indirect speech the usage is quite different. (See page 159.)

It must be his sister. (present)
It must have been his sister you saw yesterday. (past)
You should do it now.
You should have done it last week.
You ought to know better.
You ought to have known better.
It may be justified now.
It may have been justified in the circumstances then obtaining.
I wouldn't do it now.
I wouldn't have done it when I was your age.
You needn't do it at once.
You needn't have done it immediately he asked you to.
It can't be his sister.
It can't have been his sister you met at that party.
She is to sing at Covent Garden next month.
She was to have sung at Covent Garden last month but couldn't.
N.B. Both the auxiliary and infinitive change in the last sentence.

2. Must

a. The verb *must* has four principal meanings, each one of which has a different negative form.

positive	negative
i. obligation	i. *a.* prohibition
You must go to school between the ages of five and fifteen.	*You have been very ill and you must not go back to school for at least a month.*
	b. lack of obligation: it is voluntary
	You don't have to go to school after the age of fifteen unless you want to.
ii. necessity	ii. lack of necessity
You must work hard if you are going to pass that examination.	*You needn't work hard to pass that examination.*
iii. supposition or deduction	iii. negative supposition
It must be his sister.	*It can't be his sister.*

iv. desirability

You must see that film: it's wonderful.

iv. undesirability

You had better not see that film. It would only upset you.

b.   The past tense of *must* in the meaning of obligation needs some attention.

present

You must play football àt that school.

You must not play football this year.

past

You had to play football when you were at that school.

direct speech

'I was not allowed to play football that year.'

indirect speech

The doctor said he was not to play football that year.

(It is normal to omit *allowed* or *permitted* in indirect speech.)

c.   There is a distinction between *must* and *have to*. *Must* is more of an emphatic exhortation and more of an assertion of personal authority than *have to*, which is used for a necessity fixed by laws and rules and implies a detached attitude. *Must*, however, is the one used on public notices.

Compare and contrast these examples.

You must come with me this minute.

You must do as you are told. (Assertions of personal authority.)

You must think again: I cannot see you throw away your life like this. (An exhortation.)

Passengers must cross the line by the footbridge.

Passports must be shown at the frontier. (Public notices.)

You have to get a driving licence before you are allowed to drive. (An impersonal statement: that is the law.)

You have to abide by the referee's decision, whatever sport you are playing. (It is a general rule.)

Students have to find their own way to the examination centre. (That is the normal procedure. The speaker takes up a detached attitude.)

You may have to pay alimony if the divorce goes through. (That is the normal procedure. I cannot make any exceptions in your case.)

d.   Questions containing *must* may have to be answered with *need* and vice versa.

'Must you take the examination?' 'No, I needn't if I don't want to.'

'Need you leave so early?' 'Yes, I'm afraid I must.'

3. Need

(See page 50 for this verb.)

(There is a difference between *He didn't need to do it* and *He need not have done it.* In the first case he knew it was not necessary so he did not

do it. In the second case he did it and later realised that it had been a
waste of time. Compare these examples:

*When I arrived home I didn't need to get out my key because the front
door was already standing open.*

*He didn't need to say anything: I could guess what had happened by his
face.*

*He didn't need to start divorce proceedings as his wife died suddenly of
cancer.*

*I needn't have gone to the station to meet her as I found my sister had
already done so.*

*I needn't have put on my best suit to go to that party; most of the guests
were wearing jeans and sweaters.*

*You needn't have been so bad-tempered about it when you told him to be
quiet.*

You needn't have hurt his feelings by saying that, even if you thought it.

4. Be

a.   The verb *to be* is not used in the continuous form except:

i. in the passive

ii. to indicate that something you are doing at the moment is against
your real nature

iii. to suggest pretence

I don't think anything is being done about it at the moment.

I noticed that I was being stealthily followed.

You are being very stupid today.

He is being very witty all of a sudden.

Why are you being so coy?

Look how charming he is being to those children.

but:

It is terribly cold now.

At this moment the noise is deafening.

Go and see who is at the door.

b.   *Is to* and *are to* have two meanings:

i. It has been arranged

ii. Obligation

Maria Callas is to sing at Covent Garden next month. (It has been
arranged that she will do so.)

*You are to finish your homework before you come in here to watch
television* (You must do it; it is an order.)

It should be noted that in the past tense there is a distinction of meaning between *He was to come* and *He was to have come*. *He was to come
here tomorrow* means: *That was the arrangement made but whether he
will or not I don't know.*

He was to have come here yesterday means: *I know he didn't. I was
waiting for him but he didn't turn up.*

c. Be, though normally an ordinary auxiliary verb, can be used with *do* in the positive imperative—to reinforce the plea—and must be used with *do* in the negative imperative.
Do be careful, I beg you.
Don't be silly!
Don't be afraid of asking him a question!
Don't be late!

5. 'Can' and 'could'.

a. Can is used for permission and ability. For permission it remains the same in the future. For ability it changes to *will be able to.*
You can go there next year.
If you stay here for several years you will be able to speak English quite well.
b. Could is used for permission and for what it was possible to do on any occasion. If it was something you managed to do only on one occasion you must use *was able to.*
He said they could leave early if they wanted to.
Before I started school at the age of five, I could play from morning till night.
but:
Yesterday was a lovely day so we were able to go for a long walk.
Although I tried to force open the door I was not able to do so.
We weren't able to hold the barbecue we had planned because it was a pouring wet day.
c. Another meaning of *could* is *would be able to.* If I say: *By running fast he could catch the train,* it means *If he ran fast he would be able to catch the train.* If, on the other hand, I say: *By running fast he was able to catch the train,* I mean: *He ran fast and managed to catch the train.*

6. Used to

Used to should only be used as an auxiliary verb except in question tags, where *did* is now generally accepted as normal usage.
You used to go there, didn't you?
He used not to behave like that.
Used she to like him, do you think?
Your mother used to live there, didn't she?

7. 'Should' and 'would'.

There are a number of cases in which it is necessary to use *should* in all persons and others where you must use *would*. The principal uses are listed here:

Special uses of *should* in all persons.
a.   For moral duty:
You should show more consideration to your parents.
b.   For deduction:
If he left home half an hour ago he should be here any minute now.
c.   To express extreme surprise in a stereotyped construction using an inversion:
What should I see in Oxford Street but an elephant!
Whom should he run into on his honeymoon but his mother-in-law!
Who should come into the room just as I was kissing Mary but my wife!
d.   For advisability:
You really should see that film if you get a chance.
e.   As a subjunctive (see pages 53-54):
It is scandalous that you should be treated with such scant respect.
She was careful lest her behaviour should appear suspicious.
f.   In conditionals to express great improbability (see page 34):
If you should see him, please give him this.

Special uses of *would* in all persons.
a.   With *seem* and *appear* to suggest doubt:
I would seem to have been wrong on that.
b.   To indicate a typical and exasperating characteristic of someone.
Here it carries a strong stress in speaking:
You would spill ink on my new carpet!
My wife would come in just at that moment!
I would put my foot in it!
c.   For willingness:
I would help you if I knew how to.
d.   For habit in the past (an alternative to *used to*):
Every morning when I was in Corsica I would get up early and go for a swim before breakfast.
e.   For polite requests (see page 34):
He said he would be grateful if I would do that little thing for him.
Why did you ask us if we would mind leaving you alone for a moment?
N.B. Except in the above-mentioned cases it is general practice to use *should* in the first person singular and plural and *would* with the second and third persons. In fact, however, in normal conditions *should* and *would* are used indifferently in the first person.
If I did that I should/would be punished.
If we were caught we should/would be killed.

EXERCISES

a.   Insert *should* or *would* in the blank spaces.
'It is quite extraordinary that you ..... call just now because who ...... be here but Alexander, who has not seen you for ages. It ...... seem that he

has heard intriguing reports of your recent behaviour, so he is dying to meet you again. He told me that when you were together at University you ...... spend hours discussing the validity of moral codes. Of course you ...... make fun of conventional morals (it is only to be expected that you ...... at that stage of your development) but ...... you mind not shocking him too much today? It is impossible that he ...... not be keyed up by the rumours about you and if you ...... inadvertently mention to him that the accounts of your relations with his cousin are true, goodness only knows what he ...... do. I was talking to him about Helen only last week, and what ...... he do but treat me to a long harangue on the unfair treatment of women in our society! So if you ...... watch what you say I ...... be very grateful.'

b.   Put into the negative.
1. *You must go to school for ten years in England.*
2. *I have a clean handkerchief every day.*
3. *She used to live in that manor house over there.*
4. *She had her photograph taken yesterday.*
5. *I have time to deal with it now.*
6. *You must work hard to pass that examination.*
7. *That must be his cousin over there.*
8. *Be extravagant if you feel like it.*
9. *You must see that film: it is extraordinary.*
10. *I had an enormous breakfast on that occasion.*
11. *You must start work immediately.*
12. *That house used to belong to my grandfather.*

c.   Answer the following in the positive.
1. *'Need you leave so early?'*
2. *'Did you use to teach there?'*
3. *'Did you enjoy your holiday?'*
4. *'Were you able to do it?'*
5. *'Do you need to get a visa to go to Russia?'*
6. *'Need I write a bread-and-butter letter?'*
7. *'Didn't your wife use to play a lot of bridge?'*

d.   Answer the following in the negative.
1. *'Didn't you have a chance to mention it?'*
2. *'Must you take the examination?'*
3. *'Have you time to deal with this enquiry?'*
4. *'Dare he do it?'*
5. *'Did you use to like learning English?'*

e.   Put into the past, making any changes necessary to the rest of the sentence.
1. *I wouldn't do it if I were you.*
2. *You ought to know better by now.*

3. *The doctor says I must not play football for at least two months.*
4. *It must be his first visit to such a place.*
5. *He is to sing at La Scala next month.*
6. *He would do it today if he could.*
7. *It is a nice day so we can go for a walk.*
8. *You needn't do it now if you don't want to.*

f. Insert *didn't need to* or *needn't have* in the following sentences, making any necessary changes to the words in brackets.
1. *You (not need be) so rude to my sister yesterday. Why were you?*
2. *I (not need mark) all this work because I now find that the student has left.*
3. *She (not need buy) another cocktail dress as she had two already.*
4. *I (not need write) that letter after all because I received a telegram telling me what I wanted to know.*
5. *I (not need rush) to get there on time as she turned out to be half an hour late.*
6. *I (not need worry) so much about that examination as it proved much easier than I had expected.*
7. *I (not need spend) so much time clearing away the snow yesterday. It would have melted this morning anyhow.*
8. *She (not need pay) to go to that ballet because she had been given a complimentary ticket.*
9. *I (not need get) the car out for such a short journey, as I could easily walk there.*
10. *You (not need interrupt) the class to tell me that; you could have come up to me afterwards to tell me.*
11. *I (not need buy) a catalogue because you could hire one for a shilling.*
12. *I (not need pay) so much as I did for that book; I saw the same one for ten shillings yesterday.*
13. *He (not need tell) me that something was wrong: I could see it the moment he came into the room.*
14. *He (not need have) that swimming pool made in his garden. The weather has been too cold for him to use it.*
15. *If you had taken a bit more care you (not need get) your stockings so badly splashed on the way here.*

g. Put the verbs in brackets into the infinitive or gerund adding prepositions where necessary.
1. *I really do draw the line (be) expected (make) such a fool of myself in public.*
2. *You are mistaken (think) that I deceived you.*
3. *At first she accused me (be) a political fanatic, but she soon came round (realise) that my ideas were not so ridiculous as she had supposed.*
4. *Victor Hugo was condemned (spend) many years in exile.*
5. *In a desperate attempt (get) some money the wretched man resorted (blackmail) certain of his acquaintances.*

6. *In addition (be) very cunning, he is very unscrupulous.*
7. *Those men were engaged (smuggle) watches into England.*
8. *I caught my sister (listen) at the keyhole.*
9. *Aren't you being rather optimistic (want) (marry) a millionaire?*
10. *He is eager (get) started on his new job.*
11. *Russia has come a long way (reach) an understanding with the western powers.*
12. *Dostoyevski sentenced (be) shot, but a last minute reprieve saved him (meet) such an ignominious end.*
13. *Is he up (do) such a responsible job, do you think?*
14. *She is thinking (go) on the stage.*
15. *Undoubtedly some children have a flair (mimic) their elders.*
16. *Queen Victoria never really got over the shock (lose) her husband.*
17. *She was delighted (make) such an easy conquest of him.*
18. *Naturally my brother was flabbergasted (be) accused of such a crime.*
19. *He hastened (assure) her that he had no intention (hurt) her feelings when he said that.*
20. *How keen the 17th century Spanish gentleman was (protect) his good name!*
21. *Most people are furious (be) snubbed in public.*
22. *How experienced are you (do) this kind of work?*
23. *She was not enthusiastic (marry) a man so much older than herself, though her parents tried (coerce) her (do) so.*
24. *He is talking (take) Holy Orders.*
25. *Sometimes magistrates content themselves (put) young offenders on probation.*

h. Decide which of the words in brackets are right in these sentences, and use those that are wrong here in sentences of your own.
1. *I could hear someone in armour (cluttering, clattering, padding) up the stairs.*
2. *After a time my interest (flogged, flagged, lapsed.)*
3. *I was shocked at his doing such a (despicable, contemptuous, scornful) thing.*
4. *The (struggling, straggling, ragged, rugged) village (struck, stroked) me as being very unattractive.*
5. *Last year his father (bereaved, bequeathed, inherited) him £50,000, so he cannot be said to be (impecunious, improvident, destitute, hard up).*
6. *Before I (did it up, made it up, renewed it) this house was in a very (relapsed, delapidated, tumbledown, ruined, ruinous) state.*
7. *They talked for a few minutes but soon (returned, lapsed, withdrew) into silence.*

27: Indirect speech

1.   As in indirect speech you are generally informing someone else of
what happened, often in a different place from the original happening
and usually on a different day, all pronouns change, almost all verb
tenses except conditionals and past perfects change and all words
referring to a particular time or place change. This is really common
sense and applies to all kinds of sentence in indirect speech on condition that the introductory verb is in the simple past. It almost always is.
Practically the only occasion in life when the introductory verb is in the
present is when you are interpreting someone else's remarks to a very
deaf person—a comparatively uncommon situation. There are notice-
ably fewer tenses that can be used in indirect speech, as the following
list of tense changes will show.

direct speech	indirect speech
I do	*he did*
I did/I have done/I had done	*he had done*
I am doing	*he was doing*
I was doing/I have been doing/I had been doing	*he had been doing*
I shall do/I should do (conditional)	*he would do* (but see note 4 following)
I shall be doing/I should be doing	*he would be doing*
I shall have been doing / I should have been doing	*he would have been doing*
I can do	*he could do*
I could do/I have been able to do/I had been able to do	*he had been able to do*
I may do/I might do	*he might do*
I must do*/I have to do*	*he had to do*
I must not do*/I am not to do*	*he was not to do*
I needn't do/I don't need to do	*he didn't need to do*
I didn't need to do	*he hadn't needed to do*
I ought to do	*he ought to do*
I should do (It is my duty to do)	*he should do*
I used to do	*he used to do*

The commonest other changes are as follows:

this	*that*
ago	*before*

**Must and must not* are retained in indirect speech when they are applied to general
truths or laws.
The teacher explained that the angles of a triangle must make up 180°.
*The Minister of Transport said that people who had drunk too much must not be permitted
to drive.*

yesterday	*the day before/*
	the previous day
tomorrow	*the day after/*
	the following day
last week	*the previous week*
next week	*the following week*
now	*then*
here	*there*
come	*go*
bring	*take* etc.

'*I am very tired.*'
He said he was very tired.
'*Paris is a beautiful city.*'
He said Paris was a beautiful city.
'*I went there yesterday.*'
He said he had gone there the previous day/the day before.
'*I have finished this exercise.*'
He said he had finished that exercise.
'*I last saw her three weeks ago.*'
He said he had last seen her three weeks before.
'*I can see a deep valley down here at my feet.*'
He said he could see a deep valley down there at his feet.
'*You must not play here.*'
He said I was not to play there.

2. The second kind of conditional that I have classified (see pages 32 and 33) does not change in indirect speech because, however improbable it may be, it is possible and, if the tenses were changed to those of the past conditional this possibility would be removed and the meaning would be changed.
'*If he came I should be surprised.*'
He said that if he came he would be surprised.
If you say: *He said that if he had come he would have been surprised,* you are changing the meaning by removing all possibility of its happening.
'*If you saw him, you would recognise him.*'
He said that if I saw him I would recognise him.
The third type of conditional, however, being entirely impossible or unfulfilled, does change in indirect speech without changing the meaning.
'*If I were rich I would marry her.*'
He said that if he had been rich he would have married her.
'*If I were you I would not do that.*'
*He said that if he had been me he would not have done that.**

*It should be noted, however, that *were to* does not change in indirect speech:
'*I should be surprised if I were to win again.*'
He said he would be surprised if he were to win again.

Of course there are some borderline cases between these two groups where the possibility of the action happening is so remote that it can to all intents and purposes be disregarded. Here either form is permissible in indirect speech.

'If I knew how to do it, I would do it immediately.' (This implies that I do not know how to do it, but, of course, if I experimented I might hit on the right way of doing it.)

He said that if he knew/had known how to do it, he would do/would have done it immediately.

3. For statements

Many different introductory verbs may be used according to the circumstances of the case.

'I have been to Paris several times.'

He informed me/told me/boasted to me/commented/assured me/remarked/mentioned that he had been to Paris several times.

4. For questions

Many different introductory verbs may be used, generally followed by *if* or *whether*. Some grammarians consider *whether* to be preferable: others do not mind which one is used. Sometimes the infinitive can be used instead, especially in requests.

'Have you asked her to marry you yet?'

He asked me/wanted to know/enquired/wondered/was curious to know/ urged me to tell him/requested me to tell him/begged me to tell him/ entreated me to tell him/implored me to tell him/if/whether I had asked her to marry me yet.

'Will you post this for me, please?'

He asked me if I would post that for him/to post that for him/if I would mind posting that for him/to be kind enough to post that for him.

N.B. It should be remembered that there are two types of construction beginning with *Shall I ...?* One is pure future: *Shall I see you next week?* and the other is a request: *Shall I put the fire on?* In the first *Shall I* becomes *if he would.* In the second *Shall I* becomes *if he should.*

'Shall I see you next week?'

He asked if he would see me the following week.

'Shall I put the fire on?'

He asked me if he should put the fire on.

N.B. It should be noted that there is no inversion in questions in indirect speech.

'Where is the Post Office?'

He wanted to know where the Post Office was.

'What are you muttering?'

He was curious to know what I was muttering.

'Don't you like it?'

He asked me if I liked it. (The negative is generally omitted as being of no interest or importance to the other speaker.)

5. For imperatives
These have a wide assortment of introductory verbs, depending on the relationship of the people concerned. The construction is generally that of the object and infinitive.
'Do it at once, please!'

He ordered me/commanded me/requested me/begged me/implored me/ besought me/entreated me/urged me/pleaded with me/shouted to me/called out to me/screamed at me to do it at once.

6. For exclamations
In fact, as some exclamations are usually involuntary and of no interest or importance to anyone else, they can usually be omitted entirely from indirect speech. If they are necessary clumsy circumlocutions must be used. Exclamations beginning with *what* will normally need a verb added in indirect speech.
'Good heavens! What on earth are you doing?'
He expressed shocked surprise and asked me what I was doing.
'Damn! I can't find the scissors.'
He expressed his annoyance/He was annoyed at not being able to find the scissors.
'What a glorious view!'
He exclaimed what a glorious view it was.
'What terrible weather!'
He expressed his disgust at the weather.
'What a fantastic story!'
He commented on how fantastic that story was.
'Hallo! Good Lord, you look awful!'
His greeting was followed by a shocked remark on how awful I looked.
N.B. Common sense is the only guide as to when and how exclamations are to be rendered into indirect speech.

7. For suggestions
You can use a finite verb, but the verb *suggest* followed by the gerund is a useful construction.
'Let's go there now.'
'Shall we go there now?'
He suggested going there then.
'Let's have a drink.'
'What about having a drink?'
'Do you feel like a drink?'
He suggested having a drink/that we might have a drink.

8.
Although there is no need to repeat *he said* with each sentence, if the kind of sentence changes (i.e. becomes a question or imperative) it will have to be re-introduced.
'It is pouring with rain. Come inside at once!'
She shouted that it was pouring with rain and ordered me to go inside.

'*What a silly boy you are! What are you doing that for?*'
She told me I was a silly boy and asked me what I was doing that for.
'*Heavens! It's cold. What about having a whiskey to warm you up? Or do you prefer rum?*'
He remarked how cold it was and suggested that I might like a whiskey to warm me up, unless I preferred rum.

EXERCISES

a.   Put the following sentences into direct speech introducing them by a verb in the simple past. Try to vary the introductory verb as much as possible.
1.   '*I went to Rome last year.*'
2.   '*Are you going to stand about doing nothing all day?*'
3.   '*Where would you like to go tomorrow?*'
4.   '*I have seen that film already, so I don't want to see it again this evening. Why don't you ask John to go with you?*'
5.   '*I may decide not to go to Paris after all.*'
6.   '*Peter! Come here at once! How dare you play in the mud in your best clothes?*'
7.   '*A lot of skyscrapers have been built in London over the last few years.*'
8.   '*Would you mind helping me across this main road?*'
9.   '*I am going to have my portrait painted.*'
10.   '*It is raining so I think we had better find something to do indoors.*'
11.   '*Let's phone up Mary and see if she would like to come to the theatre with us this evening.*'
12.   '*Aunt Mary is coming to tea tomorrow. Do try and be on your best behaviour.*'
13.   '*Trespassers will be prosecuted.*'
14.   '*What about having a drink before we go up to change for tennis?*'
15.   '*Give my kindest regards to your sister when you see her.*'
16.   '*Can you lend me £50? I'm in a spot of bother.*'
17.   '*You mustn't play the piano now. It's after midnight and all the neighbours will be complaining.*'
18.   '*Let me know whether you can come and see me next Thursday evening.*'
19.   '*Don't you know who wrote Pickwick Papers?*'
20.   '*I do hope you'll be able to do something about it. Please try for my sake.*'
21.   '*Didn't I see you in Trafalgar Square last Saturday? Wasn't there a fantastic crowd there!*'
22.   '*Honestly, I would tell you if I knew.*'
23.   '*Where is the nearest telephone kiosk? I must ring her up this moment.*'
24.   '*Good gracious! What an extraordinary thing for him to say to you!*'
25.   '*Hallo! Fancy seeing you! What did you think of the show?*'

26. 'I'm going to join that amateur theatre. You needn't act, you know; you can just see the plays or you can help behind the scenes.'
27. 'I was enjoying the peace of the countryside when I fell and twisted my ankle.'
28. 'How about going on to a nightclub?'
29. 'I wish you were not so stupid.'
30. 'Will you make a special effort to get there on time?'

b.   Put the verbs in brackets into the right tense.

1.   I (see) the headmaster tomorrow in any case, so I (tell) him what you (just say).
2.   You (never see) such chaos as the place (be) in yesterday in preparation for today's dance. When I called round, carpets (roll) up, furniture (move) from one room to another, floors (polish), chandeliers (clean), flowers (arrange) artistically at strategic places and Mary (rush) round trying to supervise everything at once. Who (believe) it to see how orderly everything looks now?
3.   As you see, at last I (get) round to decorating the room. I (mean) to do so for ages.
4.   Can you imagine it? Next year he (work) for that firm for ten years, and yet it seems only yesterday that he (wear) his first pair of long trousers!
5.   I (try) to remember his name for the last half hour, but I (not succeed) yet.
6.   What I (see) fleeing down the corridor but a ghostly apparition!
7.   It is a long time now since he (run) away and (leave) her.
8.   In my opinion the money (steal) some time between six and seven o'clock.
9.   It seems a pity that every day our towns (expand) outwards and good agricultural land (disappear) beneath new housing estates. Who knows if at this very minute land that (till) from time immemorial (not bulldoze) to make room for new housing projects? But of course the ever-increasing population must (house) somewhere.
10.   As soon as he (finish) a hearty breakfast, he (get) up and (go) out for a long walk. We (begin) to grow anxious when he still (not return) by dinner time, but at half past eight he finally (turn) up, tired, dusty and ravenous, but in the best of good humours.
11.   What was the name of the tune that (play) as we (go) into the cinema? Ever since then it (go) round and round in my head.
12.   I (wait) here nearly half an hour now. If she (not come) within five minutes I (go) off on my own. If she (not find) me here she (have) no-one but herself to blame.
13.   I can hear cries for help. I believe someone (attack) by our bees. Quick! To the rescue!
14.   At that moment who (walk) into the room but his first wife!
15.   The matter (discuss) and (look) at from all angles. Now I (suggest) we (take) a vote on what is to be done.

16. *Only for first nights the majority of the audience at Covent Garden (wear) evening dress.*
17. *If only John (be) here to advise me!*
18. *Don't you think it disgraceful that men (make) to waste years of their lives doing military service?*
19. *Not a soul he (speak) to for days on end.*

c. Use the following words in sentences so as to bring out their meaning clearly.

a rail	easy	libel	to bruise
a railing	facile	label	to braise
raillery	fragile	liable	to praise
	brittle	lapel	to prise
lightning			to price
lightening	audacious	to imply	to prize
lighting	courageous	to implicate	

d. Choose the right idiomatic word from among those given at the end of the sentence.
1. *The film star ...... a pose for the camera-men. (struck, took, cultivated)*
2. *You had better ...... clear of him; he's a wanted man. (remain, drive, steer)*
3. *It is difficult to get people to work on public transport because ...... work is unpopular. (manual, shift, mobile)*
4. *His trial is fixed for next week, but he has been allowed out on ...... (parole, leave, bail)*
5. *The sailor opened a small ...... door in the deck (square, trap, back) and disappeared down the ...... way. (run, gang, hatch)*
6. *What a nuisance! I can't use my car because I have lost my ...... key. (starting, ignition, instrument)*
7. *That was certainly a ...... squeak: we were almost killed. (near, close, shrill) (colloquial)*
8. *They decided to give him the ...... of the doubt. (advantage, benefit, profit)*
9. *John has always been as thin as a ...... (board, wire, rake)*
10. *I couldn't open the ...... hole of my cabin (window, port, pot) but I didn't mind because the ship was air-...... (pressurised, borne, conditioned)*
11. *It is a funny kind of building really, a ...... between a farm and a hotel. (cross, medley, mixture)*
12. *It is no good expecting him to be sorry for you; he's as hard as ...... (rock, iron, nails)*
13. *The criminal attempted to ...... incriminating evidence on an innocent man. (fix, plant, depose)*
14. *As the little boat had ...... a leak (got, sprung, started) we had to ...... out (bale, pull, dive) for ...... life. (sheer, our, dear)*

15. *The firm remains open all the year except for a few days at Christmas and Easter. This is possible because the staff have ...... holidays. (deranged, staggered, postponed)*

16. *She thought I was talking about her daughter, while, in fact, I was talking about my goddaughter. We were talking at ...... purposes for a good ten minutes. (cross, mixed, involved)*

17. *She was so worried that she didn't get a ...... of sleep. (wink, nod, period)*

18. *After that piece of scandal the doctor was ...... off the register. (cut, struck, deleted)*

19. *I didn't read the ...... on the cover (libel, introduction, blurb); I ...... straight into the first chapter. (dived, plunged, ran)* (the first is colloquial)

20. *Huge waves were ...... over the promenade. (breaking, striking, beating)*

21. *This car looks a bit of an old ...... but it goes well enough. (mess, crock, hand)* (colloquial)

22. *Never count your chickens before they are ...... (killed, broody, hatched)*

23. *Martin was chosen as their ...... and had to put their grievances before the director. (interpreter, spokesman, intermediary)*

24. *The poor creatures were ...... together to try to keep warm. (squashed, bundled, huddled)*

25. *I suppose I shall have to do it, but I must say it goes against the ...... (wish, grain, current)*

28: Compound verbs K–M

Keep

1. to keep *up*
a. a house (To maintain it in good condition.)
b. someone's interest (Not to allow someone to get bored.)
2. the *upkeep* of a house (The maintenance or cost of maintenance.)
3. to keep *up with*
a. the Joneses (To aim at not being left behind them socially: to have as many 'status symbols' as they have (this often involves buying bigger and dearer things than you want or need: colloquial.)
b. I can't keep up with you. (You are going too fast for me, either physically in walking or intellectually.)

4. to keep *up with/in touch with* someone (To remain in contact.)
5. to keep *to the point* (To cut out irrelevant matter.)
6. to keep *oneself to oneself* (To be rather reserved and keep oneself aloof: not to be at all forthcoming in making social contacts.)
7. to keep *one's nose to the grindstone* (To work hard over a reasonably long period: colloquial.)
8. to keep something *up one's sleeve* (To keep something secret: colloquial.)
9. to keep *up appearances* (To try not to show how poor one is.)
10. *How are you keeping?* (How are you, these days?)
11. *to keep* on with something (To continue to work at something.)
12. to keep *house for* someone (To do the housework for someone: to be a housekeeper.)
13. to keep *one's feet* (To manage not to fall over when walking on anything slippery—ice, snow etc.)
14. to earn *one's keep* (To work in return for one's food, accommodation etc.)
15. to keep *off*
a. *Keep off the grass.* (Do not walk on it.)
b. a subject (To avoid mentioning it.)
c. mosquitoes, flies etc. (To prevent them from worrying you.)
16. to keep *out*
Keep out! (Do not enter.)
17. to keep someone *at arm's length* (Not to be very friendly.)
18. to keep a nation *down/under* (To oppress it.)
19. to keep something *from* someone
I tried to keep it from him. (Prevent him from finding out about it.)

Knock

1. to knock *about*
a. (To practise before starting a game of tennis.)
b. something (To damage it.)
c. the world (To travel extensively, roughing it without much organisation: colloquial.)
2. to knock *down*
a. someone (To knock someone flat in an accident or fight.)
b. *I knocked him down to £5.* (I haggled until he agreed to accept £5 for the article: colloquial.)
3. to knock *up*
a. someone (To awaken someone at a certain time.)
b. something (To make it oneself.)
4. to knock something *over* (To upset it accidentally.)
5. to knock *off* (To finish work: colloquial.)
6. to knock someone *out* (To punch someone so that he falls down unconscious—in boxing or a fight.)

EXERCISES

Replace the italicised part of the sentence with an expression with *keep* or *knock*.
1. I hope you will *not give up* English when you go home.
2. You must *work hard consistently* until the examination.
3. It's terribly expensive to *maintain* a large house nowadays.
4. He *is a very quiet and retiring person.*
5. Mr Winkle had some difficulty in *remaining upright* on his skates.
6. It is a good thing for young people to *see something of* the world before they settle down in middle age.
7. It is very difficult to *remain in touch with* all one's school-friends.
8. We needed a new cupboard for the kitchen so our neighbour *made one* from some wood he had.
9. I wish you would *be more concise and less discursive.*
10. I am sure she will not be able to *prevent herself from blurting out* such an important piece of news.

Lay

1. a *lay-by* (A place for parking on a major road or just off it.)
2. to lay *down*
a. *the law* (To speak with great authority—generally without any justification.)
b. one's life (To sacrifice it for one's country.)
c. one's arms (To surrender.)
3. to be laid *up with* ... (To be confined to bed on the doctor's orders because of ...)
4. to lay *off* workers (To tell workers to go home because there is no work for them.)
5. to lay *on* electricity, gas, etc. (To supply it by connecting it up to the main.)
6. to lay *out* a garden etc. (To design and construct a new garden.)
7. the *lay-out* of a garden etc. (The design of it.)
8. *outlay* (Expense.)
9. to lay *out money on* something or someone (To spend it: collo-quial.)
10. to lay *oneself out to please* someone (To go to a good deal of trouble to satisfy someone.)
11. to lay *in* a stock of (To buy reserve stock.)

Lead

1. to lead *off* (To start a discussion etc.)
2. to lead *up to* a subject (To approach it.)
3. to be led *away by* one's feelings (To be overpowered by them so

that one loses rational control.)

4. to lead someone *on to* do something (To encourage someone strongly.)

5. to lead someone *astray* (To lead someone into bad ways.)

6. a *leading* question (A question designed to elicit a particular answer.)

Let

1. to let someone *down* (To fail someone by not keeping one's promise.)

2. to let *up*

a. in one's efforts (To stop trying so hard.)

b. The rain is letting up. (It is raining less heavily now.)

3. to let *on about* something (To betray a secret that someone has confided to you.)

4. to let *the cat out of the bag* (To betray a secret unintentionally: slang.)

5. to let someone *into*

a. a room (To allow someone to enter.)

b. a secret (To tell someone it.)

6. to let oneself *in for* something (To get oneself into a position where one may have to do something unwillingly.)

7. to let *off*

a. rooms (To allow tenants to occupy them.)

b. fireworks or *guns* (To make them explode.)

8. to let someone *off* (Not to punish someone when he could justifiably be punished.)

9. to let *out*

a. clothes (To make them larger: the opposite of *to take in clothes.*)

b. a secret (To betray it by accident.)

c. a cry of pain (Not to attempt to suppress it.)

10. an *outlet* (A means by which talent, ability etc. can be allowed to express itself or by which water can be allowed out.)

11. an *inlet* (A creek: a place where the sea penetrates the coastline.)

EXERCISES

Replace the italicised part of the sentence with an expression with *lay*, *lead* or *let*.

1. People who *pontificate* are usually unholy bores.

2. I was not very impressed by the *plan* of the new town.

3. It was John's mother who *unlocked the* door *for me.*

4. When I was a small child we had no electricity in the house because it had not been *supplied* to the road.

5. It is refreshing to find a shopkeeper who really *does his utmost* to please his customers.

6. Mary is *confined to bed* with some virus infection.
7. We moored the boat in a *kind of not very rocky fjord.*
8. You have *made yourself liable to* a lot of trouble by offering to babysit for Naomi.
9. Those clothes will have to be *made looser at the seams.*
10. I dislike having fireworks *ignited* just under my nose.
11. What a vast amount of money Henry is *lavishing* on Margaret.
12. His wife *urged him* to take that step.
13. His feelings *got the better of him.*
14. Will you promise to keep it to yourself if I *tell you* a secret?
15. Socrates was accused of *corrupting* the youth of Athens.
16. The initial *expenditure* is considerable, but profits should increase so rapidly that it will be worth it.
17. In a slump a lot of labourers are *sent home.*
18. Naturally she is trying to find a job that will give her some *scope for using* her flair for sketching.
19. I will never trust him again. He has *failed me* so many times.
20. Why *haven't you punished John*? I should have thought he needed teaching a lesson.

Look

1. to look *at* (To view, to observe.)
2. to look *on/upon* someone as a friend (To regard someone as a friend.)
3. to look *on* (To be a passive spectator.)
4. an *onlooker* (A chance spectator.)
5. to look *back on* (To recall; to remember deliberately.)
6. to look *over*
a. (To check or correct a manuscript etc.)
b. (To give a view of.)
c. someone's book (To get help by seeing what he has written.)
7. to *overlook*
a. (To give a view of.)
b. (Not to notice: to miss a mistake etc.)
c. (To forgive.)
8. the *outlook* (Future prospects.)
9. *outlook* on life (Attitude to life.)
10. to look *into* something (To investigate something.)
11. to look *down on* someone (To despite someone.)
12. to look *up* to someone (To admire someone.)
13. to look someone *up* (To take the trouble to visit someone when you happen to be in his home town.)
14. to look someone *up and down* (To survey someone critically from head to foot.)
15. to look *up*
Things are looking up. (They are improving: colloquial.)

16. to look *through* something (To read something rather cursorily.)
17. to look *for*
a. (To search for something lost.)
b. (To expect or exact.)
18. to look *forward to* doing something (To expect to enjoy something.)
19. to look *like*
a. someone (To resemble someone.)
b. *It looks like remaining fine.* (It will probably remain fine.)
c. *What does he look like?* (What kind of appearance does he present?)
20. to look *after* something or someone (To take care of something or someone.)
21. to look *out over* (To command a view of.)
22. to look *to one's laurels* (To be zealous in protecting one's reputation against a rival: colloquial.)
23. *look-out*
a. *It is your look-out.* (It is your responsibility.)
b. to keep a *look-out* for someone (To watch for someone carefully.)
c. (A person on a ship whose job it is to look out for land or other ships.)
24. *Look out! (Take care!)*
25. a *look-in*
not to get a *look-in* (Not to get a chance of doing something.)

EXERCISE

Replace the italicised expressions with others containing *look*.
1. I *consider him* a friend rather than a pupil.
2. I *paid a call on Mary* when I was in Paris.
3. It is questionable whether old people *recall* their youth with nostalgia or with relief at not having to go through it all again.
4. If I am paying £20 for a meal, I *expect* something better than this.
5. I suppose St. Francis of Assisi is one of the most generally *respected* of all the saints.
6. I wonder if you would mind *reading this through* for me and correcting any mistakes?
7. The police have been asked to *probe* the disappearance of his brother.
8. John was so brilliant that no-one else in the class got *any chance of distinguishing himself.*
9. If you choose to do that, it is your own *affair*, but don't say I didn't warn you.
10. One cannot help *feeling rather contemptuous of* some people, however unethical it may be.
11. She is *excited at the idea of* seeing Paris for the first time.
12. The prospects for the car trade are certainly *better*.
13. I will *pardon* your rudeness this time, but remember how to behave in future.

14. You have a strange *philosophy of* life.
15. His villa *commands a wonderful view of* the Bay of Naples.

Make

1. to make *out*
a. (To find out or discover.)
b. (To understand.)
c. (To see in the distance with difficulty.)
d. a cheque, bill, list etc. (To write it out.)
e. (To pretend.)
2. to make *light of* something (Not to treat something seriously.)
3. to make *out a case for* (To argue logically in favour of.)
4. to make *out in.*
How did you make out in that examination? (How did you get on?)
5. to make *for* somewhere (To go directly to it.)
6. to make *up*
a. one's face (To use cosmetics.)
b. a prescription (To make the medicine from the doctor's instructions.)
c. a story (To invent it.)
d. a parcel (To tie it with paper and string.)
e. one's mind (To decide.)
f. a fire (To put more coal on it.)
g. a quarrel (To become reconciled after quarrelling.)
h. a four (To be fourth player in a game of cards or tennis.)
i. a bill (To add up the items on it and present it to the customer.)
j. a bed (To prepare a spare bed to receive a visitor.)
k. to someone (To be particularly charming because you want someone to do something for you.)
7. *make-up* (as a noun)
a. (Cosmetics.)
b. (A person's fundamental character.)
8. to be made *up of* (to be composed of.)
9. to make *up for* something (To compensate for something.)
10. to make *off* (To run away quickly.)
11. to make *over* one's property to someone (To give it someone before you die—instead of leaving it him in your will—to avoid death duties.)
12. to make *away with* someone (To murder someone: colloquial.)
13. to make *do with* something (To manage with something because one cannot afford to *get* anyhting better.)
14. *Made it! (I've managed it!* I've succeeded in doing it: colloquial.)
15. *What time do you make it?* (What time is it by your watch?)
16 to make *a clean breast of something* (To confess something fully.)
17. to make *hay while the sun shines (*To take one's opportunity when it comes.)

18. to make *a mountain out of a molehill* (To exaggerate the import-ance of something.)
19. to be *on the make* (To be anxious to get money quickly without bothering about moral scruples: colloquial.)
20. *makeshift* (Temporary and far from ideal: improvised: rough-and-ready.)
21. a world of *make-believe* (Fantasy: imagination.)

EXERCISES

a. Replace the italicised expressions with others containing *make.*
1. He *tried to give the impression* that he knew a lot about art.
2. The criminal *fled* when he saw the policeman.
3. It's my belief that he has *killed* his nagging wife.
4. Where are we *heading* for?
5. How did you *get on* in that interview?
6. As soon as the lesson was over he *went straight* to the nearest pub.
7. I haven't much food in the house. Can you *manage with* an egg and some salad?
8. I didn't *fasten* the parcel properly and it came undone.
9. I hear that he has *transferred* the bulk of his property to his son.
10. The human body is *constructed of* several million cells.
11. They had a serious argument yesterday, but I think they *are on good terms again now.*
12. You must not believe a word he says; he is always *spinning* fantastic yarns.
13. I haven't much money on me. Do you mind if I *write you out a cheque?*
14. I tried hard to *distinguish* the island but the swirling mists hid it.
15. It is no use your *turning on the charm for* me. I know what you want.
16. We had better *put some more coal on* the fire before we have dinner.
17. Sometimes it does people good to *own up to* everything.
18. You have been away a long time; you must work really hard now to *compensate* for the time you have lost.
19. You had better go and *get* the bed in the spare room *ready.* John and his wife will be arriving about six o'clock.
20. That film has a reputation for being *all out to make money.*

b. Put in the missing prepositions or particles in these sentences.
1. *The magistrate let him .... a severe reprimand.*
2. *Will you make ...... this bill, please?*
3. *Why don't you let ...... a bit? It is silly to knock yourself .... overworking.*
4. *Nobody seemed to want to start the discussion, so I asked Simon to lead ......*
5. *Look me ...... next time you are in London.*

6. *Keep it ...... yourself; don't let ...... it ...... anyone.*
7. *Money is short; a lot of people have been laid ......*
8. *He really laid himself .... satisfy his customers.*
9. *I look ...... you as my best friend.*
10. *We haven't any milk; I knocked ...... the bottle a few minutes ago.*
11. *I wish you wouldn't gallop like that. How can I possibly keep .... you?*
12. *He was asking a pound, but I knocked him .... fifty pence.*
13. *The baby let ...... a yell as she struck it.*
14. *Your make ...... isn't very good these days; you must look ...... your laurels now Jane has appeared on the scene.*
15. *You had better keep ...... the subject of divorce with her.*
16. *Didn't you know? Mary is laid .... pneumonia.*
17. *We shall be able to go out soon; the rain is letting ......*
18. *He has let ...... several rooms of the house ...... the Smiths.*
19. *When I look .... my life, there are several things I would like to have done differently.*
20. *One does not always like people one looks .... Virtue can be unsympathetic.*
21. *His brother led him .... steal the motor-bike.*
22. *His flat looks .... a disused quarry.*
23. *She's more cheerful now; things are looking ......*
24. *The Manager is looking ...... the matter: I expect something will be done soon.*
25. *I can't let ...... these trousers any more. You had better give them to someone slimmer!*

c.   Insert the right verbs in these sentences.
1. *I wish you would stop ...... my footsteps.*
2. *If you publish that you will be ...... the copyright.*
3. *I thought it best to ...... a hasty retreat.*
4. *We have ...... aground on a sandback.*
5. *He ...... himself by ...... on oath that his friends has been nowhere near the scene of the crime.*
6. *He is so unhappy in his marriage that I believe he is ...... a petition for divorce.*
7. *May I ...... my condolences on the disappointment you have suffered?*
8. *It is unwise to try to ...... favour with people by ...... to blatant flattery.*
9. *Sometimes people ...... berserk and ...... amok among a crowd of people, killing or injuring anyone that happens to be near.*
10. *She ...... into tears on hearing the news.*
11. *Some people ...... their living in very peculiar ways.*
12. *Napoleon ...... some astounding victories before he ...... his downfall.*
13. *The sight of that church tower enabled him to ...... his bearings.*

14. *His strength was ...... by the operation he had had and he died soon afterwards.*
15. *He is really a very nice fellow; you will find he ...... on acquaintance.*
16. *English subjects ...... allegiance to the Queen.*
17. *It is always advisable to ...... the contents of one's home against fire and burglary.*
18. *Titus ...... mercy on his would-be assassin; not always is mercy ...... to such people, however.*
19. *He tried to ...... on me to invest a lot of money in that concern. Some hopes!*
20. *Why are you ...... that to my charge? I had nothing to do with it.*
21. *Some people are always ...... jokes, even in the face of serious danger.*
22. *I was reading a detective story just to ...... away the time.*
23. *It will take them a long time to ...... that scandal down.*
24. *Don't ...... to conclusions; be sure of your facts first.*
25. *It is quite common for films to ...... short of one's expectations; it is rare for them to ...... them.*

d. Fill in the blank spaces with a word formed from, or related to, the word given in brackets at the end of the sentence.
1. *The family was ...... during the war. (poor)*
2. *He intends to ...... his stay in England. (long)*
3. *The ...... of the road is twice what it used to be. (broad)*
4. *That money ...... him to go to University. (able)*
5. *It is unwise to ...... your employers. (ridiculous)*
6. *Your confession ...... the whole matter. (simple)*
7. *In general foreigners ...... more than English people. (gesture)*
8. *The Minister inspired everyone with his ...... speech. (passion)*
9. *He gave me a ...... account of his journey. (fiction)*
10. *What are the ...... parts of air? (compose)*
11. *A ...... man lurched into the train. (drink)*
12. *Castiglione's courtier ...... the Renaissance ideal. (example)*
13. *'...... is next to godliness.' (clean)*
14. *You really can be ...... on occasions. (fury)*
15. *His unfortunate experiences ...... him. (bitter)*
16. *...... never drink alcohol. (total)*
17. *Who was the first person to ...... you in England? (friend)*
18. *Teachers attach a lot of importance to the ...... of words. (pronounce)*
19. *It needs courage and tact to ...... a furious snob. (peace)*
20. *The Minister was asked to ...... the position. (clear)*
21. *His rivals were plotting to ...... him. (out)*
22. *In England the ...... wind is westerly. (prevail)*
23. *You need to develop a more ...... attitude to life. (real)*
24. *There was an ...... of wild life on the island. (abound)*
25. *We have had six ...... for that job. (apply)*

26. *He has a slight ...... in his speech. (impede)*
27. *It is impossible to take Don Quixote's heroic ...... seriously. (do)*
28. *What a ...... painting! (repel)*
29. *He got ...... treatment. (prefer)*
30. *Such ...... is rarely met with. (infamous)*

29: The use of the articles in English

1.   Plural, abstract and uncountable nouns require no article if they are used in a general sense.
Liberty is a precious commodity.
Cows eat grass.
Accommodation is expensive these days.
Advice is not always welcome.
Religion is losing its hold on people.
Women have lost as much as they have gained by achieving equality.

2.   If these nouns are limited in time or place to particular examples of the thing, the definite article is required.
The liberty of the English even today is far from complete.
The cows that I bought yesterday have all died from eating the grass in my garden.
The accommodation that my brother got for that price was far from satisfactory.
The advice my wife gave me did not save me from getting into trouble.
The religion of the Aztecs was a bloodthirsty one.
The women who were agitating for the vote chained themselves to the railings outside the Houses of Parliament.

3.   Singular, concrete nouns can never be used without an article, except in idioms. The definite article is precise, specified or referring back to something previously mentioned. The indefinite article is vague, general or suggesting that it does not matter which it is.
A yard of that material costs £5.
That material is £5 a yard. *
He is a schoolmaster.
He is the schoolmaster who caused a scandal by what he said in the letter

* It should be noted that there are two common exceptions to this:
   a. to pay someone by the day
   b. Gold is weighed by the ounce.

he wrote to The Times.
The atomic bomb is a fearful weapon.
He earns £9,000 a year.
It revolves a thousand times a second.
Butter is ninety pence a pound.
A man who didn't eat for a month would die.
There used to be a beautiful old bridge over the river here, but the whole area suffered in the war and the bridge was blown up.

4.   The definite article is used with the double comparative.
The older I get, the sillier I become.
The more people go to that party, the better he will be pleased.
The more I know him, the less I like him.
The sooner the delinquent owns up, the better it will be for all of you.
The less an author has to say, the more tricks of style he will use to eke out his writing.

5.   No article is generally used with:
a.   The names of countries (unless they are really provinces or plural or are limited in time)
Italy, Persia, India, The Transvaal, The Netherlands, The United States. The England of the 15th century was very different from the England of today.
b.   The names of mountains (except those in the Bernese Oberland)
Snowdon, Everest, Mont Blanc, the Jungfrau
c.   Meals (unless they are very formal ones)
Come round to dinner one day.
Did you go to the dinner by the Lord Mayor in honour of General de Gaulle?
d.   Titles (except *the Reverend*, *the Venerable* and aristocratic titles with place names)
General Cook, Lord Byron, Cardinal Wolsey, King William I, the Reverend Charles Smith, the Duke of Beaufort, Earl Attlee, the Marquis of Bath.
e.   Streets and Squares (except for a few foreign ones)
Oxford Street, Park Lane, Berkeley Square, the Gran Via, the Champs Elysées
f.   Islands (unless they are in groups)
Ceylon, Cuba, Australia, the Channel Islands, the Hebrides.
g.   Next and *last* if they are from the time of speaking.
I am going there next week.
We spent the second week of our holiday at Avignon and the last one at Cannes.
h.   Bed, *school, hospital, church* and *prison* if these are used for the natural purpose for which they are intended and are preceded by a verb of movement. Otherwise they are used with the definite article.
I'm tired so I'm going to bed.

About 10% (ten per cent) *of people in England go to church on Sundays.*
He was caught and has been sent to prison.
He is in hospital and will have an operation tomorrow.
(The article is omitted with these words also after verbs of state, but it is inserted for unnatural purposes only after verbs of movement.)
I went to the bed to pick up some gramophone records that I had left on it.
I pursued the dog into the church.
I went to the prison to see the Governor who was an old friend of mine.

6.   The definite article is used:
a.   with rivers, seas, oceans, chains of mountains, gulfs, bays and straits
the Red sea, the Atlantic, the Alps, the Bay of Biscay, the Straits of Dover.
b.   with ships, hotels, theatres, clubs and newspapers:
the Queen Elizabeth, the Old Vic, the Times, the Hilton, the victory Club.
c.   with the points of the compass if preceded by a preposition:
He lives in the north of Sweden.
He fled to the west.
d.   before adjectives to turn them into class nouns or abstract nouns:
The millionaire lives in a different world from the pauper.
The poor are still with us.
Nurses take care of the sick.
The strong should protect the weak.
Greek education enquired into the good.
Everyone has his own ideas about the beautiful.
Poets interpret the commonplace freshly.
e.   before musical instruments
She plays the violin execrably.
I am not always in the mood to play the piano.
f.   with family names if these are made plural
Keeping up with the Joneses is absurd.
The Browns have bought yet another unnecessary household gadget.
I am going to stay with the Martins for a few days.
7.   The above-mentioned rules cover the majority of cases, but in some cases usage is everything. The following are some of the commonest cases in which singular, concrete nouns are used without an article.

to live from hand to mouth (to live in great proverty)
to make port (to reach one's destination on a ship)
to throw oneself heart and soul into something (completely)
friend or foe? (the challenge of a sentry
to turn turtle (to capsize)
to rush from pillar to post (to rush from place to place in a panic)

by word of mouth (orally)
to set sail (to start a voyage)
to fight tooth and nail (to fight very hard)
inch by inch, foot by foot etc.
by hook or by crook (by fair means or foul)
The letter has just come to hand (arrived: commercial)
by car, by train, by day etc.

(If you add an article or adjective you change the preposition.
I came in my car.
I lost my wallet on the train.
On a stormy night, people stay at home.)

by land or sea

to reply by return of post (to post a reply to a letter on the same day that it is received)

made by hand

through fire and tempest

*to take someone to task (*to criticise someone for his own good)

to cut school (to play truant from it)

to declare war on someone

to lay siege to a castle

to be at stake (in danger)

to be lying face downwards

to give ground (to retreat)

*to arrive on time (*to arrive at the scheduled time)

to be out of pocket (to have made a loss on a transaction)

to give battle (to attack the enemy)

to make way (to get out of someone's way)

to catch fire

to take breath

to put the enemy to flight

Land ahoy! (the call of a look-out on sighting land)

The river is in flood.

to be in disguise

to catch hold of

in place of

*to take something to heart (*to take something very seriously: to worry about it)

to lie in wait for

to set foot on (to step on)

*to have an eye for colour (*to have natural good taste where colours are concerned)

on suspicion of

sword in hand

to take responsibility for

on foot

to drop anchor: to weigh anchor (to pull it up)

in duty bound (because it is my duty)

on pain of death (with death as a possible punishment)

to put a job in hand (to get started on it: commercial)

bound hand and foot

to get down from table

to make peace with someone

to abandon ship

to be under arrest

to take a castle by storm

on condition that

to arrive in time (to arrive in time not to miss something)

to be in pocket (to have made a profit)

to give way (to collapse, retreat or fall down)

to talk sense

to face danger

to set fire to

to find time to

to take office (to be installed in one's job)

to be off course

to remain under cover (to remain hidden)

to take hold of

to make sense

freedom of speech

to summon Parliament

to make time for

on board ship

to turn someone out of house and home (to disinherit someone)

to do penance

in pursuit of

to send word

to sigh with relief

EXERCISES

a. Insert the correct article, if necessary, in the blank spaces

1. ...... *wealth does not always bring* ...... *happiness.*
2. ...... *weather is very peculiar this year.*
3. ...... *Russia of* ...... *Czars was very different from* ...... *Russia of today.*
4. *Does* ...... *equality mean anything if it is applied to* ...... *people?*
5. *Perhaps* ...... *bed is* ...... *most essential article of furniture in* ...... *house.*
6. ...... *longer you stay in* ...... *England* ...... *better you should understand* ...... *mentality of* ...... *people.*
7. ...... *banks of* ...... *Seine in* ...... *Paris are better laid out than those of* ...... *Thames in* ...... *London.*
8. *She works as* ...... *usherette in* ...... *cinema.*
9. ...... *London of Dickens' time comes to* ...... *life in his books.*
10. ...... *wisdom does not always come with* ...... *age.*
11. ...... *applause at* ...... *end of* ...... *concert was deafening.*
12. *He swore to fulfil his life's ambition by* ...... *hook or by* ...... *crook.*
13. ...... *debris was scattered all over* ...... *road.*
14. *May I draw* ...... *attention to* ...... *discrepancy between your figures and ours?*
15. ...... *captain never gives* ...... *order to abandon* ...... *ship until all* ...... *hope of saving it is lost.*
16. *That curtaining material cost £5* ...... *yard.*
17. ...... *freedom of* ...... *speech is* ...... *good principle, even if* ...... *abuse of it has to be curbed.*
18. ...... *books lying on* ...... *table belong to* ...... *friend of mine.*
19. ...... *intellectual curiosity is* ...... *pre-requisite to* ...... *study.*
20. *He was ordered to do it on* ...... *pain of* ...... *death.*
21. ...... *death of Shelley was* ...... *great loss to* ...... *poetry.*
22. *Flying from London to Madrid, one passes over* ...... *France and* ...... *Pyrenees.*
23. *In* ...... *olden days* ...... *knights wore* ...... *armour when they went into* ...... *battle.*
24. *I went to* ...... *wedding but could not stay for* ...... *wedding breakfast.*
25. ...... *Jungfrau is not half as high as* ...... *Everest, but is nearly* ...... *four times as high as* ...... *Snowdon. After* ...... *Himalayas, I think* ...... *Andes are* ...... *highest chain of* ...... *mountains in* ...... *world.*
26. *Do you expect me to go all* ...... *way back to* ...... *school to look for* ...... *hairpin you might have dropped there?*
27. *He stopped on* ...... *crest of* ...... *hill to take* ...... *breath.*
28. ...... *internal combustion engine has revolutionised* ...... *transport.*
29. *He plays* ...... *violin with* ...... *enthusiasm but without* ...... *tech-*

nical skill required to become famous.
30 *Do try to arrive in ...... time for ...... fanfare preceding ...... arrival of ...... Queen.*
31. *...... nonsense talked about ...... education this century outdoes anything said in ...... past.*
32. *...... policeman told me that I was under arrest and was to go with him to ...... police station.*
33. *There is ...... man at ...... front door who says he has ...... news for you of ...... great importance.*
34. *...... cake must have received ...... bump in ...... transit as ...... icing has been knocked off one corner.*
35. *He has taken ...... suite of ...... rooms at ...... Hilton Hotel.*

b.   Do what is necessary to the verbs in brackets, adding prepositions if necessary.
1. *He gives the impression (have) a great deal of self-confidence.*
2. *She has a weakness (eat) cream cakes.*
3. *I was in no way implicated (oust) your friend.*
4. *What do you say (have) a bottle of wine with our lunch? It makes one's afternoon work (go) with a swing!*
5. *I have never tried my hand (be) a waiter, but at school when we took it in turns (wait) on the staff for lunch I remember absentmindedly (offer) a bishop gravy with his fish!*
6. *He tried (mislead) his girlfriend (think) she was the only person who meant anything to him.*
7. *The ancient Greeks made no bones (use) their friends.*
8. *If you persist (spell) my name wrong, I shall make a point (write) it in block capitals and (send) it to you every day for a fortnight!*
9. *People who have no difficulty (adapt) themselves (live) in different countries are lucky.*
10. *At the risk (offend) you I will state that your chances (pass) the examination are very slight.*
11. *The Government is focusing attention (curb) inflation.*
12. *Do you mean (tell) me that you have no recollection (punch) that policeman on the nose?*
13. *I made some pretence (listen) while he told me a shaggy-dog story, but in reality I was endeavouring (think) of a good way (take) my leave without offending him.*
14. *You will not succeed (talk) me (join) the Labour Party, so you might as well give up (try).*
15. *He was charged (break) and (enter) John's house on the night of 15th May. He pleaded guilty (be) on the premises, but denied (force) an entry, (say) that he had noticed the front door (stand) open and had gone in (investigate).*
16. *During his wife's illness, he turned his talents (cook), with no very dire results.*

17. *Some children are quicker (learn) (talk) than others. I wonder if this is due (they be) more intelligent, or not.*
18. *What is the use (have) a dictionary and (be) too lazy (look) up important words?*
19. *Don't rely (he give) you back that money immediately. He has a habit (not pay) debts for months and months.*
20. *I was told off (ask) difficult questions in class.*

c. Use the following idiomatic expressions in sentences of your own.
1. *the chances are that*
2. *in all likelihood*
3. *to take the rough with the smooth*
4. *to get hold of the wrong end of the stick* (colloquial)
5. *to put one's cards on the table* (colloquial)
6. *to make ends meet* (colloquial)
7. *to work hand in glove with someone*
8. *a red-herring*
9. *to be hard-up* (colloquial)
10. *to put the cart before the horse* (colloquial)
11. *to see red* (colloquial)
12. *to pinpoint something*
13. *to be in the red* (colloquial)
14. *to be well-off*
15. *to stand on one's own feet*
16. *to take a dim view of something*
17. *to be rather under the weather*
18. *to lead someone up the garden path* (colloquial)
19. *to take something for granted/as a matter of course*
20. *there was no love lost between them*
21. *the same holds good for you*
22. *to make it worth someone's while to do something*
23. *to keep abreast of the latest developments*
24. *for the time being*
25. *to get off the beaten track*

d. Put into indirect speech with the introductory verb in the past.
1. *'Come and see what I've found down here.'*
2. *'You are a fool and you know it. How do you expect to pass the examination if you don't do any work?*
3. *'I went to the Goya Exhibition last week.'*
4. *'For God's sake tell me where she is.'*
5. *'My wife and I would like you to come to dinner next Saturday. Would about seven thirty suit you?'*
6. *'Why do you keep on asking such silly questions?'*
7. *'Be careful how you cross the road. That is a very busy corner.'*
8. *'Hide it in the bushes and don't say a word about it to anyone.'*
9. *'I intend to explore that part of London as soon as I get a really fine day.'*

10. *'Next Monday we are going to Warwick to see the castle. There is plenty of room in the car. Would you like to come with us?'*
11. *'Please try to remember where he said he was going this afternoon. If you can tell me, I may be in time to save him from getting into serious trouble.'*
12. *'Where did you find that beautiful Georgian table? Was it terribly expensive?—if you don't mind my asking.'*
13. *'What about going away for the weekend together—somewhere right off the beaten track where we shall be in an idyllic world of our own?'*
14. *'I have been waiting for a long time to tell you what I really think of you. Now is a good opportunity!'*
15. *'Be careful what you are doing with that umbrella. It is a lethal weapon in your hands.'*

e. Put the right form of *do* or *make* in these sentences.
1. *You must ...... your best and ...... the best of a bad job.*
2. *Trams have been ...... away with in England.*
3. *...... me a favour, will you, and ...... an effort to get here on time?*
4. *We haven't a proper spare bed; can you .... with a camp bed?*
5. *Some people who ...... others down ...... no bones about ...... so.*
6. *Hurry up: ...... up your face, ... up your coat and ...... out a list of things you want to buy.*
7. *Every day the au pair girl ...... the toast and coffee, ... the washing up, ... the carpets with the vacuum, ... the beds, ... the vegetables, trying not to ...... too much mess in the kitchen, cooks lunch and ...... what she likes all afternoon.*
8. *Add some more water to ...... the lemonade go further.*
9. *Snobbish people try to ...... out that they belong to a higher social class than they really ......*
10. *Don't ...... a noise; John is ...... his accounts in there.*
11. *She was very annoyed when she had just ...... the cleaning in the kitchen and her husband ...... a lot of work by walking in in muddy boots.*
12. *I wonder if people who have ...... time ...... the best writers on prison conditions?*
13. *You should ...... time to ...... the things you really want to do.*
14. *It ...... not ...... to ...... fun of your employers.*
15. *That brandy ...... me good; it's ...... a new man of me.*
16. *The insurance company ...... good the loss; in fact I think I ...... a small profit out of that accident.*
17. *Poor people must .... and mend.*
18. *His father ...... him an allowance of £70 a week.*
19. *They have certainly ...... up this station since I was last here.*
20. *How do you ...... out that I am not ...... my fair share of the work?*

21. *She will ...... him a good wife.*
22. *You shouldn't ...... fun of people ...... gymnastics. It may ......*
them good psychologically even if it cannot ...... them fine physical
specimens.
23. *...... your worst and ...... me out a liar if you want to.*
24. *The Government ...... a blunder by ...... that deal with the Amer-*
icans.
25. *He ...... a very profitable bit of business yesterday.*

f.   Use these words in sentences so as to bring out their meaning
clearly.

attic	*skit*	*treat*	*desertion*
antic	*skittles*	*treaty*	*to desert*
antique	*to scud*	*treatise*	*a desert*
antiquity	*to scuttle*	*tread*	*to get one's deserts*
		thread	*dessert*
insensible	*tout*	*threat*	
insensitive	*taut*		
senseless	*taunt*		

30: The Saxon genitive (the 's) and the use of nouns as adjectives

1.   The Saxon genitive should really only be used for real possession
as applied to people (*my father's house, John's overcoat, my sister's*
jewellery). In practice it is also used for things that happen to people
(*Caesar's murder, Napoleon's death*). Probably, however, it is better
here to say *the murder of Caesar, the death of Napoleon*. The Saxon
genitive is also used in expressions concerning time or distance (*a*
mile's walk, a few minute's delay, a year's salary, a month's holiday).

2.   Usage varies according to the person as far as adding an extra *s* to
words already ending in *s* is concerned. In general classical gentlemen
add only an apostrophe and more recent ones an apostrophe and an *s*.
Socrates' death
Euripides' drama
St James's Park
King Charles's taste in architecture
Words of one syllable are more likely to take the extra *s* than longer
words.

3.   There are a few idioms in which the *s* is not used in accordance with the general usage. The commonest are:

out of harm's way (in a safe place)
in my mind's eye (in my imagination)
to be at one's wit's end (to have no idea what to do)
to one's heart's content (as much as one wants)
to defend one's country's honour
a stone's throw away (very near)
for heaven's sake
for goodness' sake (*goodness* and *conscience* end in the same sound as 's' and do not, therefore, have an 's' after the apostrophe.)
for conscience' sake
to achieve one's life's ambition
to keep someone at arm's length
at death's door
the sun's rays
a wasp's nest
at the water's edge

N.B. The following construction, which is possible only in the first person singular, is quite common:
I borrowed a friend of mine's umbrella.

4.   Nouns can be used as adjectives for three main reasons: to indicate the *kind* of thing, to indicate the *use* to which it may be put and to indicate the *place* you would normally expect to find it.

a village church (a small, unpretentious one)
an apple tree
a mosaic floor
a shop window (a large, plate-glass one)
street lighting (not office lighting or decorative lighting)
a teacup (a cup for tea)
a coal-scuttle (a box for coal)
a kitchen broom (a broom for use in the kitchen)
a reception committee (a committee whose purpose is to receive people)
a bedroom suite (a suite designed for use in a bedroom and which you would expect to find there)
a London bus (the kind of bus normally found in London)
a cutlery drawer (a drawer designed and used for keeping cutlery in)
a garden seat (the kind of seat designed for and found in a garden)
a mouse-trap (a trap used for catching mice in)

It must be remembered, however, that usage has as much to do with the way words are used together as any tabulation of rules. It may be said, I think, that the use of nouns as adjectives is becoming widespread.

EXERCISES

a.   The two words at the beginning of these sentences can be combined in one of three ways:

i. using the Saxon genitive

ii. using a phrase with *of*

iii. as a plain sequence.

Do whichever is required. The sequence may be the other way round from that given.

1. *(hour, work) I must do another* ...... *this evening.*

2. *(education, diploma) Recognised teachers must have either a(n)* ...... *or a degree.*

3. *(moment, notice) The understudy had to take over at a* ......

4. *(hand, rail) No* ...... *was provided.*

5. *(party, politics) I find it difficult to get excited about* ......

6. *(doll, house) One of the Queen's* ...... *is on show to the public.*

7. *(summer, day) It was a beautiful* ......

8. *(wine, glass) What a pity I have broken that* ......

9. *(room, ceiling) The* ...... *was crossed with ancient beams.*

10. *(today, newspaper) I read something fascinating in* ......

11. *(break, tea) Most workers insist on having a* ......

12. *(hair, breadth) He escaped by a* ......

13. *(matter, root) The* ...... *is that he never had the slightest discipline instilled into him at home.*

14. *(worth, money) When you go out, you like to feel that you have got your* ......

15. *(ceiling, bedroom) I noticed yesterday that there was a big crack in my* ......

16. *(tray, tea) I bought her a* ...... *for her birthday.*

17. *(door, death) When I went to see him I really thought he looked as if he was at* ......

18. *(magazine, women) The sentiment in most* ...... *is so cloying that men find them unreadable.*

19. *(year, absence) He looked very different after his* ......

20. *(meeting, committee) A* ...... *has been called for tomorrow afternoon.*

21. *(mouse, church) He's as poor as a* ...... *but he gives himself the airs of a Nabob.*

22. *(cold, head) It is not so much 'flu as a very severe* ......

23. *(story, fairy) The Sleeping Beauty is one of the most charming* ...... *I know.*

24. *(story, pirate) The* ...... *enthralled his listeners.*

25. *(salt, bath) With all these* ...... *I shall smell most exotic.*

26. *(service, dinner) She bought a very elegant* ......

27. *(journey, day) He lives about a* ...... *from here.*

28. *(licence, television) I must get my* ...... *renewed.*

29. *(state, mind) It is very difficult to determine his* ...... *at the time of the crime.*

30. *(year, time) 'That* ...... *thou may'st in me behold.'*

31. *(shirt, collar) His* ...... *was decidedly frayed.*

32. *(milk, glass) He drank the ...... straight off.*
33. *(wit, end) I really was at my ...... to know what to do.*
34. *(fare, prison) ...... is not very appetising.*
35. *(house, power) A big new ...... has been built there.*
36. *(property, slum) There is still a great deal of ...... in London.*
37. *(thought, second) He answered confidently after a ......*
38. *(car, seat) Most ...... are adjustable nowadays.*
39. *(day, holiday) The boys had an extra ......*
40. *(memory, lapse) During his recital the pianist had an unfortunate*
......

b. Explain the difference between:

1. *a furniture van*
  a van of furniture
	2. *an eye-glass*
	  a glass eye

3. *a good business deal*
  a good deal of business
	4. *a shipwreck*
	  the wreck of a ship

5. *Parliament building*
  the building of Parliament
	6. *a square foot*
	  a foot square

7. *a horserace*
  a race-horse
	8. *a book-end*
	  the end of the book

9. *shipshape*
  the shape of a ship
	10. *a paper-weight*
	  the weight of paper

11. *a pay-day*
  a day's pay
	12. *a lamp standard*
	  a standard lamp

13. *plate glass*
  a glass plate
	14. *a boat-house*
	  a houseboat

15. *a workhouse*
  housework
	16 *the rush-hour*
	  an hour's rush

17. *daytime*
  a day's time
	18. *a sports field*
	  field sports

19. *a cargo boat*
  a boat's cargo
	20. *a back seat*
	  a seat back

c. Revision of basic verbs
Some of the following sentences are correct: others contain mistakes.
Decide which are right, and correct those that are wrong.
1. *I am sure I heard you coming in last night.*
2. *He thinks going to dances a waste of time.*
3. *He was let to do what he liked.*
4. *It is a film in the making.*
5. *I knew her at John's party.*
6. *I do not intend that my wife knows anything about it.*
7. *Children enjoy being sung to sleep.*
8. *If your wife insists on your doing that there is no help for it.*
9. *She prefers to stay in her flat during the evenings rather than to go out to shows.*
10. *She loves me to play chess with her.*

11. *She laughed to be expected to do such a thing.*
12. *I dared him to ask for a rise.*
13. *I shall never forget to have caught my first glimpse of Venice.*
14. *She wants that I accompany her to that party.*
15. *Does he dare say that?*
16. *I found difficulty to learn German.*
17. *Can you smell something burning?*
18. *I saw the book lie on the floor.*
19. *The matter needs looking into.*
20. *Try pushing it instead of pulling it.*
21. *She decided on taking a job in Madagascar.*
22. *He tried to talk his father into buying it for him.*
23. *I cannot have you to make a nuisance of yourself like that.*
24. *He thinks to be very clever but he isn't.*
25. *I couldn't help to laugh seeing his funny expression.*
26. *I wish you would stop to chatter in class.*
27. *The general ordered to attack at dawn.*
28. *I explained him that piece of grammar.*
29. *I shall be interested in hearing the examination results.*
30. *I would like seeing the Mayan temples.*
31. *I wouldn't advise to go there for your holiday.*
32. *Would you consider taking a job in the north of Scotland?*
33. *It is no use to make excuses now.*
34. *He has got used to be a hen-pecked husband now.*
35. *The job is yours for the asking.*
36. *You needn't to go there if you don't want.*
37. *He has little hope to fulfil his ambition.*
38. *Help yourselves with whatever you fancy.*
39. *They only succeeded by making a great effort.*
40. *I have come to wish goodbye to you.*

d. Use the following words in sentences so as to bring out their meaning clearly.

appreciative	ounce	harbour	potent
appreciable	pounce	arbour	potential
	bounce	ardour	potentate
economic	paunch		
economical	punch	impunity	elicit
	pouch	immunity	illicit
extravagant	poach	immunisation	
eccentric			

31: Compound verbs P–S

Pass

1. to pass oneself *off as* someone (To pretend to be someone.)
2. to pass something *off as* a joke (To avoid embarrassment by pretending that something was a joke.)
3. to make *a pass at* someone (To suggest or hint that you would like sexual relations with him or her: colloquial American in origin.)
4. to pass *on*
a. (To die—a euphemism.)
b. information or news (To tell it to others.)
5. to pass *out*
a. (To faint.)
b. (To finish one's initial period of training in the army, an apprenticeship etc.)
6. to pass *down* knowledge from father to son (To transmit it orally so as to exclude others from the secret of how to do it.)
7. an *underpass* (A road going under another one at a crossroad.)
8. a *pretty pass*
Things have come to a pretty pass. (They have reached a terrible state; the situation has become really serious.)

Pull

1. to pull *one's weight* (To do one's fair share of the work: colloquial.)
2. to pull *a face* (To grimace.)
3. to pull *a fast one on* someone (To play a trick on someone; to outwit someone; colloquial, American in origin.)
4. to pull *out*
a. a tooth (To extract it.)
b. *A car pulled out.* (It left the kerb after being parked there or moved towards the centre of the road to overtake.)
5. to pull *someone's leg* (To tease, joke with someone: colloquial.)
6. to pull *down*
a. a building (To demolish it.)
b. *An attack of 'flu pulls you down.* (It makes you feel weak and depressed for a long time afterwards.)
7. to pull *in* (To drive nearer the kerb so as to allow someone to overtake you.)
8. to pull *in* a man (To arrest him: colloquial.)
9. to pull something *off*
a. (To remove an object.)
b. (To succeed in an endeavour: colloquial.)

10. to pull *round* (To recover from an illness.)
11. to pull someone *round* (To cure someone of an illness.)
12. to pull oneself *together* (To control one's behaviour with an effort; to force oneself to behave rationally: colloquial.)
13. to pull *up* (To stop—used of cars, taxis etc.)
14. to pull someone *up* (To correct someone: colloquial.)
15. to pull *one's socks up* (To make more effort: colloquial.)
16. to pull *strings* (To use personal influence, e.g. to obtain a job. This expression is derived from puppetry: colloquial.)
17. to pull *the wool over someone's eyes* (To prevent someone from seeing the truth: colloquial.)
18. to pull *through* (To survive an illness.)
19. to pull someone *through* (To cure someone of an illness.)
20. to pull *over* to the side of the road (To drive nearer to kerb to allow someone to overtake.)

EXERCISE

Replace the italicised expressions with others containing *pass* or *pull*.
1. Come now: *make an effort to control yourself.*
2. I felt very faint and was afraid I would *lose consciousness.*
3. *The situation is very bad* if a husband will insult his wife like that in public.
4. The patient is still on the danger list but I think we will *recover* soon.
5. The vicar was very gratified when a stately Rolls Royce *stopped* in front of his gate.
6. Bonnie Prince Charlie successfully *disguised himself* as a servant maid and escaped back to France.
7. Am I supposed to believe you or are you *having me on?*
8. Gypsies frequently *transmit* recipes *orally within the family.*
9. The police raided the club and *arrested* several dubious characters.
10. It is rare for French teachers to *correct bad manners in their pupils.*
11. I had to tell him off for *being a slacker*
12. Far too many beautiful buildings in London are being ruthlessly *demolished.*
13. He is a fully-fledged soldier now: he *successfully completed his initial training* last week.
14. She has been *deceiving her husband* for years.
15. Congratulations on *succeeding so brilliantly in* your examination.

Put

1. to put *to sea* (To set sail.)
2. *output* ((Production, either industrial or artistic.)
3. to be put *out at* something (To be annoyed about something: colloquial.)
4. to put *off* a light (To switch it off.)

5. to put *off* doing something (To postpone doing something.)
6. to put someone *off* a bus (To tell someone where to get off it.)
7. to put someone *off the idea of doing* something (To discourage someone from doing something.)
8. to put someone *off* someone
That put me off him. (It made me dislike him.)
9. to be *hard put to it* to do something (To have some difficulty in doing something.)
10. to put *upon* someone (To sponge on someone: to live at his expense.)
11. to put *in*
a. an hour's work (To do it.)
b. (To interrupt a conversation.)
c. at a port (To call at it on the way to somewhere else.)
d. a good word for someone (To speak well of someone: to recommend him.)
e. an application (To write it and send it off.)
f. electric light, central heating etc. (To install it.)
12. to put *in for* a job (To apply for it.)
13. to put *on*
a. weight (To get fatter.)
b. airs (To behave affectedly.)
c. a light (To switch it on.)
d. clothes (To dress oneself in them.)
e. It is all put on. (It is all affectation and pretence.)
14. to put *a good face on it* (To make an effort to seem less depressed than one feels: colloquial.)
15. to put something *across*
He cannot put it across to his students. (He cannot convey his knowledge to them adequately.)
16. to put something *to the test* (To try it out to see if it really works.)
17. to put something *to* someone
I put it to you. (I am stating the position quite frankly and am confident that you will agree with me.)
18. to put *down*
a. a deposit (To make a down payment, to pay a proportion of the price of an article to reserve it.)
b. a rebellion (To quell it, to suppress it.)
c. notes (To write them down.)
d. someone as a fool (To judge someone to be a fool.)
e. I put his failure down to laziness. (I attribute it to laziness.)
19. to put *up*
a. houses (To build them.)
b. the price (To increase it.)
c. at an inn (To stay at it.)
d. someone (To accommodate someone.)
*e. a good fight (*To resist stoutly.)

f. with something (To tolerate something, to stand it, to bear it.)
20. to put someone's *back up* (To irritate someone, often unwittingly: colloquial.)
21. *a put-up job* (A crime pre-arranged to convey a misleading impression to the police.)
22. to put *one's foot down* (To assert one's authority firmly: colloquial.)
23. to put *forward* a plan etc. (To suggest it.)
24. to put someone *through his paces* (To test someone severely.)
25. to put something *like that*
If I may put it like that. (Express it in that way.)
26. to put something *into practice* (To convert ideas into actions.)
27. to put someone *up to* doing something (To give someone the idea of doing something: to draw his attention to the possibility of doing it.)

EXERCISE

Replace the italicised expressions with others containing *put*.
1. Don't go to a hotel: I can *find a bed for you* in my flat.
2. I *ascribe* his success to his unusual charm.
3. I will not be *sponged* on any longer!
4. She was very *upset* at not receiving an invitation.
5. Lope de Vega probably has the largest *number of works to his credit* of any European playwright.
6. She has *written off for* a job as a private secretary.
7. His refined accent does not ring true to me; I think it is *assumed* for the benefit of his audience.
8. We *booked rooms* at a charming old inn.
9. Who *suggested* that tax-evasion trick to you?
10. How much would it cost to *install* oil-fired central heating?
11. When he was dismissed for embezzlement he *did not find it easy* to get another job.
12. I *paid £10 in cash* and I am paying the rest off in instalments.
13. Thousands of new houses have been *erected* where that mansion and park once stood.
14. If *production* could be doubled our problems would be solved.
15. A lot of lecturers are unable adequately to *convey* their knowledge to their students.
16. English weather *deters* some foreigners *from coming* to England.
17. I am *suggesting* that you are incompetent at your job.
18. I will not *stand* this treatment a moment longer.
19. He is the kind of person who *gets on* a lot of people's *nerves*.
20. She *is a terribly affected person.*

Run

1. to run *out of* something (To have no more left.)

2. to run *in*
a. a car (To get a new car engine used to working by using it gently.)
b. a criminal (To arrest him: colloquial.)
3. to run *into* someone (To meet someone by chance.)
4. to run *off with* someone (To elope with someone.)
5. to run *over* someone (To injure someone by running your car over him accidentally.)
6. to run *over* something (To revise something quickly.)
7. to run *away* with an idea (To reach a conclusion quickly without pausing to consider other possibilities.)
Don't run away with the idea that . . .
8. to run something or someone *down* (To criticise something or someone severely and unfairly.)
9. to run *down* (To stop—used of mechanical things like clocks that have not been wound up.)
10. to run *down* one's quarry (To catch the animal or person one is hunting.)
11. to be *run down* (To be overtired and rather ill.)
12. to run *up bills* (To get more and more into debt.)
13. to run *up* a dress, curtains etc. (To sew them quickly.)
14. *a runner-up* (The challenger in a race: the next one to the winner.)
15. to run *through*
a. a book (To skim through it quickly.)
b. money (To squander it.)
16. to run *across* something (To find something by chance.)
17. to run *a business* etc. (To manage it, organise it.)
18. to be *on the run* (To have escaped from prison and not to have been caught yet.)
19. to be *in the running for* a post (To be a possible choice for a post.)
20. *in the long run*
The new tax will be effective in the long run. (It will not have much effect at first, but over a longer period of time it will be effective.)
21. a *run on*
There is a run on cigarettes. (Everyone is buying large quantities of them.)
22. a *run*
That play has had a long run. (It has been on for a long time.)
23. to run *short of* something (To have very little left.)
24. to *overrun* a country (To spread all over it—used of bad things like pests, plagues, invading armies etc.)
25. to *outrun* someone (To run faster than someone else does.)

See

1. to see someone *off* (To go and say goodbye to someone at the last moment before he leaves on a journey.)

2. to see *to*
a. *I must get someone to see to my watch.* (To mend it.)
b. *I must see to getting lunch.* (Either go and cook it myself or arrange for it to be cooked.)
c. *Invigilators see to it that candidates don't cheat.* (They make sure...)
3. to see *in the New Year* (To stay up to celebrate it.)
4. to *foresee* something (To anticipate it.)
5. to see someone *to the door* / to see someone *out.* (To accompany someone to the door when he or she is leaving.)
6. to see it *through* (To continue with a task until it is finished.)
7. to see *through* a trick (To realise that it is a trick.)
8. to see *through* someone (To realise the real personality under the veneer.)

EXERCISE

Replace the italicised expressions with others containing *run* or *see*.
1. I am sure that policy will be vindicated *in the end.*
2. Byron *squandered* a fortune.
3. I don't like people who are always *saying spiteful things about* their friends.
4. I will *make sure* that you get a ticket for *Carmen.*
5. Perhaps he will give himself up; he has been *at large* for several days now and may well be hungry.
6. When some fool introduced rabbits into Australia they soon *spread all* over the country.
7. As I have guaranteed to do that, I shall *continue with it to the end.*
8. We *have very little* sugar *left.*
9. Mr Jingle *eloped with* the spinster aunt.
10. I will begin by *reminding you briefly of* what I said yesterday.
11. When Sir Anthony Eden resigned, Mr Macmillan and Mr Butler were *possible candidates* for the post of Prime Minister.
12. I'll come to the Airport to *say goodbye to* you.
13. Whom do you think I *happened to meet* the other day?
14. We *have very little* time *left.*
15. I must *have* that armchair re-upholstered
16. I *happened to find* this old diary in the attic.
17. He *was not taken in by* that trick.
18. Irresponsible people *buy too many things on credit.*
19. *You did not deceive me for one moment.*
20. The police *trapped* the criminal in a disused coal-mine.

Set

1. to set someone *against* someone (To make someone dislike someone else.)

2. to set *off/out* on a journey (To start it.)
3. to set *out* things in a shop window (To arrange them.)
4. to set *out* one's reasons for doing something (To explain them systematically.)
5. to set *out to do* something (To attempt to do something.)
6. to set *off* a chain reaction (To put it in motion.)
7. to set *off* a brooch etc. (To make something look its best by putting it on a contrasting background.)
8. to *offset* something (To counterbalance something: to cancel it out.)
9. to set *in*
The rain has set in. (It has started to rain and it looks like continuing for some time.)
10. an *inset* (A small carving or picture set in a larger area.)
11. from the *outset* (From the beginning.)
12. to set *about* doing something (To start doing something.)
13. to set *upon* someone (To attack someone.)
14. to set *down* a passenger (To tell him where to alight.)
15. to set *up as* . . . (To establish oneself in business as. . .)
16. to set oneself *up as an authority on*. . . (To claim to know a lot about. . .)
17. to set *up* a stall, monument etc. (To erect or build it.)
18. to *upset* something (To knock it over.)
19. to *upset* someone (To hurt someone's feelings and make him unhappy.)
20. to set a dog *on* someone (To order it to attack someone.)
21. to set one's *heart on* doing something (To be exceedingly anxious to do something: to make it one's ambition to do it.)
22. to set someone's *mind at rest* (To relieve someone: to remove his sources of worry.)
23. a *set-back* (A misfortune, breakdown, bit of bad luck etc. that not only prevents you from making progress but leaves you in a worse position than you were before.)
24. to be set *back from*
That house is well set back from the road. (Well separated from it by large grounds.)
25. to set someone *back*
That set me back £5. (I had to pay £5 for it: slang.)
26. *Get set!* (All ready—used as a preliminary warning that a race is about to start.)
27. to set *one's cap at* someone (To aim at marrying someone: colloquial.)
28. to set *to and do* something (To begin something in a determined way and finish it.)
29. to set *aside* money (To reserve it for a special purpose.)
30. to set *great store by* what someone says (To value someone's opinion very much.)

Show

1. to show *up*
a. (To be noticeable against a different background.)
b. (To put in an appearance.)
2. to show someone *up* (To reveal his dishonesty.)
3. to have a *show-down with* someone (To have a real trial of strength with someone: to have a violent row to end prolonged bickering or argument.)
4. to show *off* (To try to impress people.)
5. to show *off* something (To display something to good advantage.)

Slip

1. to slip *out*
a. (To go out quickly without being seen.)
b. *It just slipped out.* (I said it without thinking.)
2. to slip *on* a coat (To put it on quickly.)
3. to slip *on* a banana skin etc. (To skid and nearly fall down because you tread on it.)
4. to slip *up* (To make quite a serious mistake.)
5. to slip *away*
a. (To go off without being noticed.)
b. *Time slipped away.* (It passed quickly.)
6. to *give* someone *the slip* (To escape from someone's charge: colloquial.)
7. to slip *off* (To go off without being noticed.)
8. to slip *off* a coat etc. (To take it off quickly.)
9. to slip *one's mind*
It slipped my mind. (I forgot it.)

EXERCISES

a. Replace the italicised expressions with others containing *set, show* or *slip*.
1. Someone has *made a real blunder* here.
2. The Spanish conquistadores *aimed at bringing* the American Civilisations under Spanish rule.
3. Florence Nightingale *was determined to be* a nurse and nothing could stop her.
4. The criminal *evaded* his escort and escaped.
5. The bandits *suddenly attacked* that caravan.
6. That letter *made me feel much happier.*
7. 'Conductor, will you please *tell me when we get to* Trafalgar Square so that I can get off there?'

8. Most mansions are *a good distance from* the nearest road.
9. That police probe certainly *revealed* a good deal of dishonesty in high places.
10. We really must *embark on* redecorating the kitchen.
11. Please understand from the *beginning* that I will not tolerate that behaviour.
12. Sooner or later there will be a real *trial of strength* between the Government and the Trade Unions.
13. It needs a strong personality to resist a woman who is really *making a determined effort to marry you.*
14. I *place the greatest reliance on* his opinions.
15. What a pity he hasn't *come* today.

b. Put the right prepositions or particles in these sentences.
1. *What time would you like to be knocked . . . . . . the morning?*
2. *Pull yourself . . . . . . and stop showing . . . . . .*
3. *The robber was given . . . . . . one of his accomplices.*
4. *She was very put . . . . not having her lease renewed.*
5. *It was certainly a risk but he pulled it . . . . . .*
6. *Will you run . . . . the off-licence? We seem to have run . . . . sherry.*
7. *He certainly put the man . . . . . . his paces . . . . . . the interview.*
8. *Who put you . . . . making . . . . . . the bulk . . . . . . your estate . . . . . . your eldest son and heir?*
9. *You will never get . . . . life unless you are prepared to put your back . . . . . . your work.*
10. *Why don't you put . . . . that job? I would be willing to put . . . . . . a good word . . . . . . you.*
11. *He has let himself . . . . a lot of trouble by running . . . . the boss's daughter.*
12. *If there is a run . . . . . . sugar my grocer says that he will see . . . . it that everyone gets a fair amount . . . . . . resorting . . . . . . rationing.*
13. *It is unkind to show him . . . . front . . . . . . the whole class.*
14. *He passed it . . . . a joke.*
15. *It is no good trying to pull a fast one . . . . . . her; she will see . . . . . . you in no time.*
16. *He set . . . . business as an antique dealer.*
17. *I didn't see her go. Where has she slipped . . . . ?*
18. *The accused slipped . . . . showing that he knew the person's nickname.*
19. *Window dressers set . . . . . . things in shop windows.*
20. *She slipped . . . . her date while her parents were glued . . . . the television set.*

c. Give the opposite(s) of:
1. a theatrical *hit*   2. *a lame* excuse

3. a criminal
5. misleading
7. to facilitate
9. expenditure
11. *post*-war
13. debtor
15. devious
17. underhand
19. *withered* leaves
21. uncouth
23. trepidation
25. the *birth*rate
27. gaudy
29. a longing

4. *gloss* paint
6. polygamy
8. *citrus* fruit
10. a skinflint
12. the *ostensible* reason
14. existent
16. a *straggling* village
18. a *fluent* speaker
20. sensible
22. The wind has *dropped*
24. ill-omened
26. a *becoming* hat
28. a *hackneyed* phrase
30. loquacious

d. Put the verbs in brackets into the infinitive or gerund, adding prepositions where necessary.

1. *The missionary applied himself (learn) several African languages.*
2. *Why do you object (I give) Mary your address?*
3. *You came here with a view (improve) your English. That at least, was the ostensible reason (come). Who knows what ulterior motive really induced (you leave) home.*
4. *What do you say (I prepare) a nice salad for lunch?*
5. *Did you have any trouble (control) those children?*
6. *She contented herself (give) him a good talking to.*
7. *Why did you mislead me (think) it was your own work?*
8. *She resents (I be) so friendly with Jane.*
9. *Some people are very prone (put) their foot in it.*
10. *Monteverdi is credited (be) the first writer of operas.*
11. *Many people who advocate (live) in the country draw back when it comes (go) (live) there themselves.*
12. *The man could not account (be) found in possession of the stolen articles.*
13. *My father certainly laid himself open (be) attacked (say) that.*
14. *Why do you scowl (be) asked (do) such a simple thing?*
15. *The thief was driven (confess) (steal) that jewellery from a flat in Knightsbridge.*
16. *The evidence points (John be) guilty (commit) the murder. It now remains (we examine) the facts with the greatest possible care.*
17. *There is no (deny) that in the last fifty years some nations have come a long way (adopt) some from of democracy.*
18. *It looks like (be) a glorious day. I really feel like (spend) it quietly in the garden. After that long journey I really don't feel up (play) tennis at the moment.*
19. *Some people are indefatigable (sit) on committees. I cannot help (be) surprised (they be) prepared (put) in so much time on such unrewarding work.*

20. *I wonder if anyone can ever be justified (use) weapons of mass destruction.*

e. Insert the right verbs
1. *I tried to . . . . . . into them the necessity for . . . . . . a decision.*
2. *I tried in vain to . . . . . . the man the slip.*
3. *When you get married you must . . . . . . farewell to your freedom.*
4. *Everyone is assumed to belong to the Union unless he . . . . . . a wish to . . . . . . out.*
5. *The gangster . . . . . . cover behind a car parked on the kerb.*
6. *The marksman waited for the pheasant to . . . . . . cover.*
7. *Did you . . . . . . with much resistance?*
8. *There is no doubt that he is innocent of the accusations . . . . . . against him.*
9. *What purpose does that . . . . . .?*
10. *One day he will be . . . . . . to account for his actions.*
11. *She . . . . . . a cry of terror.*
12. *I think it is time we . . . . . . his bluff.*
13. *If she marries him, he will certainly . . . . . . her a dance.*
14. *Quite by chance I . . . . . . on the solution to the problem.*
15. *It is about time you started to . . . . . . up to reality.*
16. *The Government . . . . an important issue out of the nationalisation of steel.*
17. *He turned pale on being . . . . . . with such incriminating evidence.*
18. *Many people have never . . . . . . into question the basis of their faith.*
19. *The police . . . . . . doubt on the authenticity of that piece of evidence.*
20. *I don't want to . . . . . . his achievements but I doubt if he is as great as you are trying to . . . . . . out.*
21. *What a pity to . . . . . . away your time on such trifles!*
22. *Another car . . . . . . level with ours.*
23. *Don't . . . . . . too much reliance on getting that job.*
24. *How long an apprenticeship do coopers . . . . . .?*
25. *Blunt people never . . . . . . matters.*
26. *Ever since then she has . . . . . . me a grudge.*
27. *Mr Pickwick easily . . . . . . angry but never . . . . . . rancour.*
28. *Gamblers . . . . . . the risk of . . . . . . debts.*
29. *You are now . . . . . . the benefit of your former thrift.*
30. *It is sometimes difficult to . . . . . . a happy medium in life.*

f. Each of the words printed in italics can be joined to one or more of the following words so that the word in italics comes first. Decide which combinations are possible and where hyphens are necessary.
1. *land*

| spot | place | mark | plateau |

2. *mountain*

| valley | tree | view | railway |

3. *day*

| dream | thought | rise | outing |

4. *village*

| manor | green | law | path |

5. *house*

| pride | coat | boat | dirt |

6. *man*

| life | hole | opinion | instinct |

7. *street*

| gutter | kerb | arab | cry |

8. *wind*

| fall | cheater | brake | organ |

9. *bee*

| queen | sting | drone | hive |

10. *pub*

| bar | lounge | crawl | room |

11. *state*

| mind | man | lottery | firm |

12. *peace*

| bid | hope | treaty | armistice |

13. *house*

| hold | breaker | cupboard | room |

14. *ship*

| hold | shape | berth | crew |

15. *clothes*

| peg | horse | wardrobe | drawers |

16. *window*

| shelf | sill | shutters | dresser |

17. *master*

| builder | work | piece | stroke |

18. *picture*

| scene | window | frame | oil |

19. *dinner*

| set | course | menu | service |

20. *hotel*

| lift | service | suite | staff |

32: Word order

1. Adverbs

The placing of adverbs causes a good deal of difficulty. The following are the most important points to bear in mind.

a. No adverb must ever be placed between a verb and its object if this can possibly be avoided.

b. Many common adverbs, especially adverbs of frequency, come between the subject and the verb.
I nearly forgot to post it.
She frequently calls round to see me.
He never remembers anything I tell him.
Intelligent students sometimes ask awkward questions.
He hardly ever comes to England nowadays.
I thoroughly enjoyed that film.
You badly need a hair cut.
The critics certainly slated that play.
She surprisingly made no objection.
I only asked; there is no need to bite my head off.
He kindly showed me the way.

c. Where there is an auxiliary verb and a principal verb, these adverbs come between the two parts of the verb. Where there are two auxiliaries, they come between them.
I have always wanted to see a Mayan temple.
I would never have thought that you would have fallen for that trick.
If you have already seen that film, there is no point in your seeing it again.
I can never find the scissors.
I shall have nearly finished/nearly have finished by six o'clock.

d. The verb *to be* has the adverb after it unless special stress is required.
That child is almost a genius.
She is always happy.
I have firmly resolved to get to work on time and never be late, but I always am late in fact. (Emphatic position.)

e. Other adverbs that are longer and less common come after the object. There is no exact rule about which can come before the verb and which cannot. Some can come in either position. In some cases usage is everything.
He does his homework conscientiously.

Few people behave disinterestedly in life.
She reached the station punctually.
He ate his soup noisily
I very much like chocolate.
I like chocolate very much.
I was frantically looking for my hat.
I was looking for my hat frantically.
They are amiably chatting in one corner.
They were chatting amiably in one corner.
She rashly decided to go there.
She decided rashly to go there.

f. Certain adverbs—such as *only*—always come immediately in front of the word they qualify. Changing their position therefore changes the meaning.
Only I spoke to his sister. (I was the only person that spoke to her.)
I only spoke to his sister. (I only talked; I did not try to kiss her.)
I spoke only to his sister. (She was the only person I talked to.)
I spoke to his only sister. (He has only one sister—the girl I spoke to.)

g. In the case of adverbial phrases *place* comes first after the verb. *Time* and *manner* come later. If there is more than one adverbial phrase of time, the particular precedes the general.
He comes to school late every day.
He ran out of the room in a panic.
He died at three o'clock on the morning of 16th June, 1832.
He very often went home late.
She was writing in her diary like a mad thing.
He sailed round the Cape of Good Hope on a wild and stormy night.

h. For emphasis adverbs can be placed at the beginning of the sentence. Except in the cases mentioned in section 11, pages 63-65, there is no inversion after them.
Perhaps you will understand one day.
Very often I feel like giving up the struggle.
On many occasions he has struck her.
Frequently you see reports of people being robbed.
Languidly he strolled down the street.
Sometimes I regret growing old.

EXERCISE

Put the adverbs in brackets at the end of the sentence into the most usual place.
1. *I go dancing. (hardly ever)*
2. *He examined the data. (meticulously)*

3. *He told me he had no intention of paying me back a halfpenny. (calmly)*
4. *They came to blows about it. (very nearly)*
5. *He looked about him. (furtively)*
6. *I enjoyed the Exhibition. (thoroughly)*
7. *I walked. (last night, home, through the park)*
8. *He denied knowing anything about it. (indignantly)*
9. *He gazed at the newspaper. (listlessly)*
10. *She forgets something. (invariably)*
11. *I was ordered to leave the room. (peremptorily)*
12. *Will you tell me how to get there? (kindly)*
13. *He viewed the whole thing. (dispassionately)*
14. *I go into a pub. (only occasionally)*
15. *I approve of your plan. (entirely)*
16. *He was late getting to the office. (awfully, yesterday)*
17. *You need a haircut. (certainly)*
18. *She refuses to believe a word I say. (cynically)*
19. *She went. (yesterday, in a huff, out of the room)*
20. *I would have believed such a thing of him. (never)*
21. *I said something to offend her. (unwittingly)*
22. *It is bad mannered to arrive. (late, at the theatre)*
23. *Some women enjoy cooking (very much)*
24. *He manages to get seats at Covent Garden. (nearly always)*
25. *He flattered her. (quite blatantly)*
26. *She started up. (involuntarily)*
27. *I am telling him off for it. (forever)*
28. *He read the book. (monotonously, aloud)*
29. *My friend arrived. (in the afternoon, at three o'clock, at London Airport)*
30. *She demanded an apology. (angrily)*

2. The indefinite article

The positioning of the indefinite article after *such, so, quite, how, too, rather* and *many* needs noticing. Here are examples of it.
I have never known such a cold spell of weather.
I have never known so cold a spell of weather. (rather a literary construction)
Such a dreadful state of affairs cannot be permitted to continue.
How difficult a time I had!
I never realised what a charming person he is.
You are too intelligent a person to be taken in by such a rogue.
It is too serious a matter to be dealt with cursorily.
That is rather a difficult question to answer.
She is rather an exacting woman.
Many a true word has been said in jest.
Many a time he did not know where his next meal was coming from.
It is quite a busy town nowadays.

3. Concessive clauses

Sometimes in expressions which would normally begin with *although* or *though* the adjective is placed at the beginning for greater emphasis.
Hungry though he was, he would not eat until I had agreed to share his meal.
Clever though he is, he will not manage to pull the wool over the examiners' eyes.
Incredible though it may seem, he had never kissed a woman before he got married at the age of twenty-five.

4. Periodic sentences

Especially in rather literary English, the usual order of 'subject, verb, object' may be varied by writing a periodic sentence—i.e. a sentence where a certain suspense is created by leaving the subject and verb until the end.
To glory and riches, power, honour among his fellows, adulation, all the pomp, ceremony and creature comforts of a mediaeval aristocrat St Francis was indifferent. The glory of God alone, the poverty of Christ himself, the simplicity of saintliness, the love of the created for all creation—these did he admire and try to make the goals of his life.

5. Exclamations

After the exclamatory word itself come the adjective (or comple-ment), subject and verb, in that order.
How cold your hand is!
What an extraordinary creature you are!
How far away those times seem now!
How good you are to me!
What an incredible journey that was!

6. Adjectives

a. In a few fixed expressions the adjective always comes after the noun.
a knight-errant
the Knights-Templar
a decree nisi
a court-martial
proof positive
from time immemorial
Mother Superior
Mother dear (*Dear Mother* etc. is used only at the beginning of letter.)

b. Occasionally the whole meaning of the sentence depends upon whether the adjectives come before or after the noun.
a pure and simple Spaniard—a Spaniard with no sexual experience and not much intelligence.
a Spaniard pure and simple—a person of pure Spanish blood.

c. Adjectives that are the result of an action come after the noun.
He dyed his suit brown. (It was brown when he finished the process.)
He dyed his brown suit. (It was brown before he dyed it some other colour.)
I tried to make the lesson easy.
He painted the ceiling black.
The acid turned the liquid red.
The Ancient Britons stained their bodies blue.

d. Adjectives come after all compounds of *some* or *any.*
I don't see anything immoral in that.
'There is nothing new under the sun.'
Anyone drunk will be asked to leave.
Do you know somewhere quiet where we might spend the weekend?
I want someone stupid and rich to marry.
There is something fishy about the whole business.

e. Adjectives indicating exact measurement follow their nouns.
Inigo Jones's undoubted masterpiece—*the double cube room at Wilton House*—*is sixty feet long, thirty feet wide and thirty feet high.*

7. Past participles

Usage differs here, but the following rules may at least help foreign students to avoid mistakes. In the first place it is necessary to distinguish between a *real* past participle (i.e. one formed from a common verb) and a *false* past participle (i.e. a word ending in *ed* but not formed from a verb at all or formed from a word that is much more common as a noun than as a verb, e.g. *a wooded hillside*—there is no verb *to wood; a terraced slope*—there is a verb *to terrace* but the word is much commoner as a noun).

a. False past participles always come before the noun.
a fair-haired girl
a bespectacled man
a battlemented castle
a pinnacled church
a walled garden
a flat-footed policeman

b. Real past participles come before the noun only if they are qualified by an adverb, at least by implication.
That is a beautifully written book.
It was a well-trodden path.
I thought it a thoroughly badly produced play.
He has a highly developed sense of humour.
He is an educated man. (This implies: *a well-educated man*)

c. If they are in no way qualified by adverbs real past participles come after their nouns, being in fact the final word of a shortened relative clause.
None of the answers given (i.e. *which were given*) *was correct.*
The money won was given to a charity.
The portrait painted was a parody of the original.
An opportunity missed is gone for ever.
The problem posed was an interesting one.

d. Among the exceptions to these rules are eight words in which, if the past participle is used as an adjective, the final *ed* is pronounced *id*.
Jagged rocks stuck up through the grass.
It was a blessed relief.
An aged person spoke to me.
'This is my beloved son in whom I am well pleased.'
We went along a crooked little street.
He was wearing very ragged clothes.
He did it with dogged determination.

8. Miscellaneous

a. Many a may be followed by an inversion, though this is not compulsory. *How many times* is generally followed by an inversion.
Many a time have I stood there waiting for a bus.
How many times have I told you not to stand on that chair!
How many times has she wept herself to sleep because of her husband's behaviour!

b. Note the position of *the* in these sentences.
If you can cope with a harder class, so much the better for you.
If he gets told off, so much the worse for him.
He did not pass the examination, more's the pity.
If you did that, the more fool you.

c. A few adjectival word groups with the words hyphenated can stand before their nouns. Students must not, however, invent such groups themselves.
I met her on a never-to-be-forgotten Friday afternoon.

He lives in some out-of-the-way village.
A party was given for all the three-year-old children on board.
He spoke in a very matter-of-fact way.
John is certainly a happy-go-lucky creature.
I don't like his hole-in-the-corner tactics.
I don't understand these new-fangled, labour-saving devices.
He gave me a 'you-can-go-to-hell-for-all-I-care' sort of look.
Here is some up-to-the-minute news.
She tried the hard-to-get technique.
It was just a run-of-the-mill play.
It made a rough-and-ready studio.
That is a very up-to-date revue.

d. Note that certain adjectives can only be used after a verb. The commonest are *ill, alive, alike, awake, asleep, aware, akin, afraid* and *afloat.* Different adjectives are used before a noun. Compare these sentences.
Predicative adjectives
The man looks ill.
Those twins look very much alike.
Some students are awake, and others are asleep.
They are very akin in some ways.
He was terribly afraid.
Attributive adjectives
Sick people go to the doctor.
They are identical twins.
Attentive students learn more than sleepy ones.
They are kindred spirits.
The frightened man panicked.

EXERCISES

a. Put the words in brackets in the right order.
1. *She wore (a hat too bright) for the occasion.*
2. *He dyed his (brown black suit).*
3. *What a beautiful (hairstyle have you)!*
4. *It was (late far too) for us to walk (alone there).*
5. *The (posed question) was a difficult one to answer.*
6. *(A many time) (I have) said the same thing.*
7. *(A so splendid gown) transformed her.*
8. *How (a thing annoying) to happen to you!*
9. *(Meal a such huge) (at night so late) did not suit me at all.*
10. *What (that was happy a time)!*
11. *He did (too far well his work) to be given the sack.*
12. *If you can do it (the much so better) for you.*
13. *Don Quixote was (devoted a too) (errant knight) to infringe the code of honour.*

14. *How many times (I have seen) such a bright hope come to nothing!*
15. *That (never have would happened) if I had been there.*
16. *It is (a too serious matter) to be dealt with cursorily.*
17. *(A many court martial) has been convened for less than that.*
18. *I hate (such a policy in the dog manger).*
19. *Only then (I did realise) (a how time difficult) he had had.*
20. *If he accepted that offer (more he the fool).*

b. Put in *do* or *make* in the right form.
1. *King Henry II had to ...... penance for his part in the murder of Thomas à Becket.*
2. *His father now ...... him a good allowance every month.*
3. *She ...... eyes at all the young men in the office yesterday.*
4. *London Transport has ...... some cuts in certain bus services.*
5. *Any complaints ...... will be forwarded to the general manager.*
6. *He had to ...... remedial exercises every day.*
7. *He was annoyed at being required to ...... a night shift.*
8. *The patient is ...... a very good recovery.*
9. *Thousands of people ...... homage to his memory at the lying-in-state.*
10. *He thinks that new course of treatment will ...... wonders for him.*
11. *When is the Prime Minister ...... a statement on that issue?*
12. *Comparatively slight damage was ...... to St Paul's in the war.*
13. *He ...... three somersaults in as many seconds.*
14. *I was never any good at ...... sums.*
15. *She did not ...... any acknowledgement of my greeting.*
16. *Trust you to ...... a hash of such a simple thing!*
17. *For a long time a great deal of research has been ...... into the causes of cancer.*
18. *Of course I was expected to ...... restitution.*
19. *Everyone ...... much of the starlet.*
20. *He ...... me an elaborate apology.*

c. Explain the difference in meaning between:
1. *He dared to ask for a rise.*
   He dared me to ask for a rise.
2. *in short*
   shortly
3. *to do someone justice*
   to administer justice
   to do justice to a meal
4. *I would have liked to do it.*
   I would like to have done it.
5. *He doesn't care to spend money on it.*
   He doesn't care about spending money on it.
6. *The Prime Minister you met last Saturday is a fool.*
   The Prime Minister, whom you met last Saturday, is a fool.

7. *to look up at someone*
   to look up to someone
   to look someone up
   to look upon someone as ...
8. *He swore to do it.*
   He swore to doing it.
9. *I had no sooner married her than ...*
   I had sooner not marry her.
10. *You are right to think that.*
    You are right in thinking that.
11. *to do some repairs*
    to make reparation
12. *I haven't had time to do it this morning.*
    I didn't have time to do it this morning.
13. *to give way*
    to give someone away
    to give away someone
    to give way to someone
14. *They went to see the nurse's home.*
    They went to see the nurses' home.
    They went to see the nurses home.
15. *He tried lighting the fire with paraffin.*
    He tried to light the fire with paraffin.
16. *My flat has a southern aspect.*
    My flat has a southern appearance.
17. *The people who were in the street were excited.*
    The people, who were in the street, were excited.
18. *I propose to go to the cinema.*
    I propose going to the cinema.
19. *to make the best of something*
    to make the most of something
20. *to believe someone*
    to believe in someone

d. Each of the words printed in italics can be joined to one or more of the following words so that the word in italics comes first. Decide which combinations are possible and where hyphens are necessary.

1. *coal*

| soot | face | scuttle | room |

2. *fire*

| outbreak | drill | screen | raiser |

3. *scandal*

| spreader | maker | item | monger |

4. *night*

| sleep | mare | dream | hunt |

5. *flag*

| pattern | stone | day | colour |

6. *snow*

| spot | flake | drop | plough |

7. *market*

| spot | gardening | sales | stall |

8. *school*

| holiday | professor | headmaster | pupil |

9. *hen*

| party | cackle | yard | house |

10. *earth*

| lump | clod | quake | pot |

11. *rain*

| downpour | drop | fall | torrent |

12. *flower*

| bed | pot | jug | stalk |

13. *moth*

| damage | bite | ball | wing |

14. *cathedral*

| bishop | close | window | throne |

15. *hand*

| grenade | shape | punch | worker |

16. *fire*

| corps | bell | brigade | squad |

17. *book*

| maker | binding | plot | worm |

18. *law*

| giver | suit | clothes | gown |

19. *foot*

| fall | hold | length | step |

20. *heart*

| whole | condition | break | state |

21. *brain*

| storm | wave | thought | washing |

22. *frost*

| bite | trace | hoar | flake |

23. *log*

| hearth | book | fire | scuttle |

24. *crack*

| width | shot | mark | trace |

25. *ship*

| board | wreck | hold | officer |

26. *pen*

| blot | quill | friend | holder |

27. *garden*

| chair | arbour | shed | wall |

28. *table*

| bench | spoon | leg | leaf |

29. *board*
| meeting | plank | floor | room |

30. *shoe*
| tree | horn | sole | make |

e. Insert any relative pronouns and commas that may be necessary in these sentences.
(Revision exercise)

1. *My brother, ... you met for the first time at the theatre yesterday, makes a lot of money as a pickpocket.*
2. *A man ...... works as hard as Charles deserves to do well.*
3. *Some actors speak too naturally, ... makes them inaudible in the back rows.*
4. *The Mary ...... you were talking to yesterday is not the one ...... I am talking about.*
5. *The village ...... you see over there used to belong to my father ...... owned a lot of land in these parts.*
6. *The knowledge ...... you get from experience is best.*
7. *London ...... is now the second largest city in the world probably means 'The City on the Lake' or 'The Lone Strong Place'. The Celts were the first people ...... founded it.*
8. *If you can't hear ...... I am bellowing put in your hearing aid.*
9. *I was so infuriated with all ...... he was saying that I walked out.*
10. *Possibly King Lear is the most intellectual play ...... Shakespeare wrote.*

33: Compound verbs S–T

Stand

1. to stand *up to*
a. someone (To resist someone, oppose him.)
b. *Those shoes won't stand up to hard wear.* (They cannot be worn often or in bad weather; they are flimsy, not strongly made.)
2. to stand *up for* something or someone (To defend something or someone, physically or morally.)
3. to stand *in for* someone (To take someone's place temporarily.)
4. to stand *by* (To hold oneself in readiness.)
5. to stand *by* someone (To support someone and remain loyal to him.)

6. a *standby* (A reserve supply.)
7. a *bystander* (A person who happens to be somewhere and so sees things happening.)
8. to stand *to lose*
He stands to lose the lot. (He risks losing it.)
9. to stand *for*
a. I won't stand for it. (Tolerate it, put up with it.)
b. He stands for freedom from want. (Defends it in principle.)
c. Parliament (To be a candidate in the elections for it.)
10. to stand *about/around* (To loiter and do nothing.)
11. to stand *out against* something
a. (To resist something in principle.)
b. (To be clearly silhouetted against something.)
12. *outstanding* (Exceptional, much better than anything or anyone else.)
13. to stand *down* (To leave the witness-box in a court of law.)
14. to stand *down in favour of* someone else (To withdraw one's application for a post so as not to stand in the way of someone else.)
15. to stand *on ceremony* (To behave very formally.)
16. *Stand back!* (Don't push forward.)
17. to stand *something*
I will not stand it any longer. (Tolerate it, endure it, put up with it, bear it.)

Stick

1. to stick *to* something (To adhere to something.)
2. to stick *to one's guns* (To refuse to modify one's view: colloquial.)
3. to stick *to* someone (To remain loyal to someone: colloquial.)
4. a *stickler*
He's a stickler for principles. (He has very strong, unshakeable moral ideas: colloquial.)
5. to stick *up for* someone (To defend someone, morally or physically: colloquial.)
6. to be *stuck* (To be puzzled; not to know how to proceed: colloquial.)

EXERCISE

Replace the italicised parts of the sentence with expressions containing *stand* or *stick*.
1. She always keeps a few tins of food as *a reserve stock.*
2. Dr Jones is *replacing* Dr Simpson while the latter is on holiday.
3. The church spire *was sharply outlined* against the red and gold sunset.

4. You must *be prepared* to put to sea at a moment's notice.
5. A good wife will naturally *come to her husband's defence* when she hears him disparaged.
6. Even a worm will turn; he will not *put up with* your nagging much longer.
7. She is very loyal person; she certainly *helped and remained with* her husband through thick and thin.
8. Hen-pecked husbands never *cross* their wives.
9. I was very relieved when the judge ordered me to *leave the witness-box*.
10. You *are in danger of losing* everything if the court finds against you.

Take

1. to take someone *out* (To invite someone out.)
2. to take *out* an insurance policy (To pay a sum of money to insure oneself.)
3. to take *(a fancy) to* someone (To like someone very much immediately: colloquial.)
4. to take *to* drink (To start drinking excessively.)
5. to take *to flight/one's heels* (to run away as fast as possible.)
6. to *undertake* to do something (To promise, to guarantee it.)
7. an *undertaking* (A difficult enterprise or a promise.)
8. an *undertaker* (A person who arranges funerals.)
9. to take *in* lodgers (To accept them into one's house.)
10. to take someone *in* (To deceive someone, cheat him: colloquial.)
11. to take *in* clothes (To make them smaller.)
12. the *intake*
a. (New pupils admitted to a school.)
b. (Consumption of food per day.)
13. to take *in* a book (To understand it properly.)
14. to take something *in one's stride* (To accept or manage something easily.)
15. to take *off*
a. trains (To reduce the service.)
b. someone (To imitate or mimic someone.)
c. (To leave the ground—of aeroplanes.)
d. someone (To remove someone to prison.)
16. to take something *down*.
a. (To write it down.)
b. (To dismantle it.)
17. to take someone *down a peg or two* (To lower someone's exaggerated opinion of himself: slang.)
18. to be taken *aback* (To be very surprised.)

19. to take *back* a remark (To apologise for having made it.)
20. to be taken *with* something (To find something very charming.)
21. to be taken *up with*
His time is taken up with his hobbies. (Filled with, occupied with.)
22. to take *up* room (To occupy it.)
23. to take *up*
a. a question (To raise it, to speak about it.)
b. golf etc. (To learn it, to begin to play it.)
24. to take someone *up on* something.
He took me up on that point. (He argued with me about it and said I was wrong.)
25. to take *up with* someone (To start a friendship with someone: colloquial.)
26. to take *after* one's parents (To inherit characteristics from them.)
27. to take something *away* (To remove something.)
28. to take someone *into your confidence* (To trust someone with your secrets.)
29. to take *on* a job or bet (To accept it.)
30. to take *on about* something
Don't take on so about it. (Don't take it to heart so much; don't take it so seriously; colloquial.)
31. to take *on*
That word has taken on a new meaning. (Developed it.)
32. to take someone *for* someone else (To mistake someone for someone else.)
33. to take *place* (To occur.)
34. to take *one's place/up one's position* (To go to one's prearranged place.)
35. to take something *into account* (To make allowances for something.)
36. to take *over from* someone (To replace someone permanently.)
37. to take *it out of* someone.
It takes it out of you. (It is exhausting.)
38. to take *it out on* someone (To make someone the victim of your anger etc, to vent your anger on someone.)
39. to *overtake* someone (To pass someone by going more quickly than he does.)
40. to take someone *for*
What do you take me for? (What kind of person do you think I am?)
41. to take *round* drinks (To offer them round the room.)
42. to take *time off* (Not to go to work without any good reason.)
43. to take *French leave* (To leave without saying goodbye or asking permission: colloquial.)
44. *Take it easy! (Relax. Don't worry.)*
45. to take someone *to task about* something (To lecture someone severely about something.)

EXERCISE

Replace the italicised expressions with others containing *take*.
1. I don't know why you *make such a fuss* about it.
2. I *showed him that his opinion of himself was exaggerated*.
3. A gullible person can easily be *made to believe anything*.
4. You should not have *agreed to* that bet if you were not prepared to pay up.
5. The aeroplane *began its flight* in brilliant sunshine.
6. She *accepted* the whole situation *quite naturally and easily*.
7. I was *flabbergasted* at his suggestion.
8. My local Member of Parliament promised to *raise* the matter at question time.
9. She *told me off quite sharply* about the state of my flat.
10. Did you *make* any notes during that lecture?
11. My friend made everyone laugh by *mimicking* Sir Winston Churchill.
12. I was very *charmed with* their new house.
13. Tennis is a very enjoyable game but it *is certainly a strenuous one*.
14. When Mr Brown retired as Managing Director last year his eldest son *replaced him*.
15. She read the telegram but did not really *grasp its contents*.
16. I cannot remember when *we first started to be friends*.
17. When did he *start getting drunk most evenings?*
18. He *assured me that I should get* the money within a week.
19. After his serious illness all his clothes were flapping around him and had to be *made smaller*.
20. He was ordered to cut down his daily *consumption* of food.
21. If you have a trying day at the office it is not fair *to vent your spleen on* your wife when you get home.
22. You did not *consider* that in reaching your decision.
23. He was threatened with dismissal for *absenteeism*.
24. She *is very much like* her father in voice and manner.
25. Everyone *is charmed with* him immediately.
26. I wonder when that scaffolding is being *dismantled*.
27. I believe that train *is no longer running*.
28. I *let him into the secret*.
29. I'm so sorry; *it is a case of mistaken identity*.
30. The wedding *was held* in a very fashionable church.

Throw

1. to throw something *at* someone (So that he is hit by it.)
2. to throw something *to* someone (So that he can catch it.)
3. to throw something *away* (To discard something.)
4. to throw *in one's lot with* a group of people (To join one's future to theirs; to become one of them.)

5. to throw *one's weight about* (To behave dictatorially and misuse one's authority: slang.)
6. to throw *up*
a. (To vomit.)
b. a job (To resign from it: colloquial.)
c. to throw *in the sponge/towel* (To acknowledge oneself beaten.)
7. to throw *off*
a. sparks (To emit them.)
b. one's pursuers (To escape from them.)
8. to *overthrow* a government (To get rid of it, generally by a coup d'état.)
9. to throw someone *out* (To remove someone forcibly.)
10. to throw *out* a hint (To drop a hint.)
11. a *throw-out* (Something discarded as below standard.)

Turn

1. to turn *in* (To go to bed: colloquial.)
2. to turn someone *in* (To hand someone over to the police: colloquial.)
3. to turn *into* (To change or transform into.)
4. to turn *out*
a. goods (To manufacture or produce them.)
b. a room (To clean it very thoroughly.)
c. *well* or *badly* (To have a good or bad result.)
d. (To leave the shelter of one's house to watch a procession, ceremony etc.)
e. one's pockets (To empty them and pull them inside out to prove it.)
f. a light (To switch it off.)
g. someone* (To expel someone and force him to leave.)
h. *He turned out to have been at school with my father.* (We unexpectedly discovered that in the course of conversation.)
5. to turn *out trumps*
He turned out trumps. (In a crisis he showed himself a nobler or braver person than anyone had suspected; colloquial.)
6. the *turnover* of a company (Total amount of money passing through its hands.)
7. to turn someone *over to* the police (To hand someone in to them.)
8. to turn *over* in bed (To change one's position and sleep on the other side.)
9. to turn *over* a page etc.
10. to *overturn*
a. (To fall over violently—like a car in an accident etc.)
b. a table etc. (To knock it over violently either in a temper or by accident.)

*This is perhaps commoner put round the other way: to turn someone *out*.

11. to turn something *over in one's mind* (To think about something deeply before reaching a decision.)

12. to turn *over a new leaf* (To reform oneself.)

13. to turn *to and do* something (To set to work and do something.)

14. to turn *to* doing something (To start doing something that becomes a hobby etc.)

15. to turn *to* someone for help (To ask someone to help you.)

16. to turn *one's hand to* something
He can turn his hand to anything. (He is very versatile; he is able to do all sorts of things.)

17. to turn *up*
a. (To arrive.)
b. a wireless (To make it louder.)
c. one's trousers (To roll them up.)
d. one's nose at something (To think that it is not good enough for one.)

18. to turn *down*
a. an offer (To reject it.)
b. a wireless (To make it softer.)
c. a street (To change direction and begin to go down it.)

19. a *turncoat* (A person who changes sides in the middle of a fight, war etc.)

20. to turn *turtle* (To capsize—used of ships.)

21. to turn *on*
a. a wireless or light (To switch it on.)
b. someone (To attack someone suddenly either physically or morally.)

22. to turn *the tables on* someone (Completely to reverse the position in relation to him: colloquial.)

23. to turn *round* (To face in another direction.)

24. to turn someone *round one's little finger* (To make someone do exactly what you want: colloquial.)

25. to turn someone *away* (To tell someone to go away because there is no room for him.)

26. to give someone *a turn*
It gave me quite a turn. (I got a nasty shock: colloquial.)

EXERCISES

a. Replace the italicised expressions with others containing *throw* or *turn*.

1. A lot of people were *sent home* because the theatre was sold out.

2. I wonder how many cars are *produced* in British factories every year.

3. When her father was ruined she had to *apply herself to finding* a way of earning her living.

4. I was surprised when he suddenly *became aggressive.*

5. I *didn't agree to taking* that job in Canada.

6. The car *somersaulted* and landed up in a hedge.

7. The Revolutionaries *got rid of* the existing government and set up a new one.
8. He managed to *evade* his pursuers.
9. The poor man was *evicted* for not having paid his rent.
10. Her family was not very keen on her marrying John but they had to admit that when trouble struck the family he *behaved admirably*.
11. He *is an invaluable handyman to have about the place*.
12. It *transpired* that the Browns had known my great-aunt.
13. He had a very good job but he has *left it* and gone abroad.
14. Quite a lot of brides have to contend against a vague fear that their fiancés may not *arrive* for the wedding.
15. I *pondered deeply about it* for some time.
16. The disillusioned teacher *decided to join* a troupe of itinerant actors.
17. She spent the afternoon *cleaning* the spare room *and putting some kind* of order in it.
18. Everyone dislikes those who *behave like little tin gods*.
19. A clever wife can usually *get her own way with her husband*.
20. He looked dreadfully ill and *I was appalled*.

b. Put in the missing prepositions or particles.
(General revision of compound verbs)
1. *How do you make ...... that I am to blame?*
2. *She made .... him ...... the dead ...... night.*
3. *Mary says that there isn't a word of truth ...... the whole thing, but I never go ...... what she says.*
4. *I feel that he is .... no good.*
5. *Mary was very upset because her fiancé had told her he was .... her.*
6. *Joan isn't here; she's .... her aunt's for a few days.*
7. *It is useless for you to be always .... me ...... it; stop nagging.*
8. *You certainly have it .... him; why are you so bitter?*
9. *This is the fourth time he has been had .... dangerous driving.*
10. *He thinks himself very hard done ......*
11. *I could certainly do ...... a bit more money.*
12. *In some countries the naïve foreigner abroad is looked ...... as someone to do ......*
13. *He cannot put ...... much time studying; all his free time is taken .... amorous adventures.*
14. *What a pity; I'm afraid the rain has really set ......*
15. *That delicate brocade upholstery will not stand .... hard wear.*
16. *I stood ...... to let her pass.*
17. *Doctors are advising everyone to cut .... smoking, if not to cut it ...... altogether.*
18. *Our failure to get a visa has cut right ...... our plans.*

19. *Everyone is cut .... having to pay higher taxes.*
20. *If that work is getting you ...... you had better give it ......*
21. *My wife has been gossiping with the neighbours for hours so we are thoroughly .... our preparations for tonight's dinner party.*
22. *She must have slipped .... being seen.*
23. *Don't run .... the idea that you can do what you like.*
24. *Strong measures are called ......*
25. *There has been such a run ...... tickets for that opera that lots of people have been turned ......*
26. *I don't feel called ...... to give them a present.*
27. *I tried to draw him ...... but he saw ...... it.*
28. *The flat has been broken ...... and ransacked; I had better call ...... the police at once.*
29. *Would you like me to put you .... the night?*
30. *How many ports do we put .... the way?*
31. *He has put .... a job as personnel manager.*
32. *I put John's success .... charm.*
33. *Please forgive me; I was carried .... my feelings.*
34. *Socrates was accused .... leading the Athenian youth ......*
35. *It was a long time before Helen came .... the operation.*
36. *You sometimes come .... the oddest things.*
37. *I was just wondering how you came ...... that mink coat.*
38. *Some people always come ...... badly ...... photographs.*
39. *The doctor assured me that, though my brother was still very ill, he would pull ......*
40. *We pulled .... the side of the road and pulled .... to have a look at the map.*
41. *How many workers have been laid .... this shipyard?*
42. *I really put him .... his paces but I could not catch him ......*
43. *I would like to know what really brought ...... that financial crisis.*
44. *The Corporation is laying ...... a lot of money ...... building a new recreation centre.*
45. *He caught ...... the slightest hope ...... saving himself.*
46. *I don't like cats because they suddenly turn ...... you and bite you.*
47. *Motorists are advised to give .... traffic ...... the right.*
48. *It is not fair; you have been holding .... me.*
49. *She gives .... her feelings too easily.*
50. *If the rain will hold .... another half hour we shall be all right.*
51. *For some reason John never seems to hold ...... a job.*
52. *When you get measles you break .... spots.*
53. *Look! At last the rain is letting ......*
54. *...... my surprise the accused was let .... a reprimand.*
55. *I promised not to let .... it ...... anyone.*

c. Replace the italicised part of the sentence with one word, without changing the meaning.

1. As soon as the police had explained the necessity for their questioning her she was quite *willing to assist them*.
2. There is rather a fashion in the theatre nowadays for making the protagonist someone who is *quite unable to express what he is really thinking*.
3. *Putting things off* wastes a great deal of time.
4. It is extraordinary that, although that girl has been at school for three years she is still *unable to read or write*.
5. He was eating his lunch *without in the least thinking of what he was doing*.
6. That argument was finally settled *in quite a friendly way*.
7. I cannot tell you *without looking in a book of reference* the exact dates of Henry IV of England.
8. If one dies *without having made a will* and has no heirs to claim shares in the estate, the money goes to the State.
9. Mr Pecksniff is the most famous example in English literature of a *person who pretends to be quite different from what he really is*.
10. Profits have *increased fourfold* this year.

d. Use the following words in sentences so as to bring out their meaning clearly.

smug	heat	abstinence
to smuggle	heath	abstention
snug	hearth	
to snuggle	health	ascetic
snag	dearth	aesthetic
snack		
smack	transitional	principal
smock	transitive	principle
smog	transitory	

e. Put the verbs in brackets into the gerund or infinitive adding prepositions where necessary.
1. *Although she is known (stand) up for women's rights on many occasions, she still cannot reconcile herself (be) treated as an equal when it comes (be) expected (look) after herself. In fact she longs (be) shown the chivalry women enjoyed centuries ago.*
2. *As I have no intention (make) any further concessions to your demands, I see no point (continue) the discussion.*
3. *Am I correct (think) that you have been married before?*
4. *I will not hear (you stay) in a hotel. why (waste) money (pay) hotel bills when I shall enjoy (have) you (stay) in my flat?*
5. *Guy Fawkes may have been betrayed (give) away the names of his instigators. Probably, too, torture was used (induce) him (reveal) their names.*
6. *Sir Walter Scott, (see) Byron as a rival poet of superior powers, abandoned (write) poetry and turned his talents (compose) historical*

novels. He must be commended (assess) his own talents as a poet so honestly.

7. (Come) to England he reckoned (be) able (get) a job quite easily. Unfortunately he found it harder (do) so than he had anticipated.

8. You must make allowances (she be) still very inexperienced as a housewife.

9. What a ridiculous amount of money he spends (try) (look) smart! He would be better advised (cultivate) his mind a bit.

10. Once you have resigned yourself (never have) a great deal of money, you can turn your attention (enjoy) the simple things of life. (Strive) (keep) up with the Joneses all the time condemns you (chafe) continually (not be) richer.

11. Why do you resent (I criticise) you? What is the point (come) to school if you are not prepared (accept) the teacher's attempts (help) you?

12. The actress claimed damages (be) shown (be) in the wrong over that. She could forgive (be) criticised but not (be) made (look) mean.

13. He has set his heart (get) on in his job and is prepared (sacrifice) his social life and his pleasures (do) so. I wonder if, when he is old and without family or friends, he will enjoy (be) rich or if he will regret (not live) his life to the full when he could.

14. Some women, without any qualifications whatever, have a gift (get) on with children. They make the best teachers in infant schools as they make the children (want) (learn).

15. It is thanks (you help) me so much that I am now capable (look) after myself. At least you have the satisfaction (know) that all your efforts have not been in vain.

34: Sentence construction

2. A compound sentence is one in which two equally complete ideas are joined together. The following are examples of some of the commonest.

and	*He came into the room and confessed everything.*
but	*They got married last year but they are not really suited to each other.*
either...or	*Either you apologise for what you have just said or it is all over between us.*
for	*I could not hear properly for the noise of the traffic was deafening.*
so	*He is very inefficient so he will have to leave.*

Whereas these listed above are always co-ordinating conjunctions which form compound sentences, certain other ones can sometimes be used in this way, though more often they are subordinating conjunctions.

I was walking down the street when I remembered that I had forgotten my umbrella. (when = and then)
Last night I went to the theatre where I saw several people I knew. (where = and there)

Certain co-ordinating conjunctions require a semi-colon before them if they come in the middle of the sentence. These, however, could also stand at the end of the sentence. *Still* is the only one that could not go at the end, and this is because it changes its meaning, according to its position in the sentence. The commonest of these are:

Nevertheless, otherwise, therefore, still, consequently, however and *nonetheless.*

I feel very sorry for her; nevertheless I do feel that she is largely to blame. (I do feel she is largely to blame nevertheless.)
You had better hurry; otherwise you will miss the train. (You will miss the train otherwise.)
You did not take your job seriously; therefore you got the sack. (You got the sack therefore.)
He is a bit reckless; still you can't help liking him.
You behaved very badly altogether; consequently certain of your friends are annoyed with you. (Certain of your friends are annoyed with you consequently/in consequence.)
The Minister resigned; however the aura of scandal remained. (The aura of scandal remained however.)
All was confusion around him; nonetheless he remained calm and unruffled. (He remained calm and unruffled nonetheless.)

2. A complex sentence is one that contains one principal clause and one or more subordinate or dependent clauses. These subordinate clauses may be of three kinds: noun clauses, fulfilling the function of a noun; adjectival clauses doing the work of an adjective; and adverbial clauses doing the work of an adverb.

a. Noun clauses
Like nouns, these can be the subject, object or complement of a verb.

subject   *That you are right* ⎰ *is quite clear.*
            The truth   ⎱ *is quite clear.*

object   *I understand* ⎰ *why he cannot come.*
            I understand ⎱ *the position.*
complement *My reason for being late was* ⎰ *that my car broke down.*
            My reason for being late was ⎱ *a breakdown.*

b. Adjectival clauses

Like adjectives, these tell you more about a noun. The commonest of
them are relative clauses but they can be introduced by other words.
This is my sister who is a painter.
This is my artistic *sister.*
The village which you see on the hill *over there is extremely old.*
That village is extremely old.
The man who did that *ought to be shot.*
The guilty *man ought to be shot.*
The place where he was killed *became a shrine.*
The historic *place became a shrine.*

c. Adverbial clauses

These can be divided into nine categories: time, place, manner, cause,
purpose, result, condition, comparison and concession. The following
sentences illustrate the commonest of each category in sentences. It
will be observed that certain of the introductory words appear in more
than one category according to their precise meaning.
i. Time
I will tell him when he comes in.
I will give him the message as soon as he comes back from lunch.
No sooner had he said it than he regretted it.
We cannot do anything until we have more precise information.
Once he has done that, he will never want to do it again.
Please let me know the moment he arrives.
By the time we get there the film will have started.
You can stay here as long as you wish.
Please close all the windows before you go to bed.
I will come and see you after you come back from your holidays.
As she was going out of the room she dropped her handbag.
Since I came to England I have not bothered to contact my friends.
While you are playing tennis I will go for a swim.
Whenever he says things like that I get annoyed.
ii. Place
In the Forces you must go where you are sent.
Wherever you go in August you find crowds of holiday-makers.
iii. Manner
You did not do as I told you.
How you managed it we shall never know.
By what means he persuaded her to leave her husband I cannot imagine.
We were at a disadvantage in that we were outnumbered.
iv. Cause
He was angry because she had refused to marry him.
I bought extra food in case any unexpected guests arrived.
She was very worried lest she should fail in the examination.
She crept in for fear that she might wake up her husband.
As you look remorseful I will forgive you.

v. Purpose

I sent you a telegram so that you would not worry if I was late.
He gave up his job in order that he might devote his life to painting.
He took his overcoat lest he should catch cold. (Rather old-fashioned)
He took his overcoat in case he caught cold.
(It should be noticed that if *so that* or *in order that* replace *lest*, *in case* or *or else* a negative must be added to the verb. E.g. ... *so that he should not catch cold.*)

vi. Result

She was so excited by the news that she couldn't get a wink of sleep.

vii. Condition

If you succeed in your plan I shall be very surprised.
Whether you succeed or not I still admire your pluck.
Unless you decide to mend your ways you will finish up in gaol.
Provided that you work hard, the prospects of promotion are good.
He was released on bail on condition that he did not make any attempt to see her.
I will lend it you on the understanding that you do not show it to anyone else.
As long as you do your best everyone will be satisfied.
Supposing he turns nasty, what will you do?
Come early or else you won't get a good seat. (= if you want to get a good seat.)

viii. Comparison

This problem is not so easy as I thought.
The situation is more serious than you think.
The more people come to the party the better he'll be pleased.

ix. Concession

Though he did his best, he was outplayed the whole game.
Although I like you, I am not in love with you.
Since you suspect something I may as well tell you the whole truth.
Even if you wanted to you couldn't do it.
She looked dazed as if* she couldn't believe what she had heard.
However much you may regret doing that, there is nothing you can do about it now.
Seeing that you are here, you may as well come in.
Whereas he should have gone to the police at once, he kept on putting off doing so.
I like her, yet I do not trust her.

3. A complex sentence may also contain an infinitive phrase (see pages 92-93) or a participle phrase. The following points should be borne in mind in using present participle phrases.

---

* N.B. After *as if* use the subjunctive of *be* if it is not a fact and the indicative if it is a fact.
He looked as if he was ill (and he was).
He looked as if he were starving (but in fact he ate well.)

a. If these come after the principal clause the two actions must be simultaneous.
He was sitting on a fence, smoking a pipe.
He came downstairs, carrying a tray.
She was sitting, reading a book.

b. At the beginning of a sentence the present participle can be used to mean *when* or *because* or *as*. It can sometimes be used for an action happening before the main one, but only if no ambiguity is possible. Otherwise *having done* will be needed.
Seeing a policeman, he turned and fled.
Coming into the room, he tripped over a rug.
Not knowing what to say, he sat there in silence.
Walking in the park, I bumped into an old friend.
Having nothing to do, he got bored.
Having come to England, he tried to get a job.
Having done it all wrong, he had to do it all over again.
Having written the letter, I felt much less angry and decided not to post it.

c. Participle phrases formed with the verb *be* can be used only in the meaning of *because:* never in the meaning of *when*.
Being a child, he could not understand.
Being very clever, he had no difficulty in getting a good job.
Being late, I ran most of the way.
(Being a child, he went to France is not correct. You must say: *When he was a child he went to France.)*

d. When and the gerund is rarely used to refer to one particular event. It is generally used in making a general statement and therefore means *whenever*.
When applying for a passport, enclose the necessary documents.
When writing a business letter begin 'Dear Sir'.
When approaching that village you must look out for dangerous bends.

e. It must be remembered that, as there is no subject in any of these participle constructions, the next word after the end of the phrase is always grammatically the subject of the sentence. Care must therefore be taken to make it logically the subject of the sentence. It is nonsense to write sentences like:
Being Monday, she was washing. (She was not Monday.)
Walking in the park, the flowers looked very pretty! (The flowers were not walking.)

f. Certain prepositional participle phrases are quite common, especially at the begining of the sentence. The following are some of the most usual:

In addition to being tactless, he was too silly to realise it.
Besides being rich, she is charming.
For the sake of looking smart, she ruined herself.
But for being a strong swimmer, he would have drowned.
Despite his being/in spite of his being very old, his brain is as clear as ever.
As for doing that, I never gave it a thought.
Hardly/barely/scarcely pausing for breath, he plunged on.
What with looking after the children, washing, cleaning, and gardening, she hadn't a minute to spare.
On hearing the news, she collapsed.

g. In rather literary English phrases with past participles can be used. These are useful occasionally but should not be overworked. They are very rare in the spoken language.
That conceded, I still do not really approve.
That point settled, we went on to the next one.
Those fears overcome, he pressed forward.
The examination finished, they burst out into the sunshine.
His guilt proved, he knew he had nothing to hope for.

EXERCISES

a. Join each group of simple sentences up into a logically constructed compound or complex sentence.

1. *I came back home. It was very late. I opened the front door. I got a shock. Burglars had ransacked the flat.*
2. *It was a stormy day. The sea was very rough. The ship was lurching from side to side. I had a most miserable time.*
3. *He is very rich. He is very mean. He never gives his friends anything.*
4. *You can see that man. He is standing in the corner. He stole my wallet last year. I remember his face.*
5. *I will lend you the money. You must pay it back within a week. I shall be very angry if you do not. I shall not speak again.*
6. *It rained very heavily. It rained for days. The level of water in the reservoir rose. The pressure on the dam grew greater and greater. In the end it burst. Many people were drowned.*
7. *It was very hot. I had taken off my shirt. I was lying in the sun. I fell asleep. I awoke suddenly. A thunderstorm woke me up.*
8. *She got out of the car. It was a Rolls Royce. She was carrying a bunch of roses. Her heel caught in a grating. She fell over. The roses scattered all over the pavement.*
9. *I was very late. I was in a hurry. I was running very fast. I collided with a policeman. He told me off.*
10. *It was very cold. The sea was cold. An icy wind was blowing. John could not swim that day.*

11. *I took out a £1 note. It was in my pocket. I showed the money to the boy. I said he could have it. In return he was to take my dog for an hour's walk.*

12. *We planned to give a dinner party. We bought lots of food. We could not cook it. We had forgotten to pay our gas bill. Our gas had been cut off.*

13. *Some boys were playing cricket. One of them hit the ball very hard. It came over the hedge into my garden. It broke a window of my greenhouse. I was very annoyed. My annoyance was quite natural.*

14. *I broke the news to her. It was very sad. It was that her son had been killed in an accident. She broke down.*

15. *The girl was riding her bicycle. It was a new one. She was not very good at riding it. She fell off. She cut her knee. I gave her some chocolate. It was to cheer her up.*

b. Correct the construction of the following sentences.

1. *Being a wet day we couldn't go for a walk.*

2. *In order to stop the train the communication cord should be pulled.*

3. *While not condemning you for it, the fact remains that you are to blame.*

4. *I opened the door, and a procession was passing the house.*

5. *She is plain and somehow attractive.*

6. *Having forgotten to buy any meat, lunch consisted of just a salad and some fruit.*

7. *I keep the tools I need for gardening in the cellar.*

8. *Being very young, I caught my first glimpse of the sea.*

9. *He came downstairs entering the kitchen.*

10. *While still a child my grandmother died.*

11. *She was standing in the middle of the garden with a doll in her hand, roaring lustily.*

12. *The manor house, which dates from Elizabethan times, is one of the largest in the district, with an old Norman church standing just beside it.*

13. *He worked very hard all the time he was in the class and failed the examination nevertheless.*

14. *Looking at those paintings our emotions were stirred.*

15. *He set up a camp stool trying to paint.*

c. Replace the italicised phrases with clauses, without changing the meaning.

1. *In spite of having a chill,* he attended the meeting.

2. *His work done,* he heaved a sigh of relief.

3. *Not being as intelligent as I had hoped,* he failed to understand what it was all about.

4. *Not being cut out for teaching,* he hated his job.

5. *To speak frankly,* I find your behaviour extremely tactless.

6. He had to do it, *willy-nilly.*

7. *On seeing a strange man in the room,* she screamed.

8. He was angry *at having that said to him.*

9. I do not understand *his saying such a thing.*
10. Do you mind *some students watching the operation?*
11. *By saying things like that* you make yourself look a fool.
12. *But for her shouting at me* I should certainly have been knocked over.
13. *Strange to say,* I knew his brother when I was at school.
14. *Curious to know what they were saying,* I clapped my ear to the keyhole, *only to find* that I couldn't hear anything.
15. She enjoys *being flattered.*
16. *His making such a fuss about it* surprised me.
17. *In order to get the job,* he hid the fact that he had been a deserter.
18. *The sentence pronounced,* the prisoner was led away.
19. *But for your prompt intervention* the police would never have caught their man.
20. It would be a pity *to throw such a nice chair away.*
21. *As well as being a playwright,* Vanbrugh was a gifted architect.
22. *Realising that his wife knew more than he had thought,* he decided to make a clean breast of everything.
23. *Once bitten, twice shy.*
24. I understand *the reasons for his not coming.*
25. *His saying things like that* annoys me.

d. Explain the difference in meaning between:
1. *How clever you are at doing it!*
   How clever you are to do it!
2. *I left them to play cards and went home.*
   I left them playing cards and went home.
3. *to hold a conversation*
   to make conversation
4. *I would not dream of it.*
   I would not dream about it.
5. *to be on the go*
   to be in the swim
   to be on the run
   to be in the running
6. *to go together*
   to get on together
7. *to care for*
   to take care of
   to look after
   to be careful of
8. *to beat someone*
   to beat someone up
9. *He likes her more than I.*
   He likes her more than me.

e. Use the following idiomatic expressions in sentences of your own:

1. *to play truant*
2. *to pluck up one's courage*
3. *in the nick of time*
4. *to mind one's p's and q's* (colloquial)
5. *to talk shop*
6. *to put someone's back up* (colloquial)
7. *to put a good face on something* (colloquial)
8. *to know the ropes* (colloquial)
9. *to lose face* (colloquial)
10. *to make heavy weather of something*
11. *to be as good as one's word*
12. *That argument doesn't hold water* (colloquial)
13. *to catch someone red-handed*
14. *if the worst comes to the worst*
15. *on the spur of the moment*
16. *to do something off one's own bat/on one's own initiative*
17. *to leave someone in the lurch*
18. *to show a clean pair of heels* (colloquial)
19. *to be on good terms with someone*
20. *to get one's own way*
21. *to be at sixes and sevens* (colloquial)
22. *to play second fiddle to someone* (colloquoial)
23. *to read between the lines*
24. *to feel the pinch*
25. *to be well up in something*
26. *It is all to the good* (colloquial)
27. *to rave about something* (colloquial)
28. *to slate something* (colloquial)
29. *to be at a loose end* (slang)
30. *to take the law into one's own hands*

f. Use the following words in sentences of your own so as to bring out their meaning.

to elude	*sprinter*	*oblivion*	*imperative*
to allude	*splinter*	*oblivious*	*impervious*
	spinster	*obvious*	*imperial*
luxurious			*emporium*
luxuriant	*comprehensive*	*historic*	*umpire*
	understandable	*historical*	
moral			
morale			

35: Miscellaneous compound verbs

It is to be noted that nouns formed from compound verbs do not always have the same meaning as the verbs themselves. the following are some of the commonest instances of this. It is also worth noting that in noun combinations with the preposition coming last, there is normally a hyphen. With the verb combinations there is not.

1. What a *set-up!* (extraordinary state of affairs)

The Government *set up* a commission of inquiry. (established)

2. The *output* of that factory has recently been doubled. (amount of stuff produced)

She *put out* the clothes to dry. (hung out)

3a. What a good *turn-out!* (number of people assembling for some event

The factory *turns out* two hundred cars a week. (manufactures)

3b. What a smart *turn-out!* (appearance)

She *turned* him *out* of house and home. (sent him away or disinherited him)

4. Take the pills two hours before the expected *onset* of sickness. (beginning)

The men *set on* (or *upon*) him and robbed him of everything. (attacked)

5. The *outcome* of the struggle was awaited with great interest. (result)

a. It *came out* that he was at school with my father. (was discovered)

b. Flowers *come out* in the spring (open)

6. He is an *undertaker*. (a person who arranges funerals)

He *undertook* to pay me the money within a week. (promised)

7. He is nothing but an *upstart*. (parvenu: person newly arrived in his social class)

We *started up* the engine. (got it going)

8. The *upshot* of the whole thing was that he lost his job. (consequence)

Prices have *shot up* in the last few years. (risen astronomically)

9a. His *intake* of food is limited. (consumption)

She *took in* the dress. (made it smaller)

9b. This year's *intake* is better than last year's. (number of new pupils)

I was *taken in* by that plausible swindler. (deceived)

10a. The *outlook* for the steel industry is improving. (prospects)

I *looked out* of the window at the snow.

10b. It's your *look-out*. (responsibility)

You had better *look out*. (be careful)

10c. He has a funny *outlook* on life. (attitude)

The house *looks out* over fields. (has a view of)

11. The *turnover* of that company is enormous. (money passing through its hands)

He is going *to turn over* a new leaf. (reform himself)

12. What *goings-on!* (scandalous behaviour)

a. Please *go on* with your work. (continue with it)

b. I wish you would stop *going on* about it. (talking and talking)

13. A few tins of food are a useful *standby*. (reserve stock)

She *stood by* him through thick and thin. (remained loyal)

14. He was suffering from a dreadful *hangover*. (a splitting headache as a result of having drunk too much alcohol)

The cliff *overhung* the road in several places. (projected forward over the road: jutted out above it)

15. That illness was a great *set-back* to him in his career. (check to progress or development)

The house was well *set back* from the road. (separated from it by something—a large park or garden)

16. What a peculiar *get-up!* (what odd clothes: colloquial)

Children *get up* to mischief. (do naughty things)

17. After the nuclear explosion there was a great deal of *fall-out*. (radioactivity)

They *fell out* last week. (had a quarrel)

18. They had a real *set-to*. (quarrel: colloquial)

They *set to* work on clearing up the mess. (began)

Note also the following compound verbs:
1. The Government is trying to *play down* the importance of the whole affair. (make it seem as unimportant as possible)
2. Boys like to *play up* new teachers. (test their discipline by being deliberately naughty)
3. I *dropped off* during that lecture. (fell asleep)
4. New teachers must *drop on* first offenders. (punish them severely)
5. Attendances have been *dropping off* (getting smaller)
6. Please *drop me off* at the next traffic lights. (let me get out of the car after being given a lift)
7. Why have you been *hanging about* there all day? (standing around doing nothing)
8. I didn't want to *kick up a fuss*. (make a scene)
9. Which team *kicked off*? (had the first kick of the game)
10. These days it is much commoner to *overcharge* (charge too much) than to *undercharge*. (charge too little)
11. That doesn't *tie up with* what I heard yesterday. (tally with; agree with)
12. When he tries to write English he always gets *tied up in knots*. (mixed up)

13. They have *patched up* their quarrel (made it up temporarily)
14. The advantages of living in a big town far *outweigh* the drawbacks. (there are more advantages than snags)
15. The Government is urging exporters to *step up* production in the near future. (increase)
16. One should beware of *overdressing*. (dressing too formally)
17. Most children love *dressing up*. (wearing fancy clothes)
18. He suddenly *rounded on* me. (started to attack me verbally)
19. A rousing cheer *rounded off* the proceedings. (brought them to a satisfactory conclusion)
20. The aeroplane *touched down* in brilliant sunshine. (landed)

There are also a number of what might be called compound nouns: that is, nouns formed from compound verbs or formed with prepositions. The following are some of the commonest which have not so far been mentioned. This kind of construction is becoming increasingly common in English.

1. The firm was given the *go-ahead* for its new factory. (permission to construct it)
2. Rich people are often surrounded by *hangers-on*. (parasites)
3. Occasionally accidents are caused, by drivers having a *blackout*. (fainting fit)
4. It was difficult to find the bandits' *hide-out* (lair)
5. Some politicians are aiming at a closer *tie-up* between European countries. (link, co-operation)
6. This is only an *offshoot* of the company. (minor branch)
7. There was such an *outcry* about it that the Government was forced to take action. (demonstration of disapproval)
8. I gave him a good *dressing-down*. (I criticised him severely)
9. Sometimes it is hard to agree about siting a *by-pass*. (a main road around a town to stop through traffic going through the centre)
10. I got caught in a sudden *downpour*. (heavy shower of rain)
11. That was a spectacular *takeover*. (swallowing up of one company by another in return for a large sum of money)
12. He must be a *throw-back* to his grandfather. (He has inherited certain characteristics from his grandfather that have not appeared in the intervening generation.)
13. My friend is on the *look-out* for a new job. (anxious to find one)
14. There has been no *let-up* in the export drive. (slowing down of impetus)
15. He was standing about on the *off chance* of earning a little money. (remote possibility)
16. That was a brilliant *send-up*. (satire or skit)
17. The actress received a tremendous *send-off*. (Lots of people went to see her off and wish her well.)
18. Everyone was disappointed at the *breakdown* of those talks. (collapse due to deadlock)

19. It is quite time there was a *shake-up* in Government circles. (a re-organisation of ministers: a Cabinet reshuffle)

20. There was some *trumped-up* charge against him. (a false accusation used as a pretext for arresting him)

21. That film got a very good *write-up*. (The critics wrote very favourably about it).

22. Naturally the dog is given the *left-overs* from lunch. (scraps of food that have been left on the plate)

23. The *build-up* of nuclear weapons has been temporarily halted. (accumulation; stock-piling; pile-up)

24. Someone gave the police the *tip-off*. (information about criminal plans to help them to catch the criminals)

25. A lot of people are getting a *rake-off* on that. (a profit somewhat unscrupulously made; a kind of bribe, but less crudely managed)

26. From time to time there is a *round-up* of the horses and cattle in the New Forest. (They are collected and checked.)

27. A lot of people were arrested in that *round-up*. (police swoop)

28. The party was a complete *wash-out*. *(failure)*

29. Some films are told in a series of *flashbacks*. (returns to an earlier period in the protagonist's life)

30. There has been another *flare-up* between those countries. (outbreak of hostilities)

EXERCISES

a. Insert the missing particle or preposition.

1. *That account does not tie .... what Brown was saying.*

2. *There was a tremendous turn ...... to give the Queen a heartwarming send ......*

3. *The manager sent ...... him and gave him a good dressing ......*

4. *Will you ...... take not to attempt to see your wife?*

5. *The ...... shot of his irresponsible goings ...... was that he was given the sack.*

6. *Tongue-twisters are designed to tie you .... knots.*

7. *Take ...... bids may result in a considerable shake ...... in administrative circles.*

8. *Don't bother to go round the corner. Drop me ...... here, please.*

9. *If you choose to behave in such an irresponsible manner it is your own look ...... if you get into trouble.*

10. *On that crucial issue every member of the House must be rounded ...... and brought in to vote.*

11. *The officer complimented the men on their smart turn ......*

12. *The police were tipped .... that bank robbery.*

13. *Is another glass of whisky the best cure for a hang ......?*

14. *This is a recent ...... shoot of the firm; the headquarters are at Ruislip.*

15. *The concert pianist was annoyed at not getting a better write ......*
16. *I always get in a muddle if a novel is told with the aid of too many flash ......*
17. *I wonder if King Harold was only an ...... start earl.*
18. *The beggar was hanging .... the ...... chance of picking up a few coins.*
19. *When the American called her homely (meaning it as a compliment) she flared ......*
20. *He was dismissed on some trumped ...... excuse.*

b. Join each group of simple sentences up into one compound or complex sentence.

1. *Shakespeare went out one night. He was poaching. He was caught. He was shut up. He came to London.*

2. *Mary works very hard. Her sister is lazy. The sister is younger than she is.*

3. *Alan was driving along a country lane. He saw an old house. It was very beautiful. He saw that it was for sale. He stopped to look at it. Finally he bought it.*

4. *She got the house very tidy. She put on her best clothes. People might call on her. She sat there all afternoon. No-one came.*

5. *Paul came in. He looked happy. I told him some important news. Immediately, he rushed out of the room.*

6. *He had a lot of money on him. He did not know what to do with it. He decided to go to a race meeting. He put his money on a horse called 'Money Galore'. He lost all his money.*

7. *The car was going too fast. Visibility was bad. The road was wet. The car skidded and crashed. The driver is in hospital with concussion.*

8. *We were having a picnic. It was by the river at Avignon. It was a windy day. Dust was flying about. We had as much dust as ham in our sandwiches.*

9. *I bought a book. It was about the Incas. I was reading it on the train. I left it on the train. I bought another copy. I nearly finished that. I left it on another train. I have never read the last twenty pages.*

10. *I called on John. He was sitting in the garden. He was asleep. I went home again. I did not disturb him.*

11. *There was once a famous burglar. He was often seen. He was never caught. He used to burgle naked. His body was covered with grease. People tried to catch him. Their fingers slipped off him.*

12. *We went to sleep. In the morning we looked out of the window. It had been snowing all night. The wind had blown the snow into drifts. We could not get out. We should have to shovel the snow away first.*

13. *We were in Spain. We were sunbathing. We got thirsty. Ian offered to get some ice-creams. He was coming back with them. He sat down very suddenly. The string of his trunks had given way!*

14. *I met his fiancée last night. It was the first time. she is rather fat. She has a round red face. She is very clever. She is very kind-hearted too. I like her.*

15. *An Underground train had just come in. We ran to catch it. We sat down. We started to read. It stopped at a station. Its name was wrong. We had gone in the wrong direction.*

c. Put into the passive.
(Revision exercise)
1. *Naturally politicians or other public speakers do not like it if people laugh at them.*
2. *Look. At last they are clearing up this bomb-site. I wonder what they will build here.*
3. *It is a pity that statue is broken but there is nothing that anyone can do about it now.*
4. *Is there anything that one may say in favour of modern mass-produced architecture?*
5. *It is no good blaming anyone for that.*
6. *It is silly for students to object to the teacher's making them work hard.*
7. *Sooner or later people grow tired of parasites who sponge on them.*
8. *That photograph needs someone to touch it up.*
9. *What were they discussing when I came in?*
10. *He sent his aunt a parrot for Christmas because he knew she liked someone to swear at her.*

d. Put the verbs in brackets into the right tense. (Revision exercise)
1. *Out of the darkness (loom) a grim fortress.*
2. *If you (tell) me all this before you (save) yourself a great deal of unpleasantness.*
3. *Only since the death of Queen Victoria women (really liberate) themselves from the rule of men.*
4. *I (rack) my brains for the last half hour to try to remember where I (see) that face before.*
5. *As soon as you (get) a letter from Margaret, please let me know her whereabouts at once.*
6. *It is high time you (realise) what a bad impression your rudeness (make) on people.*
7. *Very seldom he (make) the effort to contact his friends, yet he (always complain) that he is lonely.*
8. *Do you think it right that children (be) forced to live in such overcrowded conditions?*
9. *He (tell) me yesterday that he does not like life in England at all; still less he (want) to stay here a moment longer than is necessary, so whoever (tell) you that he (think) of becoming naturalised (talk) absolute nonsense.*
10. *We (leave) our friend's house in bright moonlight, and (expect) to have a pleasant drive home, but, as not infrequently happens in those parts, a thick fog (develop) suddenly, causing us to abandon the car and walk. We (walk) for two hours before we (arrive) home.*

11. *I am seriously suggesting that he (be) asked to resign at once.*
12. *Little he (suspect) then that his wife (spy) on him when he went out at night.*
13. *They (plod) on through the desert all day and (just begin) to give up all hope of survival when over their heads they (hear) the sound of a helicopter that (send) to search for them.*
14. *What he (do) but slap my face when I asked him if I could marry his daughter!*
15. *You (get) a letter from your fiancé soon, I daresay. Let me know how he (get) on.*

e. Use the following expressions in sentences of your own.
1. *to have time on one's hands.*
2. *I cannot say off-hand.*
3. *to be on one's beam ends* (slang)
4. *That was a close shave/near squeak* (slang)
5. *to grin and bear it* (slang)
6. *That rings a bell.* (colloquial)
7. *You will have your work cut out to do that.* (colloquial)
8. *to talk with one's tongue it one's cheek*
9. *to break the ice* (colloquial)
10. *That cuts no ice with me.* (slang)
11. *to be game for anything*
12. *to turn a blind eye to something*
13. *to palm something off on someone*
14. *to be out of one's depth*
15. *She has a way with her.*
16. *to turn the tables on someone*
17. *to face the music*
18. *cupboard love*
19. *to take something lying down* (colloquial)
20. *to beat about the bush* (colloquial)
21. *It all boils down to this* (colloquial)
22. *He looks as if butter would not melt in his mouth.*
23. *It is the thin end of the wedge.*
24. *to take something with a pinch of salt*
25. *to tell someone a few home truths*
26. *to be at the end of one's tether*
27. *to sit on the fence/to see which way the wind is blowing*
28. *to take the wind out of someone's sails*
29. *to live from hand to mouth*
30. *to pay lip-service to something*
31. *I couldn't make head or tail of it.*
32. *an eyesore*
33. *to do something of one's own accord*
34. *to be in a tight corner*
35. *He didn't mince matters.* (colloquial)

f. Insert the right verbs
1. *He was arrested for ...... a disturbance.*
2. *I ...... him to task about his laziness.*
3. *He is the kind of person who is always ...... quarrels with people on the slightest provocation.*
4. *He was touched at how his friends ...... round him to help him.*
5. *Will you ...... me an estimate for redecorating my kitchen?*
6. *All footballers must ...... by the referee's decision.*
7. *I cannot ...... out much hope of your succeeding.*
8. *On hearing that her son was safe she ...... a sigh of relief.*
9. *The conspirators ...... a plot to blow up Parliament in 1605.*
10. *That sudden illness ...... havoc with my holiday plans.*
11. *Who ...... the initiative in ...... negotiations for a cease-fire?*
12. *John did his best to ...... amends for his former rudeness to me.*
13. *Unfortunately I am not in a position to ...... your request.*
14. *The surgeon ...... the operation successfully under very difficult conditions.*
15. *How long have you been ...... under that delusion?*
16. *Michael sought to ...... my help in his scheme.*
17. *Although I ...... several broad hints that it was time for him to go, he didn't ...... any of them.*
18. *The commander decided to ...... an attack at dawn.*
19. *She ...... to being searched without protesting.*
20. *He is not at all the kind of person to ...... malice or ...... resentment.*
21. *She tried hard to ...... a fit of giggling.*
22. *They ...... a demontration against the Government's action.*
23. *Many criminals are ...... out on bail.*
24. *The Chancellor of the Exchequer did everything possible to ...... the pill of increased taxation.*
25. *We ate lots of vegetables to ...... out the rather meagre amount of meat.*

g. The same word is not always followed by the same construction. The following exercise on the government of verbs will illustrate the point.
Put the verbs in brackets into the right form (infinitive or gerund) adding prepositions where necessary.
(Revision exercise)
1*a.* Get on with the work. You *were engaged* (lay) the lawn not (stand) about gazing vacantly into space.
1*b.* The Director *is engaged* (deal) with some correspondence and cannot see you now.
2*a.* I have not had an *opportunity* (do) it yet.
2*b.* The *opportunity* (go) there with all expenses paid does not come one's way very often.
2*c.* There is not much *opportunity* (listen) to oneself speaking English.

3*a*. I am absolutely *delighted* (see) you.

3*b*. She was *delighted* (be) chosen to represent England in the beauty contest.

3*c*. She *delights* (tease) her rather solemn husband.

4*a*. He *stopped* the car (look) at his map.

4*b*. *Stop* (talk) and listen to me.

4*c*. The policeman *stopped* me (enter) the house.

5*a*. The master *forced* his pupils (work) hard.

5*b*. That document does not mean anything because I was *forced* (sign) it.

6*a*. I have never had any *temptation* (start) smoking.

6*b*. He could not resist the *temptation* (go) inside to see what it was like.

7*a*. I *stooped* (tie) up my shoelace.

7*b*. I never thought you would *stoop* (intrigue) against me behind my back.

8*a*. How much do they *charge* (repair) shoes nowadays?

8*b*. The police *charged* him (receive) goods, knowing them to be stolen

8*c*. He was put in *charge* (collect) the rents.

9*a*. The child *suffered* (feel) unwanted.

9*b*. He swore to make me *suffer* (make) him (undergo) such humiliation.

10*a*. A child must be *clever* (get) into a good grammar school.

10*b*. She is very *clever* (run) up simple, chic dresses.

11*a*. Cortes was *credited* (be) the god Quetzalcoatl returning to his people, the Aztecs.

11*b*. I gave you *credit* (have) more sense.

12*a*. I shall be *interested* (see) what becomes of him.

12*b*. I am not the least bit *interested* (watch) cricket matches.

13*a*. I *meant* (buy) some more bread but I forgot to.

13*b*. If that job *means* (travel) for nine months of the year, I am not interested in it.

13*c*. The doctor said he would find a *means* (cure) me.

14*a*. It is an easy examination and he is *sure* (pass) it.

14*b*. His self-confidence makes him *sure* (pass) the examination; I'm afraid he is in for a nasty shock.

h. Choose the right word from among those in brackets and use those that are wrong in these contexts in sentences of your own.

1. *The audience were (convulsed, repulsed, involved) with laughter.*

2. *Most pets in England are (pampered, punctured, tinctured).*

3. *This room is not really at all suitable to be a studio; it is merely a(n) (impoverished, improvised, implacable, implicit, makeshift) one for the time being.*

4. *It is not an (era, aria, area) that offers many (facilities, amenities, possibilities) to visitors.*

5. *On most railway stations there is a (bookshop, stationer's, bookstall, library).*

6. *Sherry is sometimes put into a (dissenter, decanter, commuter).*
7. *A brilliant writer can (conjure up, conjure with, invoke, evoke) a whole scene effortlessly.*
8. *My friend is more interested in (lay, secular, profane) architecture than in churches.*
9. *Sometimes (lay, secular, profane) preachers give sermons in church.*

i. (General revision exercise)
Decide which of the following sentences are correct and which are wrong. Correct those that are wrong.
1. *There is no doubt that people, who behave like that, should not be admitted to the school.*
2. *Few people like being made fools of in public.*
3. *It was very difficult for me to hear all what was being said.*
4. *He was examining systematically every corner of the room.*
5. *He said that I shall be punished if I don't do that.*
6. *You certainly lost no time to come to see me when you were in trouble.*
7. *Write an essay about the most extraordinary thing which has happened to you since you came to England.*
8. *What am I supposed to make it out of?*
9. *Do you think you are up to take the examination?*
10. *She told me to go and wash up the dinner things but I absolutely refused.*
11. *He made a big propaganda for that religious sect.*
12. *My father's country house, which you visited about two years ago, has recently been sold.*
13. *He painted his room ceiling black, hoping to make the room look lower.*
14. *He lives only a stone's throw from where he works.*
15. *Those twins are so alike that it is next to impossible to distinguish who is who.*
16. *Neither John nor Michael are able to go to the concert tonight. Would you like to go instead?*
17. *Many people in the life are dissatisfied of their lot.*
18. *Those meetings have been presided by Mrs Aveling for years.*
19. *She has kept bees for years now; it is time she knows how to handle them.*
20. *Hardly a year passes without some international flare-up.*
21. *Last Sunday was a lovely day, so I could go swimming with Mary.*
22. *He gave orders that the horses were made ready at once as he was pressed for time.*
23. *We had better take a taxi, otherwise we shall be late arriving at the theatre.*
24. *It must be fun, whizzing down ski-slopes like a bird in flight.*
25. *In such desperate straits he found himself that he was reduced to play the violin in the streets.*

KEY TO THE EXERCISES TO WHICH A DICTIONARY CANNOT PROVIDE COMPLETE ANSWERS.

CHAPTER 1

Exercise a Page 12 1. for 2. on 3. in 4. with 5. against 6. on 7. on 8. of 9. with ... about 10. for.

Exercise c Page 13 1. assorted objects (same as odds and ends) 2. decided; unlikely to change 3. 'driven out of house and home' = forced to leave their home 4. wholly 5. 'exposed to wind and weather' = liable to be damaged by the elements 6. over a large area 7. finished and forgotten about 8. 'blows fell fast and furious' = a lot of blows were delivered in anger and violence 9. assorted small objects 10. 'an out-and-out socialist' = a committed socialist 11. improvised; makeshift 12. everyone, without distinction 13. 'left high and dry' =left miserable and alone when social plans have gone wrong 14. when the right time comes 15. clean and tidy 16. 'hard and fast rules' = fixed, rigid rules 17. casual/informal (atmosphere) 18. 'more than flesh and blood can stand' = human weakness ... 19. infrequent (of buses etc); scattered (of houses etc) 20. 'make a song and dance about something' = make a fuss 21. 'try with might and main' = very hard indeed 22. hard wear which will wear it out 23. ordinary members (of parliament or a union) 24. gentle and inoffensive 25. occasionally.

CHAPTER 2

Exercise a Page 18 1. have never been 2. did not go ... was 3. is doing 4. have been living 5. was playing ... knocked 6. is making 7. have met 8. had eaten ... fell ... was dreaming ... fell ... woke 9. had been living ... decided 10. will be living 11. shall have finished 12. did you last see 13. have been longing ... have heard 14. were beaten ... they had been held ... was murdered 15. got ... found ... had run/was running 16. will soon have completed 17. will be sitting 18. is being built 19. has been built 20. are being made 21. have been sent 22. have you seen 23. was luxuriating ... rang 24. got ... found ... had been done/was being done 25. arrived ... were ... were being put ... (were being) erected ... were rushing ... were churning ... were being put ... (were being) fixed ... was/were strolling 26. was nothing done/has nothing been done/is nothing being done 27. had been working 28. will be attended to/is being attended to 29. tried ... had been working ... got .... gave 30. met ... thought ... looked/was looking.

CHAPTER 3

Exercise a Page 24 1. are continually interrupting 2. is seeing 3. was hoping ... have decided ... succeeds 4. had known ... married 5. have finished 6. is happening ... has been robbed ... is pointing ... is being chased ... will be caught 7. will be seeing 8. belongs ... was lived in 9. had been teaching ... realised ... make/made 10. went ... received ... had already relapsed ... got.

CHAPTER 4

Exercise a Page 30 1. on learning 2. for missing 3. his marrying 4. going 5. being 6. sleeping 7. to institute 8. to meet 9. me to take 10. smoking ... to smoke 11. going 12. her to be 13. sharing 14. me to book 15. my being/me for being 16. in teaching 17. for her being 18. living 19. of passing 20. against going/not to go 21. him to walk 22. in wanting ... having 23. for misleading 24. to be 25. me to buy 26. against going/not to go.

Exercise b 1. deducted ... packet 2. eligible 3. delightful/lovely ... were able to ... go for 4. inconclusive 5. disease ... contagious 6. diligently/conscientiously ... throughout 7. indefatigable 8. pull down/demolish ... restore 9. chuckling 10. sparkling/glinting

Exercise c Page 31 1. set/put 2. give 3. take ... taken 4. paid 5. attract 6. paying 7. taking ... put 8. proposed 9. give ... carried 10. took 11. fell 12. laid/put 13. keep 14. went 15. take/bear/face 16. get 17. standing 18. play 19. take 20. gives 21. win ... fill 22. make 23. paid ... prevailing 24. have 25. brought.

CHAPTER 5

Exercise a Page 33 1. is making 2. have ... shall spend 3. had asked ... would you have said 4. have finished 5. were 6. Wouldn't it have been ... had seen 7. have been 8. see ... will tell 9. had been listening ... should certainly not have heard 10. had told ... should have been.

Exercise a Page 35 1. will try 2. should be able 3. asked 4. have seen 5. would have been 6. offended/have offended 7. would be 8. would raise 9. had tried/had been trying 10. isn't snowing 11. was 12. had told.

Exercise b Page 36 1. to see/to have seen 2. But for your springing 3. But for their being 4. to see/to have seen 5. Had he not had/But for his having 6. had I not lived/but for my living 7. Had he not made/But for his making 8. to receive 9. Had the Government not intervened promptly/But for the Government's prompt intervention.

Exercise d 1. caught 2. pretty 3. panacea 4. paragon 5. loosen 6. hackneyed 7. spade a spade 8. broaching 9. thin 10. dotage 11. extenuating 12. rain 13. racking 14. trees 15. alibi 16. plain 17. buttered 18. fence ... came 19. cut 20. point.

CHAPTER 6

Exercise a Page 41 1. I must have/get my photograph taken. 2. Have/Get your breakfast brought to you in bed 3. He told me he was having/getting his portrait painted 4. It is time you had/got your house repainted 5. Unfortunately he had his house burgled ... 6. Why don't you have/get your meat delivered every day? 7. He doesn't have his flat cleaned (for him) ...' 8. I advised him to have/get a new suit made 9. Do you think I can have/get it repaired? 10. I had my pocked picked ... 11. He is having/getting his new garden laid out by a well-known firm ... 12. We must have/get them put right. 13. He had his pockets searched at the police station. 14. I hear that he has recently had his new book brought out. 15. The escaped prisoner had/got his hair dyed. 16. It is time we had/got this room decorated, 17. He had his hat knocked off in the skirmish. 18. I must have/get this jacket let out. 19. It is advisable to have/get the contents of your flat insured, 20. He had his motor-car completely wrecked in that accident.

Exercise b Page 41 1. swimming 2. in watching 3. of her changing 4. of following 5. leave 6. idling 7. to know 8. being 9. in cleaning 10. laughing 11. by getting on getting 12. to do 13 in educating 14. to go 15. not say.

Exercise c Page 42 1. priceless asset 2. barren 3. impassioned 4. regard/consider ... indispensable 5. unreadable 6. current 7. indelible 8. irrespective/regardless ... affiliations 9. iniquitous 10. injurious.

CHAPTER 7

Exercise a Page 45 1. He was left about £10,000 by his grandfather 2. The old man was set upon and beaten up 3. She doesn't like being criticised 4. Trams have been done away with in England 5. I do not think anything is being done about it 6. A concert was being given ... About fifty people were injured seriously enough to be taken to hospital. 7. He was given a cheque for the amount required. 8. He was let off with a severe reprimand. 9. Chichester Cathedral had been evacuated before the spire collapsed, so no-one was hurt 10. You are very well looked after in that hotel 11. Eventually the search for the missing man was given up 12. Some girls love being paid compliments 13. I was given this fountain-pen for Christmas 14. The news bulletin was being listened to with avid interest 15. He was curtly told to go away 16. My sister was sent a Valentine card last week 17. Some people object to being made to work hard 18. Is that television set paid for yet? 19. I hate being made fun of, though I don't mind being teased 20. Dinner is being cooked by my sister's fiancé tonight ...

Exercise b 1. fell 2. plucked 3. hold 4. put/set 5. called ... take 6. aroused/whetted/ stimulated/awakened ... tear ... satisfied 7. standing 8. held 9. face 10. fall 11. make do and mend 12. hold 13. laid 14. go ... follow 15. drawing ... solve 16. owe 17. follow 18. fulfil 19. committed ... break 20. hold 21. set 22. reached 23. achieve/fulfil/attain 24. made ... lie 25. took 26. made 27. courting 28. gaining 29. overthrown 30. blow.

Exercise c Page 46 1. has been cooking 2. was crossing ... felt ... fell ... revived ... was splashing ... glimpsed ... dived ... pulled ... would have drowned ... had been. 3. is being ... is 4. is always nagging ... does not hear 5. had been ... failed ... was ... would not have been ... do not believe ... reassured 6. will have been working ... have never known 7. have washed 8. would you have been ... had arrived ... was coming 9. promised ... had not been working ... burst ... had picked ... (had) dropped ... (had) broken 10. have you been doing.

CHAPTER 8
Exercise a Page 50 1. at being 2. painting 3. kiss 4. to go ... seeing 5. by behaving 6. sacrificing 7. your going 8. say 9. from searching 10. organising/to organise 11. investigating ... to see 12. him to be 13. liked 14. hold 15. for showing 16. at my being 17. to apologise 18. telling 19. you to be 20. him to be.

Exercise b Page 51 1. have you been ... have been looking 2. will be sitting 3. knows ... are produced ... realises ... is going 4. struck ... saw 5. turned ... had not been ... blew ... had never had 6. have been learning ... have 7. is hearing 8. are ... have been nagging ... am doing ... keep 9. have been saving ... really shall go 10. had ... Did you hear ... came ... 11. was going ... has rather put ... shall go 12. was being ... broke ... ensued 13. have been ... do not recollect 14. are you looking ... Has someone been spreading 15. have heard ... wanted ... has already done so ... shall we put.

CHAPTER 9
Exercise a Page 55 1. should have 2. were ... would do/should do 3. left 4. should be 5. have been living ... knew 6. may you enjoy 7. should repent 8. may be ... shall watch 9. made 10. should be/should have been 11. should be 12. had behaved 13. may you cling ... may you never become 14. were ... would you say 15. knew

Exercise c Page 56 1. blot 2. casual 3. party 4. ploughed 5. scratch 6. Dutch 7. counterfeit 8. levelled 9. stand 10. edgeways 11. reshuffle 12. foregone 13. slapstick 14. party 15. rude 16. pretty 17. chip 18. relapse 19. hang 20. knack 21. lap 22. object 23. raw 24. ulterior 25. past 26. cropping 27. wish 28. raw 29. creature 30. live.

CHAPTER 10
Exercise a Page 61 1. you to do 2. walking 3. going 4. skiing to doing 5. in making ... fall 6. take 7. to talk 8. about wanting/of wanting 9. me of pulling 10. telling ... moving 11. of bringing 12. not to come 13. lying 14. sunbathing 15. asking

Exercise c Page 61 1. rejuvenated 2. prevaricated 3. expatiated 4. annihilated 5. intimidate 6. incapacitated 7. placate 8. implicated 9. delegate 10. underrate 11. litigate 12. deteriorating 13. perpetrated 14. procrastinates 15. reiterate 16. resuscitated 17. reverberated 18. infuriates 19. gesticulating 20. vitiated 21. prefabricated 22. expiated 23. fumigate 24. abominate 25. rehabilitated 26. alleviate 27. facilitate 28. incarcerated 29. proliferated 30. exterminating.

CHAPTER 11
Exercise a Page 65 1. did her bad temper get ... 2. had he come 3. does one come 4. does/did Dickens show 5. did I begin 6. do I ever believe 7. do I urge 8. did he find 9. did I meet 10. have women had 11. does/did Hardy give 12. may he be called

Exercise b Page 66 1. Far out to sea lay the pirate ship 2. Nowhere else in the world can that happen to you 3. In any circumstances he would go on working 4. Round the bend sped the car. 5. Very rarely have I seen ... 6. Not a single word did he say all afternoon 7. In no way do I think he would like it. 8. On no account would I offend you 9. Perhaps you have seen it already? 10. Into the coach scrambled the children 11. The most fascinating part of the town was the Flea Market 12. Little did he think that ... 13. Nowhere else in England have I seen that kind of tree 14. Only on very rare occasions does John go to the theatre. 15. Undoubtedly Jane Austen is one ... 16. Out of the swirling mist loomed the tall figure of a man. 17. By all means let us have your ideas 18. In such a desperate situation did we find ourselves that we ... 19. With good reason is he called a fool 20. By no means is it true that ... 21. Out of the brushwood ahead of me rose a pheasant. 22. In no city he had previously visited had he been treated so abominably 23. On innumerable occasion I have told him ... 24. In no circumstances should you panic 25. Through the silence of the jungle came the ... 26. On numerous occasions I have received ... 27. Down fell a great pile ... 28. Not until his attention was drawn to certain irregularities did the director realise ... 29. Up on the backs of sturdy porters went the mass of luggage 30. Such has been the success ...

CHAPTER 12
Exercise a Page 71 1. to being 2. his getting 3. not discuss 4. dance than study 5. dancing to studying 6. playing 7. to being 8. of buying 9. go 10. into investigating 11. of forgiving ... look 12. heating ... adding 13. me of pulling 14. crying 15. of applying 16. leaving 17. tramping ... settling 18. behave. 19. her to know 20. his being ... my knowing 21. you to have 22. to going 23. being ... being 24. studying 25. collide 26. understand 27. in moping 28. cleaning 29. to shave 30. in pulling 31. die than be 32. spending 33. be 34. of being 35. you to apologise for putting

Exercise b Page 72 1. nice 2. pretty 3. turned 4. take 5. chattering 6. toast 7. ransacked/burgled/broken into 8. pitch/coal 9. sheet 10. lightning 11. gold 12. peas 13. saddled 14. pot 15. houses 16. sound 17. overdose 18. lie 19. box 20. towering

Exercise c Page 72 1. 'a cock-and-bull story' = nonsensical, unbelievable story 2. an exclamation meaning 'rubbish!' 3. 'put one's heart and soul into something ' = devote all one's attention and feeling to it 4. 'I've known him off and on for years' = with some intermissions when we didn't meet 5. a euphemism for any term of abuse 6. economise and do without things 7. the points in favour and against 8. fed up with 9. destitute 10. spirit of compromise 11. better in health and able to get out of the house 12. definitively 13. ambitious and with good prospects 14. finished and forgotten about 15. very boring (used of places) 16. haughty, giving one self airs of importance 17. generally speaking 18. 'go to rack and ruin' either fall into ruins or fall into disorganisation 19. a fight, either physical or verbal, in whch everyone takes part 20. 'head over heels in love' = very much in love 21. immediately, on the spot 22. 'the life and soul of the party' = the amusing person who makes the others enjoy themselves 23. 'He's far and away the best student' = a long way ahead of the others 24. 'the long and short of it' = to put a long story briefly 25. very uncertain: 'it's touch and go whether he will live'.

CHAPTER 14
Exercise Page 78 1. for perfecting 2. your being 3. from voting 4. for losing 5. for being 6. on being 7. on getting 8. from committing 9. hanging 10. from doing 11. for making 12. from driving 13. being 14. finding 15. on becoming ... from putting ... for making 16. from looking 17. getting 18. on improving 19. hearing 20. from doing 21. for being 22. teaching 23. on treating 24. reading 25. for playing 26. having 27. on having 28. for doing 29. reprimanding ... for treating 30. on constructing 31. for risking 32. for his being 33. on buying 34. coming 35. for giving 36. becoming 37. for libelling 38. for playing 39. from hurrying 40. for being 41. daydreaming 42. manufacturing 43. on getting 44. for asking 45. from smoking.

Exercise Page 81 1. of trusting 2. being 3. into giving 4. of winning 5. concentrating 6. of hearing 7. into giving 8. arguing 9. working/having worked 10. of your winning 11. of curing 12. at failing 13. offending ... of voting 14. of my going ... having 15. into signing 16. of snapping 17. about sponging 18. saying 19. knowing 20. of being 21. of doing ... being 22. lighting 23. your being/your having been 24. into handing 25. of being 26. of your going 27. writing 28. of committing 29. about doing 30. of paying 31. on partitioning 32. about doing 33. into buying 34. of spending 35. into accepting ... of making 36. about feeding 37. about taking 38. into thinking 39. about getting 40. of making 41. of meeting 42. being 43. into admitting 44. doing ... doing.

Exercise Page 84 1. at knitting 2. in drinking 3. against being 4. making ... with making 5. at doing 6. getting 7. at writing 8. with having 9. at being ... at being 10. at being 11. at living 12. with giving 13. in intervening 14. in reading 15. in learning 16. in not doing 17. with embezzling 18. against being 19. in denying ... having 20. in thinking ... in learning 21. in having 22. at being 23. not spending 24. going 25. playing at being 26. playing 27. being 28. in thinking 29. with being 30. in apologising 31. at raising 32. in opening 33. in asking 34. in taking 35. in educating 36. being 37. at having 38. in thinking 39. with doing 40. in singing.

Exercise a Page 88 1. my being qualified 2. helping the Africans 3. having an aperitif 4. knowing anything about the affair 5. his being guilty 6. living in the tropics 7. living abroad 8. having wealth 9. thieving/stealing 10. writing about the subject 11. seeing my point of view 12. looking elegant 13. making the party a success 14. using unnecessary violence 15. getting married 16. getting the dinner 17. committing manslaughter 18. leading a humdrum life 19. having violent fits ... 20. refusing to obey orders.

Exercise b Page 88 1. of doing 2. from living 3. of meeting 4. of clearing 5. to dying 6. of getting ... making 7. to having ... drinking ... to pub crawling 8. by making ... being 9. to stealing 10. to helping 11. of my being 12. to moralising 13. at being 14. into buying 15. of emigrating 16. from thinking 17. furnishing ... of doing 18. Being ... to making 19. by wearing 20. of being. 21. in finding 22. in asking 23. to discussing 24. to his having worked ... lived 25. By saying ... to being 26. at not receiving 27. of lowering 28. in thinking 29. about going 30. from accepting.

Exercise d Page 89 1. Do you have your house ... 2. ... the world go round 3. That money enabled them to go ... 4. He usually gets 5. If you prefer messing about to working I cannot prevent you from wasting your time 6. ... wish you goodbye/say goodbye to you 7. ... people to tell me ... 8. ... installing ... 9. ... my wife were here 10. If you have been living ... you looked ... 11. ... to living ... 12. ... if he were 13. ... he fled 14. ... me for being late/my being late 15. He was to play ... 16. If you have already seen the film ... 17. ... was glanced at by ... 18. acquitted of committing 19. to sue him did he send me 20. forgive me for being ... last time we met 21. ... is being opened 22. should you believe ... 23. ... presided over ... 24. I have been wanting ... 25. He is thinking of going ... 26. Need you really go/Do you really need to go ... 27. hope of passing 28. I would like to visit ... 29. Nelson ordered the flag to be nailed 30. So great has been the success of the Exhibition ...

CHAPTER 15

Exercise a Page 94 1. to tell 2. leave 3. for wanting to make 4. you to say 5. beg than starve 6. to publish 7. going 8. to keep 9. show ... how to do 10. to put 11. in wanting to marry 12. his son to become 13. to tell 14. him for treating 15. of attempting to make 16. at not receiving 17. To speak 18. use/using 19. in treating ... losing 20. to be ... to moralising ... liking 21. at doing 22. to reading ... going 23. at being asked to make 24. to make ... of seeing 25. to making ... scrub 26. to finish repairing 27. to maintain 28. me to give 29. being 30. you to take 31. going 32. of joining 33. to allow myself to be browbeaten into agreeing to your marrying 34. to meet ... to turn 35. her to put 36. your living 37. give ... about buying 38. with my trying 39. to my being 40. you to take 41.

helping 42. for his being 43. Their leaving 44. him to show 45. of stooping to using ... to use.

Exercise b Page 95 1. at 2. beyond ... at ... in 3. to ... on ... beneath 4. from 5. with ... on ... to 6. under ... with 7. To ... of ... by 8. with ... after 9. over ... for 10. under ... after ... in 11. In/At ... under 12. in ... for ... on ... of ... 13. for ... on 14. within ... of ... of 15. By ... to ... of

CHAPTER 16
Exercise Page 99 1. out 2. up to something 3. back me up 4. behind 5. back out 6. on at me 7. I am through with it 8. are in for 9. on to a good thing 10. be over.

Exercise a Page 101 1. have brought it upon yourself 2. break out in spots 3. brought on 4. broken off 5. break away 6. brought her round to my way of thinking 7. broken the back of it 8. break himself of the habit 9. some breakthrough 10. brings the house down 11. bringing out 12. broke down.

Exercise b Page 101 1. episcopal 2. repetitive 3. avuncular 4. beheaded 5. quarrelsome 6. despicable 7. Jocular 8. discomfort 9. remnants 10. businesslike 11. cessation 12. privacy 13. deserts 14. expulsion 15. profundity 16. abstemious 17. disused 18. elegible 19. vehicular 20. presumptuous 21. deceptive 22. predatory 23. apologetic 24. brazenly 25. retentive 26. snobbery 27. treacherous 28.cruciform 29. Brevity 30. semblance 31. breach 32. breakages 33. loan 34. resumption 35. infamy.

Exercise c Page 102 1. have been learning 2. would have died ... managed 3. is constantly interrupting 4. had been working 5. likes ... has achieved 6. had taken ... did the Minister of Transport agree 7. should still be 8. went 9. had started ... would your reaction have been? 10. has been 11. have been ... are 12. have you known 13. killed ... removed ... wiped ... was just making ... heard ... was coming ... should he do ... was 14. did he find 15. should be 16. has the success ... been ... have decided 17. should not have seen 18. should be 19. will have finished 20. did he murder ... tried

CHAPTER 17
Exercise a Page 105 1. to cut the grass with 2. to open tins with 3. to put/arrange stamps in 4. to open the door with 5. to bathe in 6. to dive in off 7. to cut bread on 8. to vacuum with 9. to stand on 10. to play games with 11. to play tennis on 12. to dig with 13. to shoot with 14. to sit in 15. to walk on 16. to wash up in 17. to cut with 18. to hold on to 19. to put/grow flowers in 20. to pack clothes in 21. to comb one's hair with 22. to get water out of 23. to screw things in with 24. to wipe one's feet on 25. to cut people's heads off with.

Exercise b Page 105 1. throw 2. staunch 3. do ... liven 4. settle 5. threw 6. harping 7. keeps/kept 8. have/exert 9. craning 10. verges 11. tipped 12. conserving/saving 13. stood 14. end 15. turned 16. weigh ... coming 17. stirring 18. downed 19. boosted 20. make ... palls 21. pander 22. appeal 23. stepped 24. tapped 25. nipped.

CHAPTER 18
Exercise a Page 108 1. Why else ... 2. Who else ... 3. How else ... 4. Who else's ... 5. ... where else 6. Someone else ... 7. What else could I use this for? 8. Where else 9. anyone else 10. ... somewhere else 11. When else ... 12. How else ...

Exercise c Page 109 1. spoon 2. weathered 3. inside 4. foul ... misadventure 5. chalk 6. contained 7. laurels 8. penny 9. loose 10. vicious 11. bargained 12. tarred 13. prime/ heyday 14. slippery ... end 15. see 16. caving 17. batted 18. half-way 19. lip 20. glut 21. jog 22. drinking 23. patched 24. gift 25. bumper

CHAPTER 19
Exercise a Page 112 1. that 2. which 3. — 4. whom 5. whose 6. that 7. that 8. what 9. — 10. which 11. that 12. —

Exercise b 1. with vivid blue eyes 2. we are running away from 3. he fell into 4. you are looking for 5. with the large house you can see ... 6. you are labouring under 7. perhaps the greatest general that has ever existed 8. I was coming by 9. with a son in prison 10. I was looking at.

Exercise c 1. in robbing 2. at losing 3. signing ... into doing 4. about going 5. at being ... to annoy 6. of misleading ... into thinking 7. about spending 8. of feeling 9. from hurting 10. at being 11. to my missing 12. at designing 13. singing 14. to seeing ... at having 15. in quelling 16. knowing ... to getting ... speaking 17. of abolishing 18. for his making 19. (with) playing 20. to his being 21. to take ... in playing 22. of wanting me to fall 23. for being 24. Doing ... of getting 25. at adapting ... to living.

Exercise d Page 113 1. crystallised 2. ratified 3. stylised 4. plagiarising 5. improvise 6. tantalised 7. specify 8. nullified 9. bowdlerised 10. mollify 11. ostracise 12. temporise 13. cauterised 14. vilify 15. jeopardises 16. petrified 17. lionised 18. rectify 19. proselytise 20. clarify.

CHAPTER 20
Exercise Page 117 1. came into 2. come down in the world 3. it came out 4. come into her own 5. come out with 6. come round to 7. does not come out 8. came across 9. come out well 10. come by 11. has come off 12. come round 13. did not come up to my expectations 14. came about 15. came off badly.

Exercise Page 118 1. cut out for 2. cut out 3. cut off 4. very cut up 5. cut down on 6. cut right across 7. He thinks himself a cut above the rest 8. cut in 9. cut down

Exercise a Page 120 1. having anything to do with him 2. doing out 3. drew back from doing it 4. draw up 5. do up ... the evenings are drawing in 6. make do with it 7. done away with 8. do without 9. hard done by 10. draw them out

Exercise b 1. through with 2. about 3. on or off 4. up to 5. down on 6. out to 7. round to 8. down 9. away on 10. down into 11. on 12. cut out for 13. away from 14. up at 15. at 16. on/upon 17. away with 18. away from 19. up with 20. off 21. by ... into 22. over 23. with 24. up 25. for

Exercise c Page 121 1. spelled/spelt 2. feathering 3. intruding 4. sour 5. lay 6. take 7. wrought 8. size 9. given ... put 10. tabling 11. practise 12. draw 13. sprang 14. played 15. issued ... go ... met 16. demand ... go 17. ascertain ... committed 18. come 19. pass

CHAPTER 21
Exercise a Page 127 1. — 2. — 3. some 4. clap/peal 5. suit 6. some 7. some ... it 8. means 9. — 10. — 11. patterns 12. state 13. rashers/slices 14. some 15. — 16. some 17. — 18. storm/volley/stream 19. lump 20. — 21. wave 22. — 23. some ... it 24. pall 25. stretch ... it 26. deal 27. some 28. any 29. patch 30. amount 31. ray 32. some 33. pane 34. — 35. stroke 36. — ... — 37. some 38. feats 39. any 40. blade

Exercise b Page 128 1. were 2. did she agree 3. was swimming ... got ... would certainly have drowned ... had not dived ... pulled 4. were curling ... was disappearing ... being 5. is being/was 6. learnt 7. does one hear 8. had left ... walked ... remembered ... has left ... went 9. had been born ... would you have liked 10. have been trying ... have not succeeded 11. did ... went 12. had been studying ... came 13. have been avoiding ... have I done 14. have made 15. would not be selling ... had not died.

CHAPTER 22
Exercise a Page 131 1. one 2. Some ... other 3. neither 4. any 5. some 6. some 7. any 8. Some 9. any 10. one 11. None 12. one 13. any 14. some ... other 15. Neither

Exercise c Page 132 1.teetotaller 2. misanthropist 3. philanthropist 4. misogynist 9. philatelist 10. believer 11. deist 12. agnostic 13. atheist 14. hostage 15. masochist 16. sadist 17. member of the congregation/worshipper 18. coroner 19. libeller 20. slanderer 21. drover 22. debtor 23. creditor 24. landscape-gardener 25. traitor 26. impregnable 27. indelible 28. unbeatable/invincible 29. inaccessible 30. unattainable 31. indestructible 32. indispensable 33. imperceptible 34. forbidden/prohibited 35. intangible 36. inexhaustible 37. illegible 38. unreadable 39. incorrigible 40. unnoticeable/inconspicuous

CHAPTER 23

Exercise Page 137 1. We bought some loaves of bread ... 2. We asked you ... 3. They have some pianos ... 4. ... ponies ... lanes 5. ... children 6. They take a pride in their ... 7. There were some poppies ... 8. They were 9. — 10. By what criteria ... these men's work 11. ... those people ... them 12. The men seem ... 13. These are genera of flowers we have 14. Those women teachers are ... their Italian ... 15. They have some châteaux ... we ... 16. — 17. Buses leave the termini ... those are the last ones 18. What are the bases of such beliefs? 19. Wives ... are ... liabilities 20. — 21.— 22. Border clashes ... 23. The robbers ... their 24. Dilettanti are ... 25. — 26. Herds of ... 27. — 28. People ... 29. Some sheaves ... were ... 30. — 31. The valleys were ... 32. Oxen are useful animals 33. — 34. Potatoes ... 35. The enemy ships fired (some) torpedoes at us. 36. — 37. International crises follow one another ... 38. — 39. Menservants are expensive luxuries ... 40. ... facts ...

CHAPTER 24

Exercise a Page 139 1. pang 2. rumble 3. splinter 4. gangs 5. whiff/puff 6. suite 7. feat ... source 8. pack 9. state 10. clump 11. bunch 12. shaft 13. gust 14. medley 15. term 16. swarms ... spell 17. herds 18. article(s) 19. rounds/slices 20. cluster 21. bundle 22. token 23. volley 24. litter 25. item ... bulletin 26. bevy 27. Teams 28. rounds 29. Board 30. sides/flitches 31. flash 32. pat 33. shoal 34. specimen 35. feats/deeds 36. nest 37. confederation 38. batch 39. wad 40 hum

Exercise c Page 140 1. insoluble 2. reprehensible 3. childish 4. décor 5. consorting with 6. whitewash 7. frivolity/facetiousness 8. prosecuted 9. pernicious 10. prescribed

CHAPTER 25

Exercise Page 143 1. got away with 2. fall in with 3. fallen for 4. fallen off 5. fall out with 6. fell upon 7. get by ... got away 8. fall out 9. get behind with 10. getting at me 11. falls away 12. get over it 13. got off with 14. got down to 15. fell through

Exercise Page 146 1. give-and-take 2. I don't go by 3. has gone down 4. have a go at writing 5. gives away 6. to go round 7. did not go down at all well with ... 8. gave way 9. gives way to ... 10. gone down 11. going in for 12. go through 13. go into 14. gave out 15. have given out 16. going over 17. give in 18. at one go 19. gone for nothing 20. go back on 21. went through 22. going up 23. gave him away 24. give way to 25. Let go of 26. given out 27. all the go 28. on the go 29. went off 30. gave off

Exercise a Page 149 1. hold with 2. withholding 3. help up 4. holding his own with 5. hold off 6. have it out with her 7. had up for 8. hold on to 9. have it in for me 10. holding out on me 11. holding them up to ridicule 12. hold out 13. hold down 14. I had it from John 15. withhold 16. does not hold together well 17. have a go at mending ... 18. uphold ... hold with 19. held it against me/had it in for me 20. holds good for ... 21. holding some shocking secret over someone's head 22. have done with it 23. held the English King up to ransom 24. hold nations down 25. I'll have nothing to do with you.

Exercise b Page 149 1. up 2. bask on 3. in in 4. up to 5. on ... with 6. over to ... into 7. way to 8. up for 9. up to 10. by 11. away to 12. by 13. through 14. away with 15. round

CHAPTER 26

<u>Exercise a Page 155</u> should, should, would, would, would, should, would, should, should, would, should, <u>would</u>, should.

<u>Exercise b Page 156</u> 1. needn't 2. don't have 3. used not to live/never lived 4. didn't have 5. haven't 6. needn't/don't need to 7. can't 8. Don't be ... don't feel 9. had better not ... isn't 10. didn't have 11. needn't 12. used not to belong/never belonged

<u>Exercise c</u> 1. Yes I must 2. Yes I did 3. Yes I did 4. Yes I was 5. Yes I do/Yes I must 6. Yes you must 7. Yes she did

<u>Exercise d</u> 1. No I didn't 2. No I needn't 3. No I haven't 4. No he daren't 5. No I didn't

<u>Exercise e</u> 1. I wouldn't have done it if I had been you 2. You ought to have known better by then 3. The doctor said I was not to play ... 4. It must have been ... 5. He was to have sung ... last month 6. He would have done it yesterday if he had been able to 7. It was ... were able to go ... 8. You needn't have done it then if you hadn't wanted to

<u>Exercise f</u> 1. You needn't have been 2. I need not have marked 3. didn't need to buy 4. did not need to write 5. needn't have rushed 6. needn't have worried 7. needn't have spent 8. didn't need to pay 9. didn't need to get 10. needn't have interrupted 11. didn't need to buy 12. needn't have paid 13. didn't need to tell 14. needn't have had 15. needn't have got

<u>Exercise g</u> 1. at being expected to make 2. in thinking 3. of being ... to realising 4. to spend 5. to get ... to blackmailing 6. to being 7. in smuggling/to smuggle (ie their purpose) 8. listening 9. in wanting to marry 10. to get 11. towards reaching 12. to be ... from meeting 13. to doing 14. of going 15. for mimicking 16. of losing 17. at making/to have made 18. at being 19. to assure ... of hurting 20. on protecting 21. at being 22. in doing 23. about marrying ... to coerce her into doing so 24. of taking 25. with putting

<u>Exercise h</u> 1. clattering 2. flagged 3. despicable 4. straggling ... struck 5. bequeathed ... impecunious/hard-up/destitute 6. did it up ... delapidated/ruinous 7. lapsed

CHAPTER 27

<u>Exercise a Page 163</u> 1. He told me he had been to Rome the previous year 2. He asked me if I was going ... 3. He enquired where I would like ... 4. He informed me that he had seen ... so he didn't want ... 4. He suggested that I ask John to go with me. 5. He warned me that he might decide ... 6. She shouted to Peter to go to her at once and told him off for daring to play in the mud in his best clothes 7. He told me that a lot of skyscrapers had been built ... 8. She asked if I would mind helping her ... 9. She informed me that she was going to have her portrait painted. 10. She suggested finding something to do indoors as it was raining 11. He suggested phoning up Mary to see ... 12. She reminded him that his Aunt Mary was coming to tea the following day and begged/urged him to be on his best behaviour 13. The notice warned that trespassers would be prosecuted 14. He suggested having a drink before we went ... 15. He asked her to give his kindest regards to her sister when she saw her 16. He explained that he was in a spot of bother and asked me to lend him £50 17. He said I wasn't to play the piano then as it was after midnight and all the neighbours would be complaining 18. He wanted me to let him know whether I could go and see him ... 19. He expressed surprise that I didn't know ... 20. She said she really hoped I would be able ... and begged me to try for her sake 21. He wanted to confirm that he had seen me ... and remarked on the fantastic crowd that was there 22. He earnestly assured me that he would tell me if he knew 23. He inquired if I knew where the nearest telephone kiosk was as he had to ring her up that moment 24. He exclaimed in surprise what an extraordinary thing that was for him to say to me 25. She showed surprise at seeing me there and asked what I thought of the show 26. She told me she was going to join that amateur theatre and explained that you didn't need to act; you could just ... could help ... 27. She explained that she was ... when she fell and twisted her ankle 28.

He suggested going on ... 29. He said he wished I were not ... 30. She begged me to make a special effort ...

Exercise b Page 164 1. shall be seeing ... will tell him what you have just said 2. have never seen ... was ... were being rolled ... was being moved ... were being polished ... were being cleaned ... were being arranged ... was rushing ... would believe ... 3. have got ... had been meaning 4. will have been working ... wore ... 5. have been trying ... have not succeeded yet 6. should I see 7. ran ... left 8. was stolen 9. are expanding ... is disappearing ... has been tilled ... is not being bulldozed ... be housed 10. had finished ... got ... went ... began ... had not returned ... turned 11. was being played ... went ... has been going 12. have been waiting ... does not come ... shall go ... doesn't find ... will have 13. is being attacked/has been attacked 14. should walk 15. has been discussed ... looked ... suggest ... take 16. does the majority ... Garden wear ... 17. were 18. should be made 19. did he speak to

Exercise d Page 165 1. struck 2. steer 3. shift 4. bail 5. trap ... hatch 6. ignition 7. near 8. benefit 9. rake 10. port ... conditioned 11. cross 12. nails 13. plant 14. sprung ... bale ... dear 15. staggered 16. cross 17. wink 18. struck 19. blurb ... plunged 20. breaking 21. crock 22. hatched 23. spokesman 24. huddled 25. grain

CHAPTER 28

Exercise Page 168 1. keep up 2. keep at it 3. keep up 4. keeps himself to himself 5. keeping his feet 6. knock about 7. keep up with 8. knocked one up 9. keep to the point 10. keep such ... from him

Exercise Page 169 1. lay down the law 2. lay-out 3. let me in 4. laid on 5. lays himself out 6. laid up 7. a kind of inlet 8. let yourself in for 9. let out 10. let off 11. laying out on 12. led him on to 13. He was led away by his feelings 14. let you into 15. leading the youth of Athens astray 16. outlay 17. laid off 18. outlet for 19. let me down 20. have you let John off?

Exercise Page 171 1. look on him 2. looked up 3. look back on 4. look for 5. looked up to 6. looking through 7. look into 8. got a look in 9. look-out 10. looking down on 11. looking forward to 12. looking up 13. overlook 14. outlook on 15. overlooks

Exercise Page 173 1. made out 2. made off 3. made away with 4. making 5. make out in 6. made for 7. make do with 8. make up 9. made over 10. made up of 11. have made it up 12. making up 13. make you out 14. make out 15. making up to 16. make up the fire 17. make a clean breast of 18. make up 19. make up the bed 20. on the make

Exercise b 1. off with 2. up 3. up ... out by 4. off 5. up 6. to ... on about it to 7. off 8. out to 9. on/upon 10. over 11. up with 12. down to 13. out 14. up ... to 15. off 16. up with 17. up 18. off ... to 19. back on 20. up to 21. on to 22. out over 23. up 24. into 25. out

Exercise c Page 174 1. dogging 2. infringing 3. beat 4. run 5. perjured ... stating 6. filing 7. offer 8. curry ... resorting 9. go ... run 10. burst 11. earn 12. won ... met 13. get 14. undermined 15. improves 16. owe 17. insure 18. had ... shown 19. prevail 20. laying 21. playing/cracking 22. while 23. live 24. jump 25. fall ... exceed

Exercise Page 175 1. impoverished 2. prolong 3. breadth 4. enabled 5. ridicule 6. simplifies 7. gesticulate 8. impassioned 9. fictitious 10. component 11. drunken 12. exemplified 13. Cleanliness 14. infuriating 15. embittered 16. Teetotallers 17. befriend 18. pronunciation 19. pacify 20. clarify 21. oust 22. prevailing 23. realistic 24. abundance 25. applicants 26. impediment 27. deeds 28. repulsive 29. preferential 30. infamy

CHAPTER 29

Exercise a Page 180 1. — 2. The 3. The ... the ... the 4. — 5. a ... the ... a 6. The — the ...

the ... the ... 7. The ... the — the — 8. an ... a 9. The — 10. — 11. The ... the ... the 12. — 13. — the 14. — the 15. A ... the —— 16. a 17. —— a ... the 18.The ... the ... a 19. — a — 20. — 21. The ... a — 22. — the 23. ————24. the ... the 25. The ——— the ... the ... the — the 26. the — a 27. the ... the — 28. The — 29. the — the 30. — the ... the ... the 31. The — the 32. A ... the 33. a ... the —— 34. The ... a — the 35. a — the

Exercise b Page 181 1. of having 2. for eating 3. in ousting 4. to having ... go 5. at being ... to wait ... offering 6. to mislead ... into thinking 7. about using 8. in spelling ... of writing ... sending 9. in adapting ... to living 10. of offending ... of passing 11. on curbing 12. to tell ... of punching 13. of listening ... to think ... of taking 14. in talking ... into joining ... trying 15. with breaking ... entering ... to being ... forcing ... saying ... standing ... to investigate 16. to cooking 17. at learning to talk ... to their being 18. of having ... being ... to look 19. on his giving ... of not paying 20. for asking

Exercise d Page 182 1. He shouted to me to go and see what he had found ... 2. He told me that I was a fool and I knew it. He asked me how I expected ... I didn't do 3. He said he had been ... 4. He implored me to tell him where she was 5. He and his wife invited me to go ... and asked if 7.30 suited/would suit me. 6. He asked me why I kept ... 7. She urged me to be careful how I crossed the road and warned me that it was ... 8. He ordered me to hide it ... and not say ... 9. He announced his intention of exploring ... he got 10. He told me that the following Monday they were going ... He said there was ... car and invited me to go with them 11. She begged me to try ... he had said ... that afternoon. She pointed out that if I could tell her, she might be ... 12. He asked me where I had found that ... and asked if I minded telling him if it was terribly expensive 13. She suggested going ... we should be ... 14. She said she had been waiting ... to tell me what she really thought of me and declared that that was a good opportunity 15. She begged me to be careful what I was doing ... and pointed out that it was ... my hands

Exercise e Page 183 1. do ... make 2. done 3. Do ... make 4. make do 5. do ... make ... doing 6. make ... do ... make 7. makes ... does ... does... makes ... does ... make ... does 8. make 9. make 10. make ... doing 11. done ... made 12. done ... make 13. make ... do 14. does ... do ... make 15. did ... made 16. made ... made 17. make do 18. made 19. done 20. make ... doing 21. make 22. make ... doing ... do ... make 23. Do ... make 24. made ... doing 25. did

CHAPTER 30
Exercise a Page 186 1. hour's work 2. education diploma 3. moment's notice 4. handrail 5. party politics 6. doll's houses 7. summer's day 8. wineglass 9. ceiling of the room 10. today's newspaper 11. tea-break 12. hair's breadth 13. root of the matter 14. money's worth 15. bedroom ceiling 16. tea tray 17. death's door 18. women's magazines 19. year's absence 20. committee meeting 21. church mouse 22. head cold 23. fairy stories 24. pirate's story 25. bath salts 26. dinner service 27. day's journey 28. television licence 29. state of mind 30. time of year 31. shirt collar 32. glass of milk 33. wit's end 34. Prison fare 35. power house 36. slum property 37. second's thought 38. car seats 39. day's holiday 40. lapse of memory

Exercise c Page 187 1. ... you come 3. was allowed 5. I met her/I got to know her ... 6. my wife to know ... 9. ... staying in ... to going out ... 11. laughed at being ... 13. forget catching 14. wants me to accompany 15. ... dare to say 16. ... in learning/I found it difficult to learn 18. lying 23. you make/you making 24. thinks he is 25. help laughing to see 26. stop chattering 27. ordered his men ... 28. I explained that piece of grammar to him 29. to hear 30. to see 31. advise you to go/advise going 33. use making 34. to being 36. want to 37. hope of fulfilling ... 38. to whatever 40. wish you goodbye/say goodbye to you

CHAPTER 31

Exercise Page 190 1. pull yourself together 2. pass out 3. Things have come to a pretty pass 4. pull through 5. pulled up 6. passed himself off 7. pulling my leg 8. pass down recipes 9. pulled in 10. pull up their pupils for bad manners 11. not pulling his weight 12. pulled down 13. passed out 14. pulling the wool over her husband's eyes ... 15. passing/pulling off

Exercise Page 192 1. put you up 2. I put his success down to ... 3. put upon 4. put out 5. output 6. put in for 7. put on 8. put up at 9. put you up to ... 10. put in 11. was hard put to it 12. put down £10 13. put up 14. output 15. put their knowledge across 16. puts some foreigners off coming 17. putting it to you 18. put up with 19. puts a lot of people's backs up 20. puts on airs

Exercise Page 194 1. in the long run 2. ran through 3. running their friends down 4. see to it 5. on the run 6. overran 7. see it through 8. have almost run out of sugar 9. ran off with 10. running briefly over 11. in the running 12. see you off 13. ran into 14. Time is running out 15. see to getting 16. ran across 17. saw through 18. run up bills 19. I saw through you 20. ran down

Exercise a Page 196 1. slipped up 2. set out to bring 3. set her heart on 4. gave his escort the slip 5. set upon 6. set my mind at rest 7. set me down at 8. well set back from 9. showed up 10. set about 11. outset 12. show-down 13. setting her cap at you 14. set great store by 15. shown up

Exercise b Page 197 1. up in 2. together ... off 3. away by 4. out at 5. off 6. round to ... out of 7. through ... at 8. up to ... over ... of ... to 9. on in ... into 10. in for ... in ... for 11. in for .. away with 12. on ... to ... by ... to 13. up in ... of 14. off as 15. on ... through 16. up in 17. away to 18. up in 19. out 20. out for ... to

Exercise d Page 198 1. to learning 2. to my giving 3. to improving ... for coming ... you to leave 4. to my preparing 5. controlling 6. with giving 7. into thinking 8. my being 9. to putting 10. with being 11. living ... to going to live 12. for being 13. to being ... by saying 14. at being asked to do 15. to confessing to stealing 16. to John's being guilty of committing ... for us to examine 17. denying ... towards adopting 18. being ... spending ... to playing 19. in sitting ... being ... at their being ... to put 20. in using

Exercise e Page 199 1. instil ... reaching 2. give 3. bid 4. expresses ... opt 5. took 6. break 7. meet 8. levelled 9. serve 10. called 11. uttered/let out 12. called 13. lead 14. hit 15. face 16. made 17. confronted 18. called 19. threw/cast 20. belittle ... make 21. fritter 22. drew 23. place 24. serve 25. mince 26. borne 27. got ... harboured 28. run ... contracting 29. reaping 30. strike

Exercise f 1. landmark 2. mountain railway 3. daydream 4. village green 5. housecoat/houseboat 6. manhole 7. street-arab 8. windfall/wind-cheater 9. bee sting/beehive 10. pub-crawl 11. state lottery 12. peace treaty 13. household/housebreaker/houseroom 14. shipshape 15. clothes peg/clothes horse 16. window sill/window-dresser 17. master builder/masterpiece 18. picture window/picture frame 19. dinner service 20. hotel staff

CHAPTER 32

Exercise Page 202 1. I hardly ever go ... 2. data meticulously 3. He calmly told me ... 4. They very nearly came ... 5. him furtively 6. I thoroughly enjoyed ... 7. home through the park last night 8. He indignantly denied 9. gazed listlessly 10. She invariably forgets 11. I was peremptorily ordered ... 12. you kindly tell 13. thing dispassionately 14. I only occasionally go 15. I entirely approve 16. was awfully late .. office yesterday 17. You certainly need 18. She cynically refuses 19. out of the room in a huff yesterday 20. I would never have ... 21. I unwittingly said 22. at the theatre late 23. very much enjoy 24.

He nearly always manages ... 25. He quite blatantly flattered her. 26. She involuntarily started up 27. am forever telling 28. aloud monotonously 29. at London Airport at three o'clock in the afternoon 30. She angrily demanded

Exercise a Page 207 1. too bright a hat 2. brown suit black 3. hairstyle you have 4. far too late ... there alone 5. question posed 6. Many a time have I said 7. So splendid a gown 8. annoying a thing 9. Such a high meal so late at night ... 10. a happy time that was 11. his work far too well 12. So much the better 13. too devoted a knight errant 14. have I seen 15. would never have happened 16. too serious a matter 17. Many a court-martial 18. Such a dog-in-the-manger policy 19. did I realise ... how difficult a time 20. the more fool he

Exercise b Page 208 1. do 2. makes 3. made 4. made 5. made 6. do 7. do 8. making 9. did 10. do 11. making 12. done 13. did 14. doing 15. make 16. make 17. done 18. make 19. made 20. made

Exercise d Page 209 1. coalface/coal scuttle 2. fire drill/fire screen/fire-raiser 4. scandal-monger 4. nightmare 5. flagstone/flag-day 6. snowflake/snowdrop/snow-plough 7. market-gardening 8. school holiday 9. hen-party/hen house 10. earthquake 11. raindrop/rainfall 12. flower-bed/flower-pot 13. mothball 14. bookmaker/bookbinding/bookworm 18.law-giver/lawsuit 19. footfall/foothold/footstep 20. heartwhole/heart condition/heartbreak 21. brainstorm/brainwave/brainwashing 22. frost-bite 23. log-book/log fire 24. crack shot 25. shipwreck 26. pen-friend/pen holder 27. garden wall 28. tablespoon/table leg 29. board meeting/boardroom 30. shoe-tree/shoe horn

Exercise e Page 211 1. whom 2. who 3. which 4. —— 5. — who 6. — 7. which that 8. what 9. — 10. —

CHAPTER 33

Exercise Page 212 1. standby 2. standing in for 3. stood out 4. stand by 5. stick up for her husband 6. stand/stick 7. stuck to 8. stand up to 9. stand down 10. stand to lose

Exercise Page 215 1. take on so 2. I took him down a peg or two 3. taken in 4. taken on 5. took off 6. took ... in her stride 7. taken aback 8. take up 9. took me to task 10. take down 11. taking off 12. taken with 13. takes it out of you 14. took over (from him) 15. take it in 16. we first took up with each other 17. take to getting drunk 18. undertook to pay me 19. taken in 20. intake 21. take it out on 22. take that into consideration 23. taking time off 24. takes after 25. taken with 26. taken down 27. has been taken off 28. I took him into my confidence 29. I took you for someone else 30. took place

Exercise a Page 217 1. turned away 2. turned out 3. turn to and find 4. turned on me 5. turned down 6. turned over/overturned 7. overthrew 8. throw off 9. turned out 10. turned out trumps 11. can turn his hand to anything 12. turned out 13. thrown it up 14. turn up 15. turned it over in my mind 16. threw in his lot with 17. turning out 18. throw their weight about 19. turn her husband round her little finger 20. (it) gave me quite a turn

Exercise b Page 218 1. out 2. away with ... in ... of 3. in ... by 4. up to 5. through with 6. over at 7. on at ... about 8. in for 9. up for 10. by 11. with 12. on/upon ... down 13. in ... up with 14. in 15. up to 16. aside 17. down on ... out 18. across 19. up at 20. down ... up 21. behind with 22. out without 23. away with 24. for 25. on ... away 26. on 27. out ... through 28. into ... in 29. up for 30. in at on 31. in for 32. down to 33. away by 34. of ... astray 35. round after 36. out with 37. by 38. out ... in 39. through 40. over to ... up 41. off in 42. through ... out 43. about 44. out ... on 45. at ... of 46. on 47. way to ... from 48. out on 49. way to 50. off for 51. down 52. out in 53. up 54. To ... off with 55. on about ... to

Exercise c Page 220 1. co-operative 2. inarticulate 3. Procrastination 4. illiterate 5.

absent-mindedly 6. amicably 7. off-hand 8. intestate 9. hypocrite 10. quadrupled

Exercise e Page 220 1. to stand up for/to have stood up for ... to being ... to being ... to look ... to be 2. of making ... in continuing 3. in thinking 4. of your staying ... waste ... (on) paying ... having ... to stay 5. into giving ... to induce ... to reveal 6. seeing ... writing ... to composing ... for assessing 7. On coming ... on being... to get ... to do 8. for her being ... 9. on trying to look ... to cultivate 10. to never having ... to enjoying ... Striving to keep ... to chafing ... at not being 11. my criticising ... of coming ... to accept ... to help 12. for being ... to have been ... being ... being ... to look 13. on getting ... to sacrifice ... to do ... being ... not having lived 14. for getting ... want to learn 15. to your helping ... of looking ... of knowing

CHAPTER 34

Exercise a Page 226 1. When I came back home very late and opened the front door I got a shock to find that burglars ... 2. It was a stormy day and the sea was very rough, so the ship was lurching from side to side and I had ... 3. He is very rich but, being very mean, he never gives ... 4. I remember the face of that man you can see standing in the corner because he stole my wallet last year. 5. I will lend you the money, provided that you pay it back within a week, but I shall be so angry if you don't that I shan't speak to you again. 6. As it rained very heavily for days, that level of water in the reservoir rose until the pressure on the dam was so great that it burst and drowned many people. 7. It was very hot so I had taken off my shirt and was lying in the sun when I fell asleep, only to be woken up suddenly by a thunderstorm 8. As she got out of her Rolls Royce carrying a bunch of roses she caught her heel in a grating and fell over, scattering roses ... 9. Being very late I was hurrying along as fast as I could when I collided with a policeman who told me off. 10. An icy wind was blowing and the sea was too cold for John to swim in that day 11. I took a pound note from my pocket, showed it to the boy and said he could have it if he took my dog for an hour's walk 12. We planned to give a dinner party so we bought lots of food, only to find we couldn't cook it as our gas had been cut off because we had forgotten to pay the bill 13. I was quite naturally very annoyed when a window of my greenhouse was broken by a ball that came over the hedge into my garden when one of the boys playing cricket hit the ball very hard 14. She broke down when I broke to her the sad news that her son had been killed in an accident 15. The girl was not very good at riding her new bicycle and fell off, cutting her knee, so I gave her some chocolate to cheer her up.

Exercise b Page 227 1. As it was a wet day ... 2. To stop the train pull the communication cord 3. Although I don't condemn you for it ... 4. I opened the door as a procession ... 5. She is plain but somehow ... 6. Having forgotten to buy any meat, I just had a salad and some fruit for lunch 7. The tools I need for gardening are kept in the cellar 8. I was very young when I caught ... 9. He came downstairs and entered ... 10. I was still a child when my grandmother died 11. She was roaring lustily and standing ... 12. ... in the district and there is an old ... 13 ... in the class but failed ... 14. As we looked at those paintings ... 15. ... stool and tried to paint.

Exercise c Page 227 1. Although he had a chill ... 2. When his work was done ... 3. Since he was not as intelligent as ... 4. Since he was not cut out ... 5. If I may speak frankly ... 6. ... whether he wanted to or not 7. When she saw a strange man ... 8. ... when he had that said to him 9. ... why he said such a thing 10. ... if some students watch ... 11. When you say things like that ... 12. If she had not shouted at me ... 13. Although it may seem strange ... 14. Since I was curious to know ... but I found that ... 15. ... it when people flatter her 16. The fact that he made such a fuss ... 17. In order that he might get the job ... 18. As soon as the sentence had been pronounced ... 19. If you hadn't intervened so promptly ... 20. ... if you threw ... 21. In addition to the fact that he wrote plays, Vanbrugh 22. As soon as he realised ... 23. Once one has been bitten, one is shy in future 24. ... why he has not come/why he did not come 25. The fact that he says things like that ...

CHAPTER 35

Exercise a Page 233 1. in with 2. out ... off 3. for ... down 4. under 5. up ... on 6. up in 7. over ... up 8. off 9. out 10. up 11. out 12. off about 13. over 14. off 15. up 16. backs 17. up 18. about on ... off 19. up 20. up

Exercise b.Page 234 1. When Shakespeare went out poaching one night he was caught and shut up, which is why he came to London 2. Mary works very hard but her younger sister is lazy 3. Alan was driving along a country lane when he saw a very beautiful old house for sale, so he stopped to look at it and, finally, bought it. 4. She got the house very tidy and put on her best clothes in case people called on her, but, though she sat there all afternoon, no-one came 5. When Paul came in, looking happy, I told him some important news which made him rush out of the room immediately. 6. Having a lot of money on him and not knowing what to do with it, he decided to go to a race meeting where he put his money on a horse called 'Money Galore', only to lose it all 7. The car was going too fast in bad visibility on a wet road, so it skidded and crashed, and the driver is in hospital with concussion 8. We were having a picnic by the river at Avignon, but the wind was blowing the dust so much that we had as much dust as ham in our sandwiches 9. I was reading a book I had bought about the Incas, but I left it on the train, so I bought another copy and had nearly finished that when I left it on another train, with the result that I have never read the last twenty pages 10. When I called on John he was sitting in the garden, fast asleep, so I went home again without disturbing him. 11. There was once a famous burglar who was often seen but never caught because he used to burgle naked with his body covered with grease so that, when people tried to catch him, their fingers slipped off him 12. We went to sleep, and when in the morning we looked out of the window we realised that we couldn't get out until we had shovelled the snow away as it had been snowing all night, and the wind had blown the snow into drifts 13. While we were sunbathing in Spain we got thirsty, so Jan offered to get some ice-creams, but as he was coming back with them he had to sit down very suddenly because the string of his trunks had given way! 14. I liked his fiancée, whom I met for the first time last night, because, while she is rather fat and has a round red face, she is very clever and kind-hearted 15. Seeing that an Underground train had just come in, we ran to catch it, sat down and started to read, but when it stopped at a station we realised that its name was wrong and that we had gone in the wrong direction

Exercise c Page 235 1. ... speakers do not like being laughed at 2. ... At last this bomb-site is being cleared up. I wonder what will be built here 3. ... nothing to be done about it now 4. Is there anything to be said in favour ... 5. No-one is to be blamed/to blame for that 6. ... object to being made to work hard 7. ... tired of being sponged on 8. ... needs touching up 9. What was being discussed ... 10. His aunt was sent a parrot ... liked being sworn at

Exercise d 1. loomed 2. had told ... would have saved 3. ... have women really liberated 4. have been racking ... have seen 5. get 6. realised ... makes 7. does he make ... is always complaining 8. should be forced 9. told ... does he want ... told ... is thinking... was talking 10. left ... expected ...developed ... had been walking... arrived ... 11. should be 12. did he suspect ... was spying/spied 13. plodded ... were just beginning ... heard ... had been sent 14. should he do 15. will be getting ... is getting

Exercise f Page 237 1. causing 2. took 3. picking 4. rallied 5. give 6. abide 7. hold 8. heaved/breathed 9. hatched 10. wrought/played 11. took ... opening 12. make 13. grant 14. performed 15. labouring 16. enlist 17. dropped ... take 18. launch 19. submitted 20. bear ... harbour 21. stifle 22. staged/organised 23. allowed 24. sugar 25. eke

Exercise g Page 237 1a to lay ... to stand 1b in dealing 2a to do 2b of going 2c for listening 3a to see 3b at being 3c in teasing 4a to look 4b talking 4c entering/from entering 5a to work 5b into signing 6a to start 6b of going 7a to tie 7b to intriguing 8a for repairing/to repair 8b with receiving 8c of collecting 9a from feeling 9b for making ... undergo 10a to get 10b at running 11a with being 11b for having 12a to see 12b in watching 13a to buy 13b travelling 13c of curing 14a to pass 14b of passing

Exercise h Page 238 1. convulsed 2. pampered 3. improvised/makeshift 4. area ... amenities 5. bookstall 6. decanter 7. conjure up/evoke 8. secular 9. lay

Exercise i Page 239 1. omit commas 3. ... all that ... 4. Put 'systematically' at the end 5. ... should be ... didn't do 6. time in coming ... 7. ... thing that 9. up to taking ... 10. Add "to" at the end 11. He did a lot of propaganda ... 13. ... the ceiling of his room 15. ... which is which 16. Michael is 17. Many people are dissatisfied with their lot in life 18. ... presided over by ... 19. She has been keeping ... it is time she knew ... 21. ... so I was able to go ... 22. ... horses should be made ... 23. Put a semi-colon, not a comma, after taxi. 25. ... straits did he find ... reduced to playing